The becoming of bodies
Girls, images, experience

REBECCA COLEMAN

Manchester
University Press

Manchester and New York

distributed in the United States exclusively by Palgrave Macmillan

Copyright © Rebecca Coleman 2009

The right of Rebecca Coleman to be identified as the author of this work has been asserted by her in accordance with the Copyright, Designs and Patents Act 1988.

Published by Manchester University Press
Oxford Road, Manchester M13 9NR, UK
and Room 400, 175 Fifth Avenue, New York, NY 10010, USA
www.manchesteruniversitypress.co.uk

Distributed in the United States exclusively by
Palgrave Macmillan, 175 Fifth Avenue,
New York, NY 10010, USA

Distributed in Canada exclusively by
UBC Press, University of British Columbia, 2029 West Mall,
Vancouver, BC, Canada V6T 1Z2

British Library Cataloguing-in-Publication Data is available

Library of Congress Cataloging-in-Publication Data is available

ISBN 978 0 7190 8918 3 paperback

First published by Manchester University Press in hardback 2009

This paperback edition first published 2012

The publisher has no responsibility for the persistence or accuracy of URLs for any external or third-party internet websites referred to in this book, and does not guarantee that any content on such websites is, or will remain, accurate or appropriate.

Printed by Lightning Source

The becoming of bodies

Manchester University Press

Contents

List of figures	*page* vi
Acknowledgements	vii
Introduction: the relations between bodies and images	1
1 From cause and effect to becoming and affect	32
2 Immanent experience	55
3 What can images do?	85
4 Looks and selves	112
5 Fighting back	141
6 Things that stay	166
Conclusion: become what you want?	195
Appendix: additional images	222
Bibliography	229
Index	241

List of figures

4.1	Sarah's art-work	117
4.2	Sammy's art-work	118
4.3	Tasha's art-work	121
4.4	Anna's art-work, front	122
4.5	Anna's art-work, back	123
A.1	Casey's art-work	222
A.2	Catherine's art-work	223
A.3	Chloe's art-work	223
A.4	Dionne's art-work, front	224
A.5	Dionne's art-work, back	224
A.6	Emily's art-work	225
A.7	Fay's art-work	226
A.8	Hannah's art-work, front	227
A.9	Katie's art-work, front	227
A.10	Tina's art-work, front	228

Acknowledgements

First and foremost, I would like to thank the girls who participated in this research for their willingness and openness in talking to me: Anna, Casey, Catherine, Chloe, Dionne, Emily, Fay, Hannah, Katie, Sammy, Sarah, Tasha and Tina. I would also like to thank Jane Harrison and John Bradshaw for making the research go smoothly. This book began as my Ph.D. research in the Sociology Department, Goldsmiths College and I would like to acknowledge the people and intellectual culture there for providing such a stimulating environment and for the direction that the research took. In particular, for their continuing encouragement, advice, enthusiasm and good-humour, thanks to Mariam Fraser and Celia Lury – I am privileged to have worked with two such inspiring people. Thanks also to Lisa Adkins, Claire Colebrook and Bev Skeggs for their help in thinking through how the project might work as a book. I'd like to thank my family and friends for their support, and the following people for their help at different stages and in different ways with the thesis and the book: Suki Ali, Jenn Barth, Karl Broome, Angela McRobbie, Ada Nwosu, Iyabo Osho, Clare Pritchard, Lucy Rhoades, Alison Rooke, Marsha Rosengarten, Gisa Weszkalnys and Rachel White. For helping me out and keeping me going in ways which exceed this project, thanks especially to Monica Moreno, Jen Tarr, Debra Ferreday and Matt Moran. This book is dedicated to Paul Nightingale.

This research was funded by the ESRC, Studentship Award Number RA42200134103.

Some of the Introduction and Chapter 3 has previously been published as 'The Becoming of Bodies: Girls, Media Effects and Body-Image' in *Feminist Media Studies*, Vol. 8, No. 2, 2008, 163–179. Some of Chapter 6 has previously been published as '"Things That Stay": Feminist Theory, Duration and the Future' in *Time and Society*, Vol. 17, No. 1, 2008, 85–102.

Introduction: the relations between bodies and images

The term 'the becoming of bodies' refers to a conviction that bodies must be conceived as processes which are constantly moving rather than as discrete, autonomous entities. This is not a particularly novel claim to make: within feminist theory, and social and cultural theory more generally, attention is increasingly drawn from 'form' to 'process' (see for example such diverse work as Barad 2007; Buchanan and Colebrook 2000; Butler 1993, 2004; Deleuze 1992; Fraser *et al.* 2005; Grosz 1999a; Merleau-Ponty 1962/1989, 1968/1977; Rose 1986). However, to be concerned with bodies as processes is not necessarily to be concerned with bodies as *becomings*. That is, while the concepts of 'process' and 'becoming' share a logic of movement and are in many ways inseparable, they are not interchangeable. The difference between process and becoming that I point to and explore in this book designates a distinction between a notion of process which argues that bodies are constantly moving and are never complete(d) and a notion of becoming which argues that bodies are constantly in the process of *enfolding*. This book takes a feminist Deleuzian perspective in order to explore the becoming of bodies through their enfoldings with *images*. In Chapter 1 I argue that 'the fold' is one way in which Deleuze (1993/2003), through Leibniz, conceives 'things' and 'the world' as a continual and reciprocal enfolding; the thing is folded in the world and the world is folded in the thing. For Deleuze it is through enfolding that things and the world become. As such, I suggest that what is at stake is not so much the things or the worlds themselves as the relations between them; enfoldings are the *relations* of becoming. Taking up this notion, this book argues that bodies cannot be understood as discrete, autonomous entities, not only because they are always in process but also because their movement is always through their *relations* in the world; bodies are not autonomous from the world.

This book addresses not the becoming of bodies and the world in general but the becoming of particular bodies through particular relations with particular aspects of the world. The particular bodies in focus are those of thirteen 13 and 14 year old white British girls who participated in empirical research on their experiences of their bodies through images. The enfoldings of the relations between bodies and images that I consider here, then, are the specific relations between these girls' bodies and images that they deem important and significant. In exploring the becoming of bodies not only in theoretical terms but also empirically, one of my aims is to ground Deleuzian theory in concrete (or 'actual') bodies. While bodies have clearly been at stake in recent feminist work which engages with Deleuze (see for example Braidotti 1994, 2002, 2006; Bray and Colebrook 1998; Grosz 1994, 2000, 2001; Kennedy 2004; Munster 2006; Parisi 2004; Pisters 2003),[1] there has been little work to date which takes up Deleuzian concepts in relation to empirical research[2] (see Fisher and Goodley 2007; Potts 2004 as exceptions[3]). In exploring the relations between these girls' bodies and images through key Deleuzian concepts of becoming, enfolding, relationality, affect, intensity and assemblage, I consider what Deleuze's work opens up for feminist theoretical and empirical work and what its limitations are. That is, Deleuze's theory is explored not only in the abstract but also in practice.

My interest here is in examining how becomings of bodies are made possible, and impossible, through their relations with images. My focus on the relations between bodies and images is part of an extensive tradition within feminism. Feminist theory, for example, has long been occupied with the relations between girls' and women's bodies and mirror images (de Beauvoir 1949/1997), and images in art (Betterton 1987, 1996; Pollock 1987; Adams 1996), photography (Kuhn 1995; Lury 1998), film (Doane 1992; Mulvey 1989; Rose 1986; Stacey 1994)) and popular culture more widely (McRobbie 1999; Walkerdine 1997; Walkerdine et al. 2001).[4] Recently, much feminist empirical work has attended to the relations between girl's and young women's bodies and images in 'the media'[5] (Duke 2000; Durham 1999; Goodman 2002; Goodman and Walsh-Childers 2004; Grogan and Wainwright 1996; Grogan et al. 1996; Nichter 2000). Outside of academia, there is also much contemporary interest in this topic: within journalism and news media more generally (controversy over 'size 0' and obesity), government (the Body Image Summit 2000) and consumer groups (the Dove campaign for real beauty), for example. This chapter begins with a discussion of one of these sites, the Body Image Summit, and moves to examine two feminist empirical research projects[6] on different aspects of the relations between young women's bodies and media images. My intention here is provide an overview of the prevalent ways in which girls' and women's bodies, images and the relations between them are commonly conceived, understood and researched. The point of this discussion is not so much to critique the arguments and conclusions of these three projects, as to unpack the ways in which such arguments and conclusions can be made. My suggestion is that, despite their different contexts and aims, a model of media cause and effect underpins these arguments, a model which itself rests upon a framework of subject(ivity) and object(ivity). Thinking through feminist theory on women's spectatorship of images which disrupts a clear distinction between subject(ivity) and object(ivity), and introducing Deleuze and Guattari's (1987) notion of molecular becoming, I argue for an understanding of bodies and images outside of a framework of cause/effect, subject/object. Approaching the relations between bodies and images from a feminist Deleuzian position which takes seriously an ontology of becoming, I argue that bodies and images are not separate and separable entities (subjects and objects) and as such do not act on each other in terms of (linear) cause and effect. Instead, bodies and images are processes which are inextricably entwined and which become through each other. This Introduction therefore acts as a frame of reference for the book and begins to explain and explore its central thesis; bodies become known, understood and lived through their relations with images. It concludes by sketching the trajectory of the book and outlining the concerns of the following chapters.

Media cause-and-effect

The Body Image Summit was held in June 2000 by the British government to investigate and intervene in the links between images in the media and fashion industries and an increase in girls and women involved in practices of dieting, eating disorders, self-harm and generally feeling unhappy with their bodies.[7] Its key aims were to identify and address the concerns that young women felt about their bodies because of images they were presented with. Participants in the Summit were 'leading figures in the worlds of fashion, modelling and women's media' (Cabinet Office Press Release, 20.06.2000), including government ministers, magazine editors, fashion stylists and journalists, representatives of business and academics. In her address to the Summit, Tessa Jowell, the Minister for Women at the time, explained that the 'pressure' felt by 'young women, . . . their mothers and grandmothers' to be thin 'can undermine self-esteem and confidence, which in turn can have an impact on their health and well-being' (Cabinet Office Press Release, 20.06.2000). On the one hand, Jowell described the Summit as 'not about telling women, the fashion industry or the world of film and media what to do and how to do it. We are certainly not saying these industries are responsible for causing eating disorders amongst young girls' (Cabinet Office Press Release, 20.06.2000). On the other hand, however, the Summit was responding to concerns raised by women about 'body image and media' during two previous government consultations. While Jowell was careful not to hold responsible media and fashion industries for eating disorders, recognising 'the important contribution these industries make to the economy', magazine images in particular were seen as a significant factor in the pressure to be thin: 'young women themselves, their mothers and grandmothers have all told us they want to see more women with a wider range of body shapes and sizes and more women from ethnic minorities as models in magazines' (Jowell, Cabinet Office Press Release, 20.06.2000).

Jowell's statement was supported by the young women who contributed to the Summit, as a poem presented to the Summit by the Northolt Young Women's Project demonstrates:

Clothes to fit all
Not extra small
Tops to fit all size breasts
Mags to increase our self confidence
Give the diet page a rest
We want normal to be popular
We'd be much happier
Feel better about ourselves
Realistic women on our TVs
And catwalks please
And less on the shelf.

The Body Image Summit marks an important landmark in Britain to attend to asymmetrical gender relations which place women of all ages under pressure to be thin. It addresses the ways in which these relations are represented and reproduced in and by media and fashion and proposes more realistic images of women from all ethnic backgrounds to counteract the harm to women's health, well-being and everyday experiences of their bodies. In some ways, then, the Summit takes up and expands so-called 'second wave' feminism's criticism of media images for their sexism and call for more positive representations of women (see, for example, King and Stott 1977). The Summit can be understood as a good example of feminism's 'success' (McRobbie 2007) in mainstreaming notions of unequal gender relations and representations and forcing government policy to take seriously women's issues.

As indicated above, my interest in discussing the Body Image Summit is not to take issue with its aims, arguments or conclusions but to consider the conceptual models on which they are based.[8] In these terms, the Summit can be understood as beginning from the assumption that a negative link existed between how young women felt about their bodies on the one hand and media and fashion industry images on the other and concluded, perhaps unsurprisingly, that young women felt under constant pressure to be thin due to 'impossible images'. One solution to the problem of these 'impossible' media and fashion images, as both Jowell and the Northolt Young Women's Project point out, is their replacement with images of a 'wider range of body sizes' so that 'normal' women are represented 'realistic[ally]'.

While the Summit was a policy organised and oriented initiative, and therefore operated within a problem-solving remit, it is noticeable that its arguments are echoed in much recent feminist academic research on the relations between girls' and women's bodies and images at stake in a number of disciplines.[9] For example, from a psychological perspective, as part of a wider project (see for example Grogan *et al.* 1996), Sarah Grogan and Nicola Wainwright (1996) conducted a study of young women's body image and body (dis)satisfaction using group interviews with white working and middle class girls aged 8 and 13. Grogan and Wainwright argue that girls as young as eight recognise and internalise cultural pressures to be thin. Some of the questions asked in the group interviews specifically concerned models in magazines and media role models (1996: 668) and the girls who participated raised issues of weight and body shape, exercise (and body building especially) and food as particularly worrying and discussed their dissatisfaction with their bodies. For example, when asked by the interviewer, 'is there anything you like to do to change your body shape?', two 8 year old girls described that they felt fat and replied that they would like to lose weight (1996: 668), and three 13 year old girls were dissatisfied with their stomachs (1996: 668). For Grogan and Wainwright, this is evidence that 'girls of these ages have already internalised adult's ideals of slimness' (1996: 668) and, further, that 'women from primary-school age onwards are sensitive to cultural pressures to conform to a limited range of acceptable body shapes' (1996: 672).

Drawing on feminist work in media and cultural studies, Grogan and Wainwright focus on girl and teen magazines in particular and argue that images in such magazines:

> have powerful effects on their readers, serving to foster and maintain a 'cult of femininity', supplying definitions of what it means to be a woman. It is a matter of concern that the images presented in teen magazines

present such a restricted range of models for young women. If women's body image can be bolstered by alternative sources of information, they may be more resilient against influences such as teen magazines, because young women who grow up with a positive body image are less likely to be affected by cultural messages (Grogan and Wainwright 1996: 672, references omitted).

For Grogan and Wainwright here, girls' bodies need to be 'more resilient against influences such as teenage magazines' in order to be 'less likely to be affected by cultural messages'. They suggest that 'alternative sources of information' are one way of 'bolster[ing]' 'women's body image' because they would feature a less 'restricted range of models for young women' and would thus 'supply' a greater range of feminine ideals. In this way, the argument Grogan and Wainwright make and the solution they pose resonate with the arguments and proposals of the Body Image Summit. Young women are vulnerable to images in the media, and especially in magazines, and often report body dissatisfaction because of this. To counteract such dissatisfaction, the restricted range of bodies that young women are presented with should be replaced by or supplemented with a greater diversity and/or with alternative sources of information; 'young women who grow up with a positive body image are less likely to be affected by cultural messages'.

From the perspective of sociology and media and cultural studies, Grogan and Wainwright's psychological position on the relations between girls' bodies and magazine images might be considered problematic. David Gauntlett (2005), for example, indicates how psychological studies on media effects are notoriously silent around the question of how such effects are or can be measured. Moreover, Grogan and Wainwright do not address questions of 'readership' and 'interpretation'. What does it mean for an 8 year old and a 13 year old white working or middle class girl to read a magazine? Do they interpret the same material differently? Are they affected by cultural messages differently? Questions such as these derived from cultural studies work on audiences and feminist research on gender, race and adolescence occupy a central place in Lisa Duke's (2000) study of girls' interpretations of the feminine ideal in teen magazines. Duke's research questions specifically address why and how girls read magazines (are magazines satisfying the girls' needs and desires? Do they read fashion and beauty critically?) and the role of race in 'influenc[ing] the way these middle-class girls interpret teen magazines' images and text' (2000: 374). Duke's article is based on a longitudinal study which traces girls' interpretations of magazines from early to late adolescence (2000: 375). Three groups of middle-class girls participated in the research. The first group comprised of ten white girls interviewed aged 12–14 and again aged 16–18 and the second and third groups comprised of sixteen African-American girls, eight of whom were aged 12–14 and eight of whom were aged 17–18 (2000: 375).

Duke's starting point is that '[m]edia have been implicated in establishing atypical standards of appearance as the social norm and encouraging girls' preoccupation with their looks' (2000: 369). Adolescent girls, because they 'experience significant physical and developmental change', are especially vulnerable and 'media like teen magazines serve as guidebooks on acceptable appearance, gender roles, and relationship formation. . ., replacing parents and augmenting or surpassing peers as primary information sources' (Duke 2000: 369). In Duke's interviews, both black and white girls discuss how magazine images are unachievable but nevertheless powerful in their ability to 'put a picture in your head' (2000: 377). However, Duke's study indicates that:

> Most African-American girls . . . were uninterested in striving for or achieving the ideal feminine physique, as the magazines portray it. Similarly, there was little interest in makeup and grooming advice that was seen as inappropriate for Black girls, due either to formulations intended for White girls, or African-American girls' belief that cosmetics were superfluous to being attractive. (2000: 382)

For Duke, whereas the white girls in her study evaluated and defined themselves by their appearance, the African-American girls deemed personality and character more significant (2000: 382). Duke argues that the feminine ideal of beauty and slimness is less important to African-American girls, partly because of the exclusion of images of black girls and women in magazines and partly due to African-American culture, which has a 'more realistic, inclusive view of the female physical norm . . . reinforced by elder female family members, who were said to view heavier girls as healthier, and by African-American men, who prize "thick" or amply filled out girls as sexually appealing and desirable' (2000: 385). Duke's argument here is that the African-American cultural valuation and appreciation of a 'more realistic, inclusive . . . female physical norm', directs African-American girls' interest away from 'striving for or achieving the ideal feminine physique' depicted in teen magazines.

Duke's research attends to questions of race, readership and interpretation which are overlooked in both the psychological study and the Body Image Summit. However, the research begins with the influence of media, and in particular teen magazines, and the consequent vulnerability of girls and young women. As such, magazines are seen as causes which effect, to a greater or lesser extent depending on racial and cultural background, girls' bodies. Central to the argument I am making here, then, is that, in spite of their different orientations and disciplinary backgrounds, the three projects have in common an evocation of and a reliance on a model of media effects. That is, the Body Image Summit, Grogan and Wainwright's psychological argument and Duke's media and cultural studies research, somewhat implicitly and in different ways, conceive and research the relations between the girls' and young women's bodies and (media) images in terms of cause and effect: images effect bodies in (usually) negative ways. For these three projects, which work with different levels of complexity, images are understood to be causes and bodies are read in terms of the effects that images have on them.[10] The criticisms of media effects models are well documented and extend from the problem of measuring effects in any meaningful way to the lack of creative methods used to research the interactions between people and media (Gauntlett and Holzwarth 2006) to the assumed passivity of the audiences and/or consumers (see for example 'classic' media and cultural studies work on audiences such as Hall 1980) to the concentration on specific 'types' of images to the detriment of other images that might also be significant (see Chapter 3).

While these criticisms are important and accurate, my interest here lies in the ways in which the media effects model rests upon a two-fold distinction which maps bodies and images onto subjects and objects. That is, the model of media cause-and-effect underpinning the projects discussed above distinguishes between bodies and images and conceives bodies as subjects and images as objects. Bodies/subjects and images/objects are understood as different and separate entities and it is through this difference and separation that the model of cause and effect is able to emerge. As mutually incompatible entities, images/objects have (negative) effects on bodies/subjects. In identifying this distinction between body/subject and image/object, I consider how such a distinction is ultimately unsustainable. In the following section, I concentrate on feminist theories of spectatorship which have demonstrated the impossibility of clearly and finally distinguishing between subject(ivity) and object(ivity), women's bodies and images.

Feminist theory, subjects and objects

Feminist work on images, looking and spectatorship is wide-ranging, but can be grouped around an interest in women's relationship to visual culture. Such work throws into tension the separation of bodies and images and the mapping of bodies and images onto subject(ivity) and object(ivity). For Griselda Pollock (1987), arguments which separate bodies and images are fundamentally flawed. Pollock draws attention to the 'confusion and mystification' (1987: 41) of what 'images of women' (Pollock 1987: 41) mean and suggests that the term relies on an unhelpful, and ultimately unsustainable, separation of 'women' and 'images' where women are treated as 'real' and images as 'representations' (Pollock 1987: 41). In understanding images as representations Pollock argues there is 'a common misconception to see images as merely a reflection, good or bad, and compare "bad" images of women (glossy magazine photographs, fashion ads, etc.) to "good" images of women ("realist" photographs, of women working, housewives, older women, etc.)' (Pollock 1987: 41). What is important in the context of this discussion is that the distinction between what is real and what is representation, between women and representation, is a dichotomy which relies upon a separation of subjects and objects; women are subjects which are distinct to and in antagonism with images which are objects. This opposition of subjects and objects is, as many feminists argue, dependent upon a masculine notion of the subject as secure and stable and able to forge, or not, relations with objects.[11]

Rosemary Betterton (1996), for example, argues that this dichotomy is difficult to maintain if considered from the position of women who, as part of what she considers a visual culture characterised by the pervasiveness of images of the female form, are everywhere constituted as objects. For Betterton in an earlier essay (1987), such objectification means that women cannot experience themselves as purely subject because they are also always capable of being objectified, of becoming objects. Betterton examines this state of, potentially, being both subject and object through a focus on the processes of looking and spectatorship which she argues are based upon a notion of the masculine subject who gazes at an object that is (spatially and temporally) distinct. Theories of women as spectators traditionally position women within this masculine model which Betterton argues structures them within one of two negative states: 'On the one hand, women as spectator is offered the dubious satisfaction of identification with the heterosexual masculine gaze, voyeuristic, penetrating and powerful. . . . On the other hand, it is argued, women's pleasure is bound up with a narcissistic identification with the images of the female body, usually shown to be desirable but passive' (Betterton 1987: 219). For Betterton, the pleasure that might be involved in looking as women at images of women has been understood as restricted either by women's coercion into adopting a masculine vision or through a narcissistic relationship with the image in which women can only reinforce their own passivity. Indeed, writing in relation to mirror images, Simone de Beauvoir (1949/1997) points to both the restricted nature of women's look and the narcissism which positions women as object rather than subject.[12] De Beauvoir argues, 'woman, knowing and making herself object, believes she really sees *herself* in the glass. A passive and given fact, the reflection is, like herself, a thing; and as she does covet female flesh, her own flesh, she gives life through her admiration and desire to the imagined qualities she sees' (1997: 643).

De Beauvoir's argument here questions the masculinist distinction between a body/subject who is, spatially and temporally distinct from image/object from the position of a woman spectator who 'believes she really sees *herself* in the glass' and thus 'gives life' to 'the imagined qualities she sees'. For de Beauvoir there is no distinction between the woman who looks and the woman who becomes. Taking up these points, in the following discussion I focus on the feminist psychoanalytic theory on film and art by Adams (1996), Doane (1992) and Rose (1986), and Lury's conception of mimesis in relation to photographs, to examine in more detail two ways in which the distinction between subject/object, body/image is understood to be unstable. Despite coming from different theoretical positions, what both of these sets of arguments – and indeed many other feminist theories of visual culture – have in common is their understanding of the relations between women's bodies and images as unavoidably and irretrievably dissolving the conventional, masculine, temporal and spatial gap between subject(ivity) and object(ivity). It is through this dissolution of the gap between body/image subject/object, which feminist theory points to, that I move to consider Deleuze's notion of molecular becoming.

Psychoanalysis, sexual difference and spectatorship
Within feminist psychoanalytic film and art theory, Freud's model of narcissism is often a starting point for development and critique. In 'On Narcissism' (1914/1995) Freud understands narcissism as a necessary developmental stage occurring between a child's 'primitive auto-eroticism' and 'object love' (1995: 545). From initially conceiving narcissism in relation to serious psychological conditions such as schizophrenia, Freud widened his concept to the erotic life of humans in general. Originally, all subjects have two choices of object love – themselves and their mother. This 'primary narcissism' is present and possible in us all. However, Freud then frames narcissism within a model of sexual (mapped on to gender) difference and argues that object choice can develop along two paths. In Freud's model, a person may love,

(1) according to a narcissistic type
    (a) what he himself is (ie himself)

(b) what he himself was
  (c) what he himself would like to be
  (d) someone who was once part of himself
(2) according to the anaclitic/attachment type
  (a) the woman who feeds him
  (b) the man who protects him
     and the succession of substitutes who take their place. (1995: 555–556)

The paths are then split along the lines of sexual/gender difference as Freud identifies the anaclitic 'normal' type as characteristic of the male and the narcissistic type being more prevalent in the female. For Freud, it is during the process of developing from a girl to a woman that the female deviates from a normal object choice to narcissistic love where what should be an object choice – a subject detached from herself – is replaced with her own self:

> With the onset of puberty the maturing of the female sexual organs, which up until then have been in a condition of latency, seems to bring about an intensification of the original narcissism, and this is unfavourable to the development of a true object choice with its accompanying sexual overvaluation. Women, especially if they grow up with good looks, develop a certain self-contentment which compensates them for the social restrictions that are imposed upon them in their choice of object. Strictly speaking, it is only themselves that such women love with an intensity comparable to that of the man's love for them. Nor does this lie in the direction of loving, but of being loved; and the man who also fulfils this condition is the one who finds favour with them. (Freud 1995: 554–555)

Freud's position here can clearly be criticised from a variety of feminist perspectives for its understanding of girls as deviating from a masculine conceptual norm. What is interesting for this discussion and for the empirical analysis in later chapters, however, is the way in which subjects and objects are figured. Freud develops his conception of narcissism according to biological sexual difference ('maturing sexual organs' for example) where girls' bodies are the source of narcissism. Mapped onto this pubescent body are certain social conditions that 'restrict' the object choice that a girl/woman can make. Both because of, and to compensate for, the restrictions of the biological and the social, girl/woman turns to herself to love, indeed, turns herself into (transforms into) her object choice. With this narcissistic choice, woman becomes an object. She is, according to Freud, incapable of pure subjectivity because she is unable to love another subject/object; she may only love herself (and be loved by a man). Freud's understanding of subjectivity, then, requires others (subjects/objects) with whom to enter into mutual relations (of love for example), that is, to be a subject/object and not just an object involves a symbiotic relationship (preferably) between a man and a woman. Bodies therefore become objects when they are not in mutual relations with other bodies; to be an object is to be unable to love, and therefore unable to enter into relationships with others. Subjects and objects are, in Freud's model, differentiated from each other by relationships of distanciation where 'normal' object choices involve loving that which is not self and where 'narcissistic' object choices involve loving that which is self.

For Freud, there are certain spatial and temporal gaps between subjects and objects, between bodies and images for example, that must be maintained in order to love anaclitically. That these gaps are preserved by males but not by females is because of biological, psychical and social differences between them. These gaps are understood by Freud through the distinction he makes between seeing and knowing, premised on gender and sexual difference and the first sight of the opposite sex's genitalia. Mary Ann Doane (1992) takes up Freud's distinction between seeing and knowing and describes it in terms of a boy child's first sight of a girl child's genitalia as unaccompanied by any 'primitive knowing' or understanding. This is in contrast to a girl child's first sight of a boy child's genitalia where she is immediately aware that she is without, is lacking (1992: 232–233). Doane understands this sexualised and gendered difference between seeing and knowing as a spatial and temporal gap which exists for a boy child but not for a girl child. For a boy child there is an inherent gap between looking and knowing, indeed how he looks *determines* how and what he knows. There is, then, a distinction between his body and his knowledge of the world. However, for a girl child Doane argues there is no causal relationship between looking and knowing. For girls, looking and knowing are *simultaneous*; there is no spatial or temporal gap. A girl becomes her body at the moment she realises that she is lacking, that she is not a boy.

Doane applies this female lack (of a penis/phallus and a gap) to women's spectatorship of images of women. She argues:

> For the female spectator there is a certain over-presence of the image – she *is* the image. Given the closeness of its relationship, the female spectator's desire can only be described in terms of a kind of narcissism – the female look demands a becoming. It thus appears to negate the very distance or gap specified . . . as the essential precondition for voyeurism. (1992: 231)

For women, then, there is no gap between her body and the image – 'she *is* the image'. The concept of 'the gap' belongs to the masculine notion of the subject as distinctly separate from the object.[13] In Doane's terms, 'the woman can never ask her own ontological question' (1992: 241, n4). That the man is able to ask is due to his constitution as subject with the ability to separate himself from objects and from his identity. Woman, however, is *both* subject and object and *embodied*: the rational disembodiment, the gap between seeing and knowing, required to look at, understand and describe the self is not (as widely) available as a privilege to women.

Doane's figuring of the lack of distance between women and images reworks Freud's concept of narcissism through a feminist psychoanalytic perspective. By drawing attention to how 'the gap' depends on a masculine notion of subjectivity and objectivity, Doane demonstrates that the development of a 'normal' object choice is structured more difficultly for girls. Moreover, according to Doane's argument, feminine narcissism is more complex than self-love because to look is not simply to see and know but to *become* – 'the female look demands a becoming'. Looking is not a narcissism that is static and stagnant, a circular reinforcement of self-appreciation for example, but involves some movement, some possibility. Narcissism, then, is a relation of the self to the self that cannot be understood in terms of (masculine) models of distance nor in terms of subjects versus objects. Narcissistic women are, according to Doane (and Betterton) subjects *and* objects and not, as in Freud's model, subjects that transform themselves into objects. Narcissistic women are not *represented* in images but *are* images; there is no spatial or temporal distance through which a representation can be produced. There is no gap between body and image.[14]

The relevance of Freud's model of narcissism for thinking through the relations between women, as subjects, and images has also been discussed by other feminist psychoanalytic theorists. Jacqueline Rose (1986), for example, examines the 'instance of perception' whereby the boy and girl child recognise themselves as different (1986: 218) in terms of the centrality of cinematic images of women in providing an answer to, 'at its simplest, the question of "how we *see* ourselves"' (Rose 1986: 199). Rose suggests that one way of understanding this instance of perception is 'to make of it nothing *other* than a moment of perception which is immediately effective in its results, which means that the sight itself (with the associated connotation of inferiority) has an immediate psychological effect on the child' (Rose 1986: 218). However, she goes on to argue:

The other way of reading this moment is to see that it has absolutely no meaning outside a structure of sexual difference (the point at which boys and girls must define themselves *as* different) within which socially and historically the male term is privileged. (Rose 1986: 218; see also Rose 1986: 202)

For Rose, this second reading is more valuable than the first because a psychoanalytic reading of film must not only refer to 'the act of perception' but must also account for 'the structure of sexual difference' (Rose 1986: 218).[15] Rose suggests that such a psychoanalytic reading is able to address 'the way in which the woman gets set up, not simply as a certain *image*, something which can be criticised historically or sociologically, but as a *guarantee* against the difficulties of the cinematic system itself' (Rose 1986: 220). Rose's focus on the cinematic system refers to an arrangement beyond film itself and therefore reworks the position of the spectator; 'in narrative cinema the spectator identifies with the camera itself and is seduced into a regime of specularity, caught by the very apparatus itself and then identifying, necessarily, with the positions of desire and sexuality which each individual film puts into play' (Rose 1986: 216–217). The 'regime of specularity' is, for Rose, structured by sexual difference and the possibilities of identification with a position of desire and sexuality for women is, therefore, problematic; in classical cinema, women are both 'set up . . . as a certain *image*' – as 'other, dark continent' (Rose 1986: 211) – and, 'at the same time . . . sexuality is frozen into her body as spectacle, the object of phallic desire and/or identification' (Rose 1986: 211). As such, there is a 'genuine double bind':

For, if it is in relation to this phallic reference that woman is defined as different or outside and the organisation and cohesion of cinematic space is always also the securing of that reference, then the other side of this – the disturbance or trouble behind the cohesion itself – cannot be brought back into the cinematic space *for* women without thereby confirming the negative position to which she was originally assigned. (Rose 1986: 211)

According to Rose, woman is simultaneously outside of and part of the cinematic image and thus, as Doane and Betterton point out in different contexts, the predicament of a specific feminine spectatorship emerges. Working through the psychoanalytic concept of desire, Rose suggests, 'woman's sexuality is inseparable from the representations through which it is produced ('images and symbols *for* the woman cannot be isolated from images and symbols *of* the woman . . . it is the representation of sexuality which conditions how it comes into play)' (Rose 1986: 67, reference omitted). The 'gap' between subject and object, woman's sexuality and image, does not exist.

The relationship between representation and sexual difference is also considered from a feminist psychoanalytic perspective by Parveen Adams (1996). Like Rose, Adams turns to the concept of desire in order to examine the problem of the regime of spectatorship; that is, like Rose, Adams considers that '[i]t is not the image of woman as such that is crucial, but how the image organises the way in which the image is looked at' (Adams 1996: 2). In her discussion of Della Grace's *The Three Graces* (see Adams 1996: 123–139), Adams suggests that the photograph disturbs 'the usual way in which the representation of women operates. The system of this photograph breaks with the meaning of the Woman, the meaning which feminism denounces and disclaims in its destiny of being-object-for-the-male-look' (Adams 1996: 123). Indeed, Adams argues that 'in the photograph there is a move away from the woman as object. This allows a female subject of the look, a woman of satisfaction, a woman spectator, and a woman who *makes*' (Adams 1996: 123). Organising her argument around the Lacanian concept of the phallus, Adams contends that 'the phallus is the central reference point [of the photograph] because *no one* possesses the phallus' (Adams 1996: 124). Addressing the problem, also raised by Rose, of 'the experience of sexual difference, the way subjectivity is propped upon the experience of objects, exemplary among which is Woman as object' (Adams 1996: 126), Adams argues that 'the question of the representation of the woman is not just her role as the object, but her relation to the object look' (Adams 1996: 126). Della Grace's photograph is important to Adams because the role of the woman as object is displaced by the 'object's' look:

> Within traditional representations the figures look in a line which either circulates endlessly or where the line of the look travels out of the circle and out to one side of the frame. In this photograph the figure in the centre seems to look at us before we register her look. At the same time she remains rooted in her circle. Our eyes have been misled. We can look, but there is no invitation. Rather our look is seen. This look that sees seems to break the traditional circle around the feminine object. It disrupts the smooth circuit of the scopophilic drive. The path of sublimation is disrupted. (Adams 1996: 130–131)

Adams describes the figure in the centre as working to 'empty' the place of the image. That is, 'the image that is produced is not exemplary; it should not become the mark of a representation of the new woman. That would be a phallic move in itself' (Adams 1996: 131). Rather, Adams proposes 'to keep the place of the object as open as we can tolerate. Only within that tolerance can new objects emerge'

(Adams 1996: 131). For Adams, then, the emptiness of the image disrupts the binary between subject/object and enables the possibility of modes of feminine spectatorship other than those which women are usually structured within. What is also important to note in both Adams' and Rose's argument is the idea of the fractured subject; their psychoanalytic perspectives sees women spectators as, fundamentally, non-unitary. The notion that there is a clearly defined, autonomous subject who is able to look at a separate bounded image is made redundant.

Mimesis and the photographic image
Feminist psychoanalytic theory on film and art has suggested, in different ways through a focus on sexual difference, that the spatial and temporal gap conceived between subjects and objects, bodies and images, is or can be disturbed for women spectators. Theoretical accounts of the relations between bodies and photographic images has also demonstrated how this gap is difficult to maintain in contemporary culture. For example, Celia Lury's (1998) work on 'prosthetic culture' conceives the gap between subjects and objects that has conventionally been framed in terms of space and time, as disappearing through new prosthetics of experimentation and extension. Lury concentrates her analysis on the ways in which photography has both contributed to and is part of the development of an experimental, prosthetic culture. Of particular importance here is her argument that 'the photograph, more than merely representing, has taught us a way of seeing, and that this way of seeing has transformed contemporary self-understandings' (1998: 3, reference omitted). These contemporary self-understandings, Lury suggests, have shifted culturally from an understanding of subjects as 'possessive individuals' to thinking instead of experimentation as a defining feature of identity. Whereas possessive individualism took identity to be a property of the individual and attempted to make 'the person', 'the individual' and 'self-identity' fit together seamlessly, the experimental individual has the capacity to take up different and multiple, mechanical or imaginary, prosthetics or extensions, through photographic images for example. As such, Lury sees the central premise of possessive individualism, 'I think, therefore I am' transformed to *'I can, therefore I am'*, for the experimental individual.

The emphasis on what is possible – the 'I can' – of which the photographic image is a vital part, is crucial for the disappearing of the gap between subjects and objects. In particular, Lury argues that the gap may be closed through the photograph's ability to freeze, frame and fix its objects and thus confuse the temporality that both the viewer and image exist as. Two processes of framing, freezing and fixing occur in prosthetic culture that disrupt and confuse the temporalities of subjects and objects. First, a process of *'outcontextualisation'* whereby the framing of an image not only disrupts the context of the featured object but also alters the viewer's perspective of it, 'encouraging the view that the object can be seen from all positions at once' (Lury 1998: 3). The outcontextualisation of an image does not rely on an organic or original context of an object which is then shifted, manipulated and positioned within a different context, but rather refers to the ways in which the image is in continuous movement and flux; the image does not 'belong' in any one space or time but rather is always being removed, reworked and reintroduced as different situations. In the same way, the apparent 'view from everywhere' which the outcontextualisation of an image creates does not mean that an image's object can be seen in its entirety but rather that there is *no singular way of seeing the object or image*.[16] The object and the image are therefore never depleted or fully consumed but instead exist simultaneously as both their own and different temporalities and spatialities. There is an excess of the image.

A second process that operates through the photograph is *'indifferentiation'* where the ability of an image to freeze and fix its objects enables a distortion of temporality and the 'disappearance or infilling of the distance between cause and effect, object and subject' (Lury 1998: 3). The experimental individual is necessarily partial – that is not unified – and as such does not occupy a consistent, coherent, distinct spatiality or temporality. The diverse ways that individuals might experiment and extend themselves through prosthesis means that there is no conventional spatial or temporal gap between subjects and objects. This, then, is a critique of the model of cause-and-effect, whereby images and bodies are understood as spatially and temporally separate and capable of having effects on each other: 'bad' images = 'bad' bodies. According to Lury's argument, the temporal and spatial differentiations of bodies and images cannot be maintained.

Central to Lury's understanding of the disappearing gap between subjects and objects is the notion of *mimesis*. Lury distinguishes between two different 'types' of mimesis: (i) 'perfection-seeking homeostasis' where mimesis is understood as the imitation of itself and where ultimately the representation can replace its referent (1998: 5) and (ii) 'blind imitation' where mimesis is 'understood as a relation of adaptation, affinity and reciprocity between self and context' (1998: 6). The first is a technique of possessive individualism where mimesis has a referent to imitate (even if it can ultimately replace it). As such, identity as a property may be the imitation of the individual; the individual and the identity correspond but are separate. This sense implies that something prior exists that can be mimicked. In contrast, Lury understands the second definition of mimesis as a technique of the experimental individual. This definition, which is developed from Walter Benjamin's notion of mimesis as the impulse to 'become and behave like something else' (Lury 1998: 5) is not so much imitation as it is *metamorphosis, transformation or binding into the environment*. In this second sense, the distinction between individual and environment, subject and object, body and image, is blurred, dissolved or infilled. Mimesis is not the imitation of an original but a relation of 'being like', of adapting to context:

> mimesis does not necessarily confirm or construct the notion of relation between an origin and the copy at all. It is a relation of being similar, not a relation of likeness in which something (the copy) is similar to something else (the original). Nor is it a relation of being similar or secondary to the copy. The relation at issue here cannot be contained within a closed system *whichever direction of motivation* is privileged . . . for its reversibility is not symmetrical; it is not necessarily a relation of either reflection or transparency. It is blind imitation that makes possible situated knowledges (Lury 1998: 226).

This blind imitation, then, is not a kind of knowingness, is not the imitation of something in order to pass for example,[17] but is rather, Lury argues, a '"relating to" or "yielding into"': as Benjamin writes, "Every day the urge grows stronger to get hold of an object at very close range by way of its likeness, its reproduction"' (Lury 1998: 32, references omitted). Lury discusses Michael Taussig's development of this notion of mimesis through challenging 'the tyranny of the visual notion of the image' which he argues should be replaced with an understanding of vision as 'the active yielding of the perceiver in the perceived – the perceiver trying to enter into the picture and become one with it, so that the self is moved by the representations and into the represented' (Taussig in Lury 1998: 31–32).[18] Mimesis here, then, is a way of seeing that disappears the spatial and temporal gaps between subjects and objects as bodies and images 'move' and 'yield into' each other; looking is not what takes place *from* a subject to an object but is the *in-between* which makes the distinctions difficult to know.

In relation to photographic images, Lury argues that the body of/in photography has historically been constructed as white and male (1998: 100). The gap that exists between this body and the photograph in possessive individualism is being disappeared through new experimental prosthetics, new ways of seeing for example, where subjects and objects, bodies and photographs, yield into each other. Lury suggests that the subject of prosthetic culture is distinct from yet in certain ways dependent upon the subject of possessive individualism; it is a rational, sovereign and disembodied – masculine – subject. The masculine subject is disembodied, both from 'himself' (the separation of the person, the individual and the self-identity) and from objects. The disembodiment of masculine subjectivity in prosthetic culture makes it possible to experiment with the gap between subjects and objects without objects necessarily becoming embodied. There is a kind of distance that potentially remains, or is made to remain. Lury questions whether the same kind of experimentation is possible for women who have historically been excluded from the construction of the possessive individual. Rather than extension and potential through images, Lury raises the possibilities instead of fear, trauma and self-annihilation for women and asks:

> Do the historical links between the photographic image, trauma and modernity make it impossible for women to see themselves in contemporary culture? Has the possibility of a specifically feminine relation to mimesis been lost in the disappearance of context: does the individual who internalises the exterior, or makes the immediate mediated, necessarily construct a masculine self-identity? (1998: 101)

For Lury here then, relations of mimesis between the photographic image and women's bodies disappears the distance between masculine bodies and images and, potentially, 'make it impossible for women to see themselves'.

Bodies, images and becomings

Feminist theory has critiqued the spatial and temporal gap between women's bodies and images by demonstrating that the distinction between subject(ivity) and object(ivity) cannot be maintained from the position of women's spectatorship. In this sense, Doane's, Rose's, Adams' and Lury's arguments understand the relations between bodies and images outside of a representational model and outside of a model of media effects. It is not, for example, that images represent women – and should represent them better – but that, in different ways for these authors, images make possible for women particular ways of seeing and knowing bodies. Bodies and images, then, are not separate but rather bodies are known, understood and experienced through images. Drawing on this unsettling of the distinction between bodies and images, subjects and objects, in this section I turn to consider Deleuze and Guattari's (1987) notion of *molecular becoming*. Deleuze and Guattari's work is an explicit attempt to disrupt dichotomies and as such is productive as another way in which to approach the relations between bodies and images without mapping them onto pre-existent distinctions and without understanding them in terms of cause-and-effect. Chapter 1 examines in detail the key concepts from Deleuze's work which underpin this book, but here I begin to outline the concept of becoming and what it does to the possibilities of understanding and exploring bodies and images.

Becoming is a central concept for Deleuze – in fact it can be termed an ontology (see Chapter 2) – and thus is difficult to pin down to any one of his works. In *A Thousand Plateaus* (1987), Deleuze and Guattari conceive of becoming as a philosophy which disrupts the binary oppositions upon which traditional Western philosophy has rested. Becomings are lines, processes or productions that challenge Being (one or the other) by concentrating instead on the in-between; '[t]he only way to get outside the dualisms is to be-between, to pass between . . . never ceasing to become' (Deleuze and Guattari 1987: 277). On the one hand, then, Deleuze and Guattari place Being which they argue is concerned with a molar politics, an attempt to find a form. On the other hand, becoming is concerned with *molecularity*; the world is molecular, fibrous, constantly becoming through all its different elements and things. Central to the notion of becoming is a process of transformation, not of forms transforming into another or different form but of constantly processual, constantly transforming relations. Deleuze and Guattari write, '[f]ibers lead us from one to the other, transform one into the other as they pass through doors and across thresholds' (Deleuze and Guattari 1987: 272).

According to a philosophy of becoming, bodies are understood not by their form but through what Deleuze (1992) terms their longitude and latitude. By longitude, Deleuze refers to the relations of speed and slowness, motion and rest of a thing. This might, for example, be the particles that compose it from any one specific point of view. By latitude, Deleuze is referring to the set of potential affects that defines a thing at any one moment (1992: 629), that is of what a body might be capable.[19] By proposing longitude and latitude rather than form as the ways in which to understand bodies, Deleuze aims to replace History, that is linear time, with geography.[20] Indeed, this is the point that Deleuze and Parnet (1977/2002) make in relation to the women's movement:

> We think too much in terms of history, whether personal or universal. Becomings belong to geography, they are orientations, directions, entries and exits. There is woman-becoming which is not the same as woman, their past and their future, and it is essential that women enter this becoming to get out of their past and their future, their history. (2002: 2)

For Deleuze and Parnet here, the woman's movement, concerned as it is with History, is molar and therefore can never reach its objectives of social change precisely because it is not a 'movement' but rather is concerned with 'being' a 'woman' in relation to a system that is about 'being' a 'man'. In conceiving History as such, Deleuze equates (linear) temporality with transcendence as he suggests that any notion of planning or progress implies a supplementary dimension; 'the plan' for Deleuze is always a theological plan, an attempt to organise, from above, through the transcendence of a thing (1992: 624–625). In contrast, for Deleuze, geography (longitude and latitude) and becoming are understood in their immanence, not as a plan or a development but as a composition of and for itself. The immanence of spatiality is conceived as a *plane* and it is through this plane that Deleuze urges us to understand the life and the living (of a) body:

> What is involved is no longer the affirmation of a single substance, but rather the laying out of a *common plane of immanence* on which all bodies, all minds and all individuals are situated. This plane of immanence or consistency is a plan, but not in the sense of a mental design, a project, a program; it is a plan in the geometric sense: a section, an intersection, a diagram. (Deleuze 1992: 625)

According to Deleuze here, a plane of immanence is not concerned with uniting things within 'a mental design, a project, a program' but rather with mapping the relations between infinitely related moments.[21] Becoming for Deleuze is not definable by its form or smooth evolution but rather is to be understood in terms of its movement as 'a complex relation between different velocities, between deacceleration and acceleration of particles. A composition of speeds and slownesses on a plane of immanence' (Deleuze 1992: 626).

One way to think about Deleuze's argument further at this point is through the notion of becoming-woman, mentioned in the quotation above from Deleuze and Parnet. Deleuze's work, where gender is at once 'absent and present' (Driscoll 2002: 191), has been debated by some for its appropriateness for feminism. In particular, the concept of becoming-woman has been especially controversial for feminists because it 'is a feminisation that takes the specificity of woman away from women' (Driscoll 2002: 191). Becoming-woman is for Deleuze and Guattari necessary to all becomings. It is, as Luciana Parisi (2004) puts it, 'the first step towards the destratification (declination) of the body from the sexed and gendered organism, subject and signifier' (2004: 198). Becoming-woman is the fundamental move to 'get outside the dualisms [and] be-between' (Deleuze and Guattari 1987: 277) and thus 'entails a micropolitics that goes beyond the male-female, man-woman binarism. Yet, this micropolitics involves men and women' (Parisi 2004: 198). The difficulty for some feminists with this concept, then, is that the 'woman' in 'becoming-woman' does not designate a woman 'as defined by her form, endowed with organs and functions, and assigned as a subject' (Deleuze and Guattari 1987: 275). The force of a feminism based on what Deleuze and Guattari term 'molar politics' – that is in concepts such as identity, subject(ivity), rights – is dispersed. As such, becoming-woman seems to suggest 'woman' 'must also be the first to disappear' (Jardine cited in Grosz 1994: 161).

There is much discussion of the relationship between Deleuze's work and feminism (see for example Braidotti 1991, 1994, 2002, 2006; Grosz 1994; Fraser 1997; Colebrook 2000) and of becoming-woman (see for example Grosz 1994; Conley 2000; Olkowski 2000; Driscoll 2002; Parisi 2004) and, while I do not want to repeat this here, it is worth noting at this point the ways in which the concept is understood to be important to feminism. For Deleuze and Guattari, 'becoming-woman' is a 'becoming-minoritarian', that is an 'in-between' movement which disrupts and refuses conventional categorisation and signification. As such, for Catherine Driscoll, '[b]ecoming-woman is a deterritorialisation of the organised body precisely because it uses gender against that organising signification' (2002: 195). Or, as Parisi argues, drawing on other Deleuzian feminists:

> becoming-woman deploys an important tactics of differentiation of a body beyond the tradition of representation. Becoming is no longer subjected to 'being' (the law of identity), but directs itself against man or the human as the origin of all concepts and politics . . . For feminism, this becoming does not propose a becoming of the subject woman, but a becoming towards differentiation, the challenge of inventing new virtual (potential) bodies. (2004: 199)

For this book, it is also worth noting that the multiplicity of a molecular woman is enacted through the girl: 'the molecular women is the girl herself' (Deleuze and Guattari 1987: 276). What this suggests is that there is not a linear causal relationship between girl and woman (there is no smooth, linear evolution from girl to woman) but that, in her molecularity, the woman *is* the girl. The girl, therefore, 'is defined by a relation of movement and rest, speed and slowness . . . She is an abstract line, or line of flight. Thus girls do not belong to an age, group, sex, order or kingdom: they slip in everywhere, between orders, acts, ages, sexes: they produce *n* molecular sexes in the line of flight in relation to the dualism machines they cross right through' (Deleuze and Guattari

1987: 276–277).[22] One point that is worth taking through a reading of this book is Deleuze and Guattari's definition of the girl as molecular, that is as 'not belong[ing] to an age, group, sex, order or kingdom'. The 'girls' at stake here, then, are understood not in terms of 'Being' (a particular age, sex, gender, class, race for example) but in terms of becoming; a becoming which 'slip[s] in everywhere, between orders, acts, ages, sexes'. The girl is 'everywhere'.

Moreover, as I have outlined already, the emphasis of this book is not so much on 'the girls' themselves as the relations between bodies and images. My interest here is in exploring the ways in which *bodies* become through images. Indeed, this focus on bodies also suggests one of the ways in which, whilst drawing on its unsettling of the subject/object distinction, the Deleuzian approach that I take up is distinct from feminist psychoanalytic perspectives. In drawing attention to geography, the significance of Deleuze's work for an understanding of bodies is that notions of symbols, signs and symptoms, the models of depth, and the centrality of sexual difference, are re-worked.[23] In the important book in which she moves from an understanding of bodies from the 'inside-out' to the 'outside-in', Grosz (1994) explains this shift as such:

> the body is not a mode of expression of a psychical interior or a mode of communication or mediation of what is essentially private and incommunicable. Rather, it can be understood as a series of processes, organs, flows, and matter. The body does not hide or reveal an otherwise unrepresented latency or depth but is a set of operational linkages and connections with other things, other bodies. The body is not simply a sign to be read, a symptom to be deciphered, but also a force to be reckoned with.
> (Grosz 1994: 121)

Grosz goes on to explain that, according to a Deleuzian approach to bodies, 'one does not need to read meaning onto bodies and their behaviour; rather one can survey the linkages between bodies of different kinds. Instead of aspiring to a model of signification, which links the subject's psyche to signifying chains, to the order of the signifier, that is, in which the body is the medium of signification, Deleuze sees his project as that of the mapmaker, the drawer of lines and spaces on a flat surface' (Grosz 1994: 121). It is such an understanding of bodies – as force, connections, immanence, rather than as subjects to be understood through signification – that informs this book. This theoretical framework is discussed in more detail in Chapter 1 and, in particular, I return to the concept of immanence, or flatness, in Chapter 2.

Deleuze and Guattari's notion of becoming clearly indicates an alternative way of conceiving the world outside of binary oppositions. It is, partly at least, because of this potential to replace the dichotomy of man/woman, masculine/feminine, subject/object, with flows, processes and becoming, that Deleuze's work is increasing important to feminist theory. Chapter 1 unpacks in more detail the relevance and usefulness of Deleuze's work for an empirical study of the relations between bodies and images, but here it is worth noting that, understood through becoming, bodies and images cannot be separated into discrete units of Being, but rather are always-already fibrous, in relations of change and transformation. Understood as a geography, as situated on a common plane of immanence, the relations between bodies and images can be traced not in terms of hierarchical, deterministic, linear effects (images have negative effects *on* bodies, for example) but as productive, constitutive, transformative; bodies and images are always-already in relations (on the plane of immanence) and it is through these relations that bodies become. The rest of this chapter is an overview of the ways in which the book takes up, develops and explores the relations between the bodies of the girls who participated in my research and images through this Deleuzian notion of becoming. As such, one of the aims of this book is to attempt to shift the focus of feminist empirical work in this field from questions of media cause and effect towards a consideration of how bodies are known, understood, experienced – how bodies *become* – through images.

The becoming of bodies: girls, images, experience

This book is concerned with the becoming of thirteen girls' bodies through images and a number of Deleuzian concepts thread their way through the chapters. These concepts are developed through the empirical material in order to consider how the relations between bodies and images might be reconceived. Chapter 1 introduces the conceptual underpinnings of the book and discusses in detail what Deleuze's philosophy might offer to the empirical study of the relations between girls' bodies and images. The chapter begins by expanding the discussion above to consider becoming as an *ontology* and then moves to outline the key concepts of the book: *assemblage* and *BwOs* (Deleuze and Guattari 1987); *enfolding* and the *actual/virtual* coupling (Deleuze 1993/2003); *relationality*, *intensity* and *affect* (Deleuze 1992). These concepts – which emerge through an understanding of bodies as becomings – are taken up in following chapters and re-worked through the empirical material. My aim in this chapter is to begin to make firm connections between the theory of Deleuze on the one hand and the subject matter of the relations between girls' bodies and images on the other. This chapter therefore does not work on an entirely theoretical or abstract level, but rather ends with an account of some of the shifts involved for feminist empirical work in turning to an ontology of becoming.

Chapter 2 is concerned with laying out the methodology of the book and exploring the links between bodies, images and *experience*. The chapter begins with a brief overview of the centrality of experience to feminist methodology and to feminist work on bodies and embodiment, focusing primarily on some of Donna Haraway's work (1991, 1992, 1997). Pulling through this history of feminist work on experience, I develop a methodology of experience which draws on the concepts of assemblage, relationality, intensity and affect discussed in Chapter 1. I suggest that experience is not what has happened in 'the past' and what remains locked there, but rather that *moments of intense experience* move and become re-experienced as different temporal and spatial moments. Intensity becomes a crucial way to understand both the capacity of moments of experience to move, and the relations between experience and images and I suggest that experience is a methodology of approaching and studying the becoming of bodies through images. My concern in this chapter is also to consider the ways in which the empirical material produced through my research can be interpreted and analysed. Drawing on Deleuze's notion of 'transcendental empiricism' (Deleuze 2001a, 1968/2001b; Deleuze and Parnet 2002) where there is a commitment to tracing and exploring the actualisation of the virtual, I suggest a way of understanding the becoming of bodies where experience seeks to account for the ways in which the world and a body are folded into each other. Furthermore, a transcendental empiricist project demands that 'data' is not fitted into a pre-existent conceptual framework but rather that concepts or 'problems' (Deleuze 1991) are 'created', or 'invented' through the becoming of a thing. I suggest that the concepts introduced in Chapter 1 provide creative ways of thinking through the relations between bodies and images outside of a model of subject(ivity)/object(ivity) or of cause-and-effect.

Chapters 3–6 involve discussions and analyses of the empirical research and in each I address the relations between bodies and images not through the subject/object distinction but instead through different Deleuzian concepts or problems. In Chapter 3 I develop the ontology of becoming through a focus on images; what can images do to the possibilities of the becoming of bodies? The aims of this chapter are, then, to begin to think through how images are understood by the girls and what knowledges and experiences these understandings of images make possible for the girls' bodies. What and how do the girls' bodies become through images? To examine these questions the chapter begins with an exploration of what 'images' meant to the girls and then moves to discuss the girls' experiences of their bodies through (i) photographic images; (ii) mirror images and (iii) media images. I argue that the girls understand these types of images through notions of accuracy, 'truth', movement and possibility in relation to different temporalities. From the analysis of these images, the chapter moves to consider how the girls found it difficult to ultimately determine the boundaries of images. Bodies are not (only) experienced through relations with one type of image but through relations with multiple and diverse images. As such, following the proposal that relations cannot be planned for in advance (Deleuze 1992) but rather are produced through this research and that bodies are the assemblage of multiple and diverse 'organs', the chapter concludes by exploring what other kinds of images might be involved in a body's becoming. This chapter therefore sets up ideas concerning the possibilities, and impossibilities, of images that are explored in the following three chapters.

In opening up what an image might be and in exploring not 'bodies' and 'images' but the relations between them, I argue that bodies become through how they are known, understood and lived as multiple and diverse moments of temporal and spatial experience. Chapter 4 explores the ways in which the girls understood their bodies as assemblages (or BwOs) of *looks* ('how I look') and *selves* ('who I am') through both verbal and visual interview material. The notion of *intensity* is developed here to draw attention to the ways in which, as an immanent assemblage, the organs of a body are not equal or equivalent. Some organs are more intense than others: looks and selves, for example, can be of different intensities and yet can still assemble as aspects of 'a' body. Intensity is therefore a concept to explore the ways in which organs are experienced – how some organs might be prioritised over others, for example – without placing them in a hierarchy or attributing some kind of depth to them. I argue in this chapter that looks and selves are assembled in different ways and that the intensity of looks or selves makes possible, and impossible, particular becomings of a body. I also argue that the concept of intensity provides an alternative way of approaching the question of power. Drawing on the notion that bodies are involved in and constituted through affective relations, this chapter suggests that attending to intensive experiences involves the tracing of the actualisation of the virtual, or, to introduce another 'coupling', the organisation of intensity into extensity. The question of how and why some experiences become intense involves examining the 'wider series' that the girls' bodies become through. Looks, for example, are an extensive social and cultural organisation into which intensive experiences are fitted and made meaningful.

Chapter 5 develops the concepts of *affect* and intensity to consider in more detail how the girls' bodies become through relations with other bodies. Taking up some of the girls' descriptions of being unable to 'fight back' to comments from boys, this chapter explores the becoming of bodies through the gendering of relations of affect. It considers how gender might be understood not as pre-existing the relations through which the girls' bodies become but rather as an extensity which limits and/or expands the possibilities of becoming. The question of power is addressed here, then, in terms of the capacities that gendered relations produce. The focus on affective capacity is intended to draw attention away from 'the girls' (as 'subjects', for example) and, as suggested in previous chapters, pull it instead towards *the relations between bodies*; how are the girls' bodies affective capacities of affecting and being affected? Through considering the gendering of relations of affect, this chapter explores the *ethics* of an affective understanding of bodies. What does a notion of bodies as constituted through affective relations with other bodies do to gender and how might this be understood, in Deleuze's terms, as an ethics?

Chapter 6 moves to examine more explicitly the *temporalities* of the becoming of bodies by focusing on images of their bodies that the girls describe as 'staying'. 'Things that stay', then, refers to the girls' discussions of images of bodies which do not remain in the space and time in which they were first experienced but which rather move and are re-experienced. The chapter draws on the notion of time as *intensive* rather than extensive, and on Bergson's notions of *intuition* (1903/1999) and *duration* (1908/2002) which suggest that the temporality of bodies is to be grasped through the rhythm that is specific to that body. I explore here the girls' experiences of their bodies through comments which have different durational capacities; some comments stay, others do not. This chapter begins by examining what comments stay and introduces Bergson's concepts of intuition and duration in more detail. The chapter then considers the ways in which comments stay through memory and discusses how the girls' explain the endurance of comments through (i) deliberate remembering and (ii) the shocks of memory. Through this discussion of memory, the relations between the past, the present and the future are explored and are argued to be not linear or uni-directional – that is extensive – but intensive. The past does not determine the present and the future but rather the past, present and future assemble in ways which disrupt a model of linear progression.

The Conclusion takes up this focus on temporality, and on the future of feminist theory in particular (Grosz 2000), to think critically about what an ontology of becoming makes possible for a feminist Deleuzian study of the relations between bodies and images. In keeping with the exploratory approach of *The becoming of bodies*, rather than attempting to answer this question in any coherent way, the Conclusion examines what is opened up by understanding bodies and images as relations of becoming. The discussion is focused around a consideration of the centrality of sex, gender and heterosexuality to feminism, and, especially, to feminist research on the bodies of girls and young women. I discuss two key traditions within feminism – social constructionism and social construcitivism (primarily the work of Butler 1990/1999, 1993) – and consider how these approaches could have been inhabited for this research. My suggestion here is that, in accounting for bodies through sex, gender and heterosexuality, feminist social constructionism and feminist social constructivism position bodies as already knowable, that is as knowable through sex, gender and heterosexuality. Moreover, both approaches are underpinned by the dichotomy of structure and agency; in social constructionism through the notion that power is either within the structure which construct agents or within the agent who can resist the structure and in social constructivism through the conception of power as produced through the complex interweaving of structure (or discourse) and agency (or the matter of bodies) in time. This chapter argues that this book has worked through an alternative framework where power is neither presumed in advance and mapped onto bodies (sex, gender and heterosexuality for example) nor understood as located within or produced by the agency of subjects (or objects) or the structure of the social and cultural. Instead, I have highlighted issues of becoming and relationality and have paid attention to the *emergence* of power through relations. My intention in this book, which is made explicit here, is to demonstrate how, from the position of a feminist Deleuzian empirical study, the becoming of bodies are not endlessly open and exciting but rather are made possible, and indeed impossible, through relationality. As such, bodies cannot become what they want but neither is the becoming of bodies to be presumed in advance. Instead, the becoming of bodies is a decidedly *empirical* project which explores bodies in their making and seeks to create appropriate concepts in relation to this making.

Notes

1 Indeed, at least some of the increasing interest in issues of bodies and embodiment across the social sciences, arts and humanities can be explained by the concurrent interest in Deleuze and Deleuzian concepts.
2 Partly, by 'empirical' I mean sociological and cultural research based on interviews, ethnographies or observation. However, empiricism takes on a

particular sense in Deleuze's work and it is also in this sense that I refer to empirical here. See Chapter 2 for a discussion of empiricism.
3 It is also worth noting that in the examples cited here, Deleuze's work has been taken up in relation to science.
4 These references are indicative only and do not cover the wide range of feminist theoretical work that has been and is being carried out on specific images and on visual culture more generally.
5 Placing 'the media' within inverted commas here is intended to draw attention to the problem of grouping images from different mediums – magazines, television, film, popular music for example – under the umbrella term 'the media'. I am grateful to Imogen Tyler for bringing this point to my attention.
6 It should be noted that I discuss two research studies here as examples because they are indicative of the questions and conclusions of much feminist empirical research, and because of the number of methodological features they have in common with each other and with my research (see Chapter 2). See Coleman (2008b) for a discussion of these research studies in relation to some of the empirical material discussed in Chapter 3.
7 Information on the Body Image Summit was from a website (www.cabinet-office.gov.uk/women's-unit/WhatWeDo/BodyImage) which is no longer live. I last accessed this site in the autumn of 2001. For recent British statistics on dieting and eating disorders, see for example the Eating Disorders Association's website: www.b-eat.co.uk/Home, accessed 15th August 2007.
8 For other discussions of the Body Image Summit, see for example Cussins 2001 and Orbach 2003.
9 These disciplines include psychology (Grogan 1999; Grogan and Wainwright 1996; Grogan *et al.* 1996), psycholanalysis (Orbach 2003), educational studies (Willett 2007), anthropology (Nichter 2000), sociology (Frost 2001), cultural studies and media studies (Duke 2000; Durham 1999; Goodman 2002; Goodman and Walsh Childers 2004) and health and medical studies (British Medical Association 2000).
10 This argument could also be reversed with the 'cause' being the subject and the 'effect' being the representations produced, for instance as in some feminist arguments that a media run by and for men will produce certain images of women as opposed to a media run by and for women.
11 In Chapter 1 I consider how, despite his conception of subjects and objects existing in the flesh of the world, Merleau-Ponty's phenomenology maintains the notion of the subject as secure and as moving out into the world of objects.
12 De Beauvoir's argument is that women are trapped in the immanence of objects/objectification, in contrast to the subjective transcendence of men. See also Iris Marion Young (1998) who argues that 'feminine bodily existence remains in immanence, or better, is overlaid with immanence' (1998: 265). I return to this distinction between immanence and transcendence in Chapter 2 through Deleuze's work on empiricism.

13 Indeed, Luce Irigaray (1977) argues that the relationship that women have with images can never be comprehended through formalistic structures of language which she argues are inherently masculine. Utilising Freud's and Lacan's assertions that woman is fundamentally constituted through lack, Irigaray insists on a new feminine language in which woman is neither excluded nor exists outside. Masculine language relies upon the unity of the subject (and the unity of the object that it is distinct from and opposed to), a unity which Irigaray argues is impossible for the feminine which is always at least two, always constituted through being not-masculine/subject. She writes, in ways which raise similar points to Doane and Betterton, 'The masculine can partly look at itself, and describe itself for what it is, whilst the feminine can try to speak through a new language, but cannot describe itself from the outside or in formal terms, except by identifying itself with the masculine, thus losing itself' (1977: 65).

14 There are other notable feminist psychoanalytic perspectives that rework Freud's model of narcissism within film studies that should be noted. See for example Laura Mulvey's (1989) classic feminist 'cinepsychoanalytic' perspective which states that cinematic pleasure is structured around male desire where the male subject is the viewer who looks at female images. Female desire is either absent (lacking) or must work through the masculine subject (see Kennedy 2004: 43–44 for a critique of this position and more generally for a Deleuzian alternative of cinematic pleasure). Jackie Stacey (1994) also critiques masculine psychoanalytic understandings of narcissism by placing narcissistic relations within a social context which she argues draws attention to the significance of *others* in the knowing of one's self. In particular, she emphasises Freud's assertion that the original narcissistic stage is one which both girls and boys must develop through. By arguing that narcissistic relations are a developmental stage for *both* girls and boys, and by insisting on narcissism as a relation between the self and other, rather than the self and self, Stacey argues that there is a kind of dynamism and movement in the narcissistic look and attempts to 'rescue' narcissism from its derogatory or ab-normal meanings for girls and women.

15 Rose's argument here is in the context of the introduction of psychoanalytic concepts into cinema and film theory as part of a deliberate move away from semiology. For Rose, '[s]exuality, and specifically sexual difference, are therefore the terms which need to be centred in the analysis and consideration of cinema if those concepts from psychoanalysis are to have any meaning (we need to ask why this detaching of the concepts has in fact taken place), and if the movement away from a classical semiology is to have its proper effects' (Rose 1986: 218).

16 Indeed, the term 'view from everywhere' that I use here is taken from Haraway's (1991) work on situated knowledges but taken up in a slightly different way. Whereas Haraway's term refers to a masculine notion of objectivity which believes, as it were, that everywhere can be viewed, and

which should be replaced by strong, locatable, partial 'views from somewhere', I am using the term as a condition of the outcontextualisation of an image where an image can be viewed *as if* from everywhere but never wholly, completely or organically.

17 As Carole-Ann Tyler points out in relation to the political ineffectiveness of mimesis, imitation and masquerade, 'No matter how self-consciously we deconstruct identities, no matter how self-consciously we perform our selves, we are still "doing" them. What's more, we demand that the Other recognize both our identities and our "cynicism" about them – the Other is at once our credulous dupe and "the subject who is supposed to know" that we know better' (1994: 222).

18 Here, then, representations are not of the same quality as the representations in, for example, the Body Image Summit. In Taussig's formulation, representations (images) are not inherently and impossibly separate from what is 'real' (bodies) but rather can be merged with and lived.

19 I return to this particular definition of a body as its affective capacities below, and in Chapter 2.

20 It is important to note here that it is *linear* time (History) that Deleuze opposes and not time or temporality in general. Indeed, temporality, understood through Bergson's (1908/2002) notion of duration, is crucial to becoming. See Grosz (1999a) and Chapter 6 here for a more detailed discussion of the temporality of becomings.

21 Cf. Badiou (1994) who argues that Deleuze's concept of the fold understands multiplicity in terms of univocality.

22 The centrality of the little girl to becoming-woman is worked out through the psychoanalytic account of Oedipalisation, where the girl functions both to oppose and define the boy's development. For Deleuze and Guattari, the girl is 'outside' the binary of male and female because 'she is neither a-sexed nor is she ready for sexual reproduction' (Parisi 2004: 198). It is for this reason – that the girl can be understood as escaping the molar order – that Jardine suggests that it is possible to read Deleuze and Guattari's notion of becoming-woman as requiring 'woman' to 'disappear' (see above). Despite resting on Oedipalisation, Parisi suggests, '[t]his principle is not to be considered as a psychoanalytic discourse but as an event: a singular organisation of desire that invests all spheres of organisation of power (biocultural, bio-political, bio-economical)' (2004: 199).

23 See Coleman (2008c) for a discussion of some of the research material of this book through Bergson's method of intuition, where immanence is preferable to signification.

1

From cause and effect to becoming and affect

If the concern of the Introduction was to situate the argument I make in this book, this chapter is an explanation and exploration of its conceptual underpinnings. I begin by drawing on and developing the discussion of Deleuze and Guattari's notion of molecular becoming in relation to other key Deleuzian concepts: assemblage and Bodies with Organs (BwOs); the fold, the virtual and the actual; relationality, affect and intensity. Perhaps unsurprisingly, given their philosophical basis, defining these terms is at first an abstract task. However, as well as detailing these concepts as philosophical terms, in this chapter I aim to demonstrate their productiveness for reconceiving the relations between bodies and images. The chapter therefore moves to suggest becoming not only as a concept but also as an *ontology*. I outline some of the shifts involved in moving feminist empirical research on the relations between bodies and images from a model of subject(ivity)/object(ivity) to an ontology of becoming.

Assemblage and BwOs

For this book, Deleuze's philosophy of becoming needs to be thought in relation to a number of other concepts. In *A Thousand Plateaus*, for example, Deleuze and Guattari (1987) take up the *multiplicity* inherent to molecular becomings, and which replaces the notion of the subject (and object), and conceive bodies not as unified, organic human beings, or subjects, but instead as *assemblages*. Writing in terms of the movement (the longitude and latitude) of a body, Deleuze and Guattari characterise an assemblage as 'precisely this increase in the dimensions of a multiplicity that necessarily changes in nature as it expands its connections' (1987: 8). An assemblage is thus the multiplicity of a body and a moment at which a becoming transforms. This understanding of a body as an assemblage is a critique of the body as a subject on which power is exercised and made to work:

> You will be organised, you will be an organism, you will articulate your body – otherwise you're just depraved. You will be signifier and signified, interpreter and interpreted – otherwise you're just a deviant. You will be a subject, nailed down as one, a subject of the enunciation recoiled into a subject of the statement – otherwise you're just a tramp. (Deleuze and Guattari 1987: 159)

Deleuze and Guattari oppose this body-as-subject because of how certain ways of living are prioritised through a body's organisation as an organism. They take apart this organisation of a body as an organism through their concept of the *Body without Organs*. A BwO is not, perhaps confusingly, a body that has no organs but is rather a body that is not organised as an organic subject, as an organism. They explain the BwO as such:

> We come to the gradual realisation that the BwO is not at all the opposite of the organs. The organs are not its enemies. The enemy is the organism. The BwO is opposed not to the organs but to that organisation called the organism. (1987: 158)

For Deleuze and Guattari, then, the BwO is an attempt to consider how else a body might be understood – how it might become – other than as an organised organism. Indeed, for Deleuze and Guattari, the BwO is an attempt to demonstrate that there is nothing inevitable or inherent about a body being organised as an organism, as a subject. A body instead is an assemblage on a plane of immanence of different organs, different moments, different elements and things. A BwO is a body which resists its organisation according to certain dominant truths, beliefs and plans.[1]

One way in which Deleuze and Guattari understand a BwO as opposing not the organs but the organisation of the organs into an organism is by conceiving a BwO not as a closed, unified entity (a human being or subject) but instead as a body which is always part of something else, always something other than what it is. As they say, 'the BwO is never yours or mine. It is always *a* body' (1987: 164). Deleuze and Guattari argue that a BwO dismantles the body of subjectivity through the connections it makes with other bodies. A BwO is not necessarily a human body but is any body of assembled organs. Connections between BwOs, then, are not necessarily connections between human bodies but can be between any bodies. A body is not an entity but is a *process*, is always *becoming* through the connections it makes with multiple and different bodies. Moreover, as a process a body does not necessarily prioritise the human element in the process of becoming; other elements, other organs, become just as important (or unimportant) as the process becomes.

In dismantling the body of subjectivity, Deleuze and Guattari argue that the subject, and not the body, is made redundant:

> Dismantling the organism has never meant killing yourself, but rather opening the body up to connections that presuppose an entire assemblage, circuits, conjunctions, levels and thresholds, passages and distributions of intensity, and territories and deterritorialisations measured with the craft of a surveyor. (Deleuze and Guattari 1987: 160)

It is this opening up of a body to different connections, different assemblages, different possibilities, which is so productive in Deleuze and Guattari's conception of a BwO. A BwO is not a bounded entity which has relations with other bounded entities. A BwO is not, for example, a subject that has relations with objects or a subject that reaches out towards objects (as phenomenology would suggest – see below). Subjectivity is not necessary to understand a body and is therefore not prioritised. Instead, what the concept of the BwO enables is a consideration of the multiple and diverse ways in which bodies are assembled and through which they become, a consideration that allows a focus on specific bodies while at the same time 'presuppos[ing] an entire assemblage'.

Enfolding and the actualisation of the virtual

One way to understand this focus on a specific body whilst simultaneously presupposing an entire assemblage is through the concept of *the fold* (Deleuze 1993/2003). In his book on Leibniz's philosophy of the Baroque, Deleuze develops the fold through 'the monad':

> As an individual unit each monad includes the whole series: hence it conveys the entire world, but does not express it *without expressing more clearly a small region of the world, a 'subdivision', a borough of the city, a finite sequence.* (2003: 25)

Here, Deleuze offers the monad as 'an individual unit' whose relation with the world is expressive. The monad is an individual unit which 'includes the whole series', that is, the monad is that which expresses a 'finite sequence' of the 'entire world'. With the monad, Deleuze conceives the world in terms of folds. The world is living – as Deleuze states, '[t]he question always entails living in the world' (2003: 137) – but the world is not that which provides the substance for the incorporation of subjects (and objects). That is, the world is not 'a single substance' (2003: 24) but rather the world is infinity expressed in the finite monad. The monad is both part of the world but is also differentiated from the world. It expresses most clearly a particular aspect of the entire world. In Deleuze's terms, this differentiation is through a *fold of expression*. The monad expresses the world of which it is part and the world is expressed in the monad. In this sense, the world is folded in the monad which expresses it.

This does not mean, however, that the world only exists as that which is expressed in a monad. The world is infinite and so there are an infinity of monads that express a 'small region of the world', as Deleuze writes,

> each monad expresses the world, but 'cannot equally well express everything; for otherwise there would be no distinction between souls'. We have seen how Leibniz was able to implement the conciliation on his own account: each monad expresses the world
>
> $$\frac{1}{\infty}$$
>
> but clearly expresses only one particular zone of the world
>
> $$\frac{1}{n}$$
>
> (with each *n* having a specific value). (2003: 130, reference omitted)

That the infinity of the world is expressed in each monad does not account for the entirety of the world. Indeed, through the fold, Deleuze offers in addition to infinity, a notion of *virtuality*:

> In all cases it is true that the world only exists folded in the monads that express it, and is only unfolded virtually as the common horizon of all monads, or as the outer law of the series they include. (2003: 74)

This shift from infinity to virtuality can be understood through the discussion above of the gap between subject and object which is disappeared through molecular becoming. For Deleuze, 'folds replace holes' (2003: 27). That is, 'folds' are not the attempt to erase gaps but rather folds are the continual rhythms through which the virtuality of the world is expressed. As a rhythm, there are no gaps. And, as a rhythm, the world is not the one all-encompassing substance. Deleuze states that Leibniz recognises,

> the determination of a being-for-the-world instead of a being-in-the-world. The condition of closure holds for the infinite opening of the finite: it 'finitely represents infinity'. It gives the world the possibility of ...[2] beginning over and again in each monad. The world must be placed in the subject in order that the subject can be for the world. This is the

torsion that constitutes the fold of the world and of the soul. And it is what gives to expression its fundamental character: the soul is the expression of the world (actuality), but because the world is what the soul expresses (virtually). (2003: 26)

Through the concept of the fold Deleuze argues that the world exists as a virtuality made actual through monadic expression. For Deleuze here, the world is an infinite virtual which is expressed in the finite actuality of the monad. The virtual 'holds for the infinite opening of the finite'. In being-for-the-world, the monad makes finite the infinite but in so doing opens this finite to infinity. The world is a virtual unfolding which begins again in each monad. *The monad actualises the virtual*:

> The world or the hazy line of the world resembles a virtuality that is actualised in the monads. The world has actuality only in monads, which each convey it from each monad's own point of view and on its surface. (2003: 104)

The world is the virtual which, through its folding in (or as) the monad, is actualised. However, Deleuze goes on to state that the virtual/actual 'coupling . . . does not resolve the problem' of the fold:

> There exists a second, very different coupling of the possible-real. For example, God chooses one world among an infinity of possible worlds: the other worlds also have their actuality in monads that are conveying them. . . . Therefore there exists an actual that remains possible, and that is not forcibly real. The actual does not constitute the real; it must itself be realised, and the problem of the world's realisation is added to that of its actualisation. God is 'existentifying', but the Existentifying is, on the one hand, Actualising and, on the other, Realising. (2003: 104)

Here, then, Deleuze proposes the 'coupling' of the possible/real in addition to the virtual/actual. The understanding of the virtual/actual in relation to the possible/real is not straightforward. That is, the virtual/actual cannot be mapped onto the possible/real. On the contrary, the possible and the real are worlds that are distinct from, even if they exist in relation to, virtual and actual worlds. According to Deleuze here, the virtual is the world that God has chosen. Thus, despite the world's infinity, the virtual is finite; it has been chosen 'among an infinity of possible worlds'. The possible is therefore the other worlds that God has not chosen. Deleuze argues that these possible worlds 'have their actuality in monads that are conveying them'. Monads, then, actualise both the virtual and the possible, or, better, monads *have the capacity of* actualising both the virtual and the possible. This emphasis on the capacities of monads is because '[t]he actual does not constitute the real; it must itself be realised'. Put another way, 'there exists an actual that remains possible, and that is not forcibly real'. Monads, then, can actualise the virtual and the possible but there can be an actuality in the monad that is not realised; the monad cannot realise. So, what can realise?

The beginnings of the answer to this question are offered by Deleuze in the following quotation:

> The world is a virtuality that is actualised in monads or souls, but also a possibility that must be realised in matter or in bodies. (2003: 104)

Here, distinctions are made not only between virtuality and possibility on the one hand and actualisation and realisation on the other but also between *monads or souls* and *matter or bodies*. Monads or souls actualise virtualities and matter or bodies realise possibilities.[3] But why is this so? In his development of the concept of the fold, Deleuze identifies 'two floors' which, despite the distinctions between them being unable to hold (2003: 119), differentiate the fold in two ways. On the upper floor are monads and souls which are 'like private apartments that are not connected to one another, that do not act upon each other, and that are variants of the same interior decorator'. And, '[o]n the floor below we find the material universe of bodies, like that of Commoners who are forever expressing movement, propagating waves, and acting upon each other' (2003: 100)[4]. The reason that Deleuze provides for the ability of matter and bodies to realise possibilities is their movement, propagation and affects on each other. This is a *relational activity* of matter and bodies, rather than a singular unity that is characteristic of monads and souls, that Deleuze explains in terms of phenomena.

> The world is a virtuality that is actualised in monads or souls, but also a possibility that must be realised in matter or in bodies. It is curious, we might argue, that the question of reality is posed in respect to bodies that, even if they are not appearances, are simple phenomena. Yet what happens to be a phenomenon . . .[5] in the strict sense is what is perceived in the monad. When, by virtue of the resemblance of the perceived to something = x, we ask if bodies might not be acting upon each other in ways such that our inner perceptions correspond to them, we are thus asking the question of a realisation of the phenomenon or, better, of a 'realising' of the perceived, that is, *of the transformation of the currently perceived world into an objectively real world*, into an objective Nature. (2003: 104–105, my emphasis)

According to this quotation, perception, what is perceived in the monad (or soul), is realised in bodies through the ways in which 'they act [. . .] upon each other'. That is, bodies transform a 'currently perceived world into an objectively real world'. Bodies then, are both 'simple phenomena' and what transform phenomena. In this sense, Deleuze's understanding of bodies is not so much a definition of bodies as a conception of a body's capacities, of what a body can do. He goes on to state that: *'It is not the body that realises, but it is in the body that something is realised, through which the body itself becomes real or substantial'* (2003: 105, my emphasis). The body does therefore not exist prior to that which it realises. That is, the body does not exist prior to its realisation of the world. Conceived through the fold, the body is that which exists as an expressive relation to the world, as that which makes the world real but in so doing does not foreclose the possibilities of the world, of realising a different world or of realising the world differently.

Phenomenology, flesh and the fold

Deleuze's concept of the fold is clearly difficult. To unpack it in more detail, and to demonstrate further how the relations between bodies and images are approached through a feminist Deleuzian perspective, a comparison with phenomenology's notion of the flesh is helpful. Merleau-Ponty's (1962/1989, 1968/1997) phenomenology is an attempt to theorise the relations between the subject and the world through the prioritisation of the body and, consequently, to displace the Cartesian logic of the mind over the body. As Elizabeth Grosz (1994) puts it, the body is 'the condition through which I am able to have a relation to objects' (1994: 86). In this sense, as with feminist theories of spectatorship, Merleau-Ponty disrupts the clear distinction between subject and object. In particular, Merleau-Ponty's prioritisation of the body sees the body not as an isolated subject but as defined through its relations with objects. Discussing the visible and sight, for example, Merleau-Ponty (1968/1997) describes the body as that which 'unites us directly with the things through its own ontogenesis' (1997: 136):

> What there is then are not things first identical with themselves, which would then offer themselves to the seer, nor is there a seer who is first empty and who, afterward, would open himself to them – but something to which we could not be closer than by palpating it with our look, things we could not dream of seeing 'all naked' because the gaze itself envelops them, clothes them with its own flesh. (Merleau-Ponty 1997: 131)

Seeing, then, for Merleau-Ponty, designates a process in which things are not separate from the seer; things are what are seen by the seer, what are 'enveloped' with flesh, and the seer him- or herself is what is seen by things. The body is both the body of a subject and an object for other bodies that surround it. The subject/object relationship is therefore not causal but inherently meaningful, that is the relationship between the subject and object is not uni-directional with the subject simply defining the object for it is the subject's situation in relation to the object that defines the object and that also defines the subject.

Indeed, in her discussion of a phenomenological conception of the body, Grosz draws attention to this positioning of objects in identifying the *spatiality* of the subject/object relationship where the body both occupies space and is defined by its bodily situation in relation to objects as they exist in space. This 'space' in which the body and object exist is known and understood through this bodily situation in space where the object does not have to be 'whole' or 'real'. As Grosz puts it:

> It is as an embodied subject that the subject occupies a perspective on objects. Its perspective represents the position within space where it locates itself. Its perspective dictates that its modes of access to objects are always partial and fragmentary, interacting with objects but never grasping them in their independent and complete materiality. (1994: 90–91)

The body in phenomenology is therefore a 'being-in-the-world', an immediate spatial existence where 'being' and 'meaning' are always inextricably bound up with each other (Eagleton 1983: 55).[6] The body's spatio-temporal positioning in the world is an immediate and intimate experience which conditions both the body and the world. This immediacy, this inability to distinguish between the body and the world it inhabits, is developed by Merleau-Ponty in his concept of the *flesh*. The concept of flesh

> is not matter, is not mind, is not substance. To designate it, we should need the old term 'element', in the sense that it was used to speak water, air, earth, and fire, that is, in the sense of a *general thing*, midway between the spatio-temporal individual and the idea, a sort of incarnate principle that brings a style of being wherever there is a fragment of being. The flesh is in this sense an 'element' of Being. Not a fact or a sum of facts, and yet adherent to *location* and to the *now*. (Merleau-Ponty 1997: 139–140)

Merleau-Ponty's 'flesh' is thus what he terms an 'ultimate notion' (1997: 140), not another compound nor simply the material of the body but as thinkable in itself. This is an ontology of flesh: the flesh does not just refer to the material of the body, but to the world in general; 'the body belongs to the order of things as the world is universal flesh' (Merleau-Ponty 1997: 137). As such, Merleau-Ponty cannot make any clear distinction between the subject and the world as the world is of the same flesh as the body and is therefore also a living thing; '[w]here are we to put the limit between the body and the world, since the world is flesh?' (Merleau-Ponty 1997: 138).

Kathryn Vasseleu (1998) describes this concept of flesh as

> Merleau-Ponty's term for the prototypical structure of all subject-object relations. In every instance of this relation, flesh defines a position which is both subjective (a subjective reality) and objective (objectifiable for others), and also simultaneously as subjectivity which is internally divergent within itself. In other words, flesh expresses the inscription of difference within the same. (1998: 26)

In this sense, the flesh is understood not as a foundation nor as foundational but as the interrelations of the outside and the inside, as a single thing folded back onto itself, as intermingling and integration. The flesh has the capacity of reversibility, a 'double sensation' which allows at once 'the position of both subject and object, the position of phenomenal and objectual body' (Grosz 1994: 100). Vasseleu points to Merleau-Ponty's example of the way in which one of a subject's hands touches the other so that both are at once touching and touched, subject and object of perception. Through this example, Vasseleu explains, '[t]he body is therefore a hinge; an articulation of the world; an *entre-deux*. Alternatively, it is a fold – never reducible to the difference in which it is created' (Vasseleu 1998: 27). Vasseleu argues that this reversibility, this double sensation or fold of the oneness of flesh depends upon the multiple, or the two as opposed to the singular. This idea of the two is not a binary opposition of one or the other but necessarily involves both. That said, it is not the *combination* of the two but the *in-between* of the two as in the two eyes, the two ears, the two lips (Irigaray 1977); '[i]t is not I who feel or see, but feeling and seeing are an anonymous sensibility which inhabits us both. The concordant operations of the other's body and my own are one intercorporeal being, which supports a perceptual faith in the common world' (Vasseleu 1998: 31).[7]

With Merleau-Ponty's phenomenology there appears to be a difference between subjects and objects which is left implicit. That is, it is the body that perceives and that has the capacity to move towards an object that pre-exists it. Despite being of the same stuff, there is, then, a distinction between subjects and objects.[8] In Grosz's terms, phenomenology works from the inside-out, the reversibility of the flesh is asymmetrical as it is '[t]he subject [who] brings to the world the capacity to turn the world back on itself, to fold over itself and the world, introducing that fold in which the subject is positioned as a perceiving, perspectival mobility' (Grosz 1994: 102). Although the notion of the flesh seeks to incorporate the 'double sensation' of interiority and exteriority (of feeling and of being felt for example), ultimately it is the body which orientates and positions itself in relation to objects. It is the body of the subject that has the power to grasp, albeit partially, and to finally turn away from or expel the object from its field of perception. The body, rather anything else, places the subject in the world. As Merleau-Ponty suggests, 'if the body is a thing among things, it is so in a stronger and deeper sense than they: in the sense that, we said, it is *of them*, and this means that it detaches itself upon them, and, accordingly, detaches itself from them' (Merleau-Ponty 1997: 137). As such, despite the intentions to dispel the mind/body dualism by locating transcendence in the lived body, the dualism of subject/object persists. Moreover, this difference between subjects and objects is hierarchised; Merleau-Ponty does not simply recognise the subject and object as different but *prioritises* the subject over the object by only awarding subjects the capacity of positionality, perception and movement. His concept of vision, for example, is uni-directional as it is subjects rather than objects that determine and define visibility. Any notion of the dynamism of the relationship between the body and the object is thus inequitable as it is only the body which has the ability of activity and animation.

Significantly for this discussion, Merleau-Ponty's phenomenology can also be critiqued from the position of Deleuze's concept of the fold, where the fold is a particularly intense expression of the world. Interestingly, in their explanations of phenomenology, both Vasseleu and Grosz describe the flesh in terms of folds and folding. Vasseleu explains the body as 'a hinge . . . a fold – never reducible to the difference in which it is created' (see above) and Grosz accounts for the subject as having 'the capacity to turn the world back on itself, to fold over itself and the world, introducing that fold in which the subject is positioned as a perceiving, perspectival mobility' (see above). The concept of the fold which Deleuze develops differs from both of these descriptions of the phenomenological fold. For Grosz, the phenomenological fold accounts for the (albeit asymmetrical) reversibility of the subject's capacity of 'doubleness', of the human body 'as a "being of two leaves", one of which is an object in a world of other objects, the other of which is a perceiver of these objects. It is doubled back on itself' (1994: 102). Vasseleu's comments on the body as a fold also deal with this 'being of two leaves':

> Living flesh is the modality of the body inscribed within sensibility. This body is not an internal or external projection, but *a sensibility inextricable from its inhabiting of a world . . . Through sensibility (the double touching) my body inserts itself between the two leaves of the world, which itself is inserted between the leaves of my body.* (Vasseleu 1998: 27, my emphasis)

According to Vasseleu here, the flesh is a living substance which incorporates the body into the world but which is capable of differentiating itself into 'two leaves'. It is between these two leaves that, through sensibility, the body 'inserts itself'. Leaving aside the problem of the primacy of the subject over the object, discussed above, the issue of difference is raised in the notion of doubleness, of two leaves. For Vasseleu, as 'a fold' which is 'never reducible to the difference in which it is created', the body is an *insertion* into the living flesh of the world. The body is thus both part of the flesh of the world but it is part of this flesh through its insertion into it. The body exists in some way external or prior to the flesh of the world into which it inserts itself. The body is thus at once part of flesh but also differentiated from it.

While this specificity of a body, that is its function as in some way differentiated from the world, is not necessarily opposed to Deleuze's notion of the fold, what is problematic about the phenomenological fold is the understanding of flesh and of bodies differentiated through *insertion*. One consequence of Deleuze's understanding of the world is that differentiation does not involve gaps; the folding of the body and the world is as a rhythm. The notion of 'gaps' is complicated because phenomenological flesh attempts to negate gaps by conceiving all of the world and all of the things in the world as of the same substance. Things (subjects and objects) are differentiated through the 'folding' of 'two leaves', through a double sensitivity. The two leaves are simultaneously a sameness and difference, an 'insertion' into flesh. Merleau-Ponty's 'fold' is the incorporation of gaps (at least for masculine subjects).

Relationality, intensity and affect

The lack of gap between body and world that Deleuze's concept of the fold suggests does not imply that there is no *difference* between different bodies and between bodies and the world. Deleuze's concept rejects the notions of insertion and of a single substance and instead proposes a plane of immanence on and through which different elements assemble, enfold and become. In this section I consider how *affective relations* are key to a Deleuzian approach and to the way in which enfolding does not ignore difference. As I suggested in the Introduction, what Deleuze's work draws attention to is the relations through which things (bodies and images for example) are constituted. In his essay on ethology (1992), or what he terms the 'affective capacity' of things, Deleuze argues that it is through relations that things become. Deleuze begins the essay with Spinoza's definition of a body as (i) 'composed of an infinite number of particles . . . [of] relations of motion and rest, speed and slowness' and (ii) as affective; 'a body affects other bodies, or is affected by other bodies' (1992: 625). Taking up these points, Deleuze develops an explanation of ethology as 'first of all the study of the relations of speed and slowness, or the capacities for affecting and being affected that characterise each thing' (1992: 627).[9] Deleuze argues that if bodies are understood in terms of their capacity to affect and be affected, 'many things change. You will define an animal or a human being not by its form, its organs and its functions and not as a subject either; you will define it by the affects of which it is capable' (1992: 626).

What is important here – and what is picked up in Chapter 2 – is that a body's capabilities cannot be known before or outside of its relations; *it is the relations of affect that produce a body's capacities.* As Deleuze says, 'you do not know beforehand what good or bad you are capable of; you do not know beforehand what a body or a mind can do, in a given encounter, a given arrangement, a given combination' (1992: 627). If this is the case, if we do not know beforehand what a body, or an image, can do, the question arises of how we know, in advance of the relations through which they become, that bodies are subjects and images are objects. Moreover, in understanding a body in terms of what it is capable of doing, where these capabilities are produced through the relations that that body is involved in, it becomes difficult, if not impossible, to determine where a body ends and an image begins. If a body becomes through its relations with images, where is the limit between the body and the image? What is image and what is body? In asking these questions the emphasis of an exploration of the relations between bodies and images falls not so much on the bodies and images themselves as on the relations. According to Deleuze's affective approach, what models of subject(ivity)/and object(ivity) conceive as gaps are instead conceived as relations; *gaps are reworked as relations.*

In order to explore further the centrality of relations to affect, it is necessary to consider the ways in which the concept of affect has recently become important to many social and cultural theorists working from a range of disciplinary and interdisciplinary perspectives. In the rest of this section I focus only on the work of four contemporary theorists of affect; Eve Sedgwick (2003), Brian Massumi (2002a, 2002b), Sara Ahmed (2001, 2004) and Vinciane Despret (2004). It is not my intention to give an overview of what affect 'means', nor to trace the different trajectories of the concepts that these theorists work with, either from Deleuze or from each other. Rather, my aim here is to explore the potential of the connections that might be made between affect, relationality and bodies and, perhaps more importantly, to consider what these relations might do to the possible ways in which (women's) bodies and images have been understood.

In a discussion of psychologist Silvan Tomkins' definition of affect as distinct from drives, Eve Sedgwick (2003) explains that both the affect and drives systems are embodied and interconnected with cognitive processes and that the distinction between them is about specificity and generality. 'The difference . . . is between more specific and more general, more and less constrained: between biologically based systems that are less and more capable of generating complexity or degrees of freedom' (2003: 18). Sedgwick explains that Tomkins conceived drives as having narrowly constrained aims; for example, a drive only satisfies its own aim (breathing does not satisfy hunger), and this aim is constrained by time (a human must breathe within the next minute to live) and by its 'range of objects . . .: only a tiny subset of gases satisfy my need to breathe' (2003: 18). Unlike drives which must satisfy their constrained time and object aim, affects have a greater freedom. An affect like anger, for example, can last for a moment or for a lifetime and can be attached to any object without having a necessary or self-evident link: 'Affects can be, and are, attached to things, people, ideas, sensations, relations, activities, ambitions, institutions, and any number of things, including other affects. Thus one can be excited by anger, disgusted by shame, or surprised by joy' (Sedgwick 2003: 19).

In terms of this book, the distinction between drive and affect systems can be thought in relation to the model of cause-and-effect that is critiqued above. A drive has a cause that aims towards an effect; I am hungry, I must eat. The aim traverses, but maintains, the gap between cause and effect as a necessary and inevitable link; being hungry necessarily results in eating. An affect, however, does not rely on or work through a necessary link that may or may not fill a gap; an affect can attach itself to – can affect and be affected by – any object. The 'gap' between cause-and-effect is not necessary, inevitable or logical. Instead, the gap between cause-and-effect *is* affect, is the space and time of possibility where things can affect and be affected. *What affect does, then, is produce 'gaps' as relations.* Whereas the model of cause-and-effect begins from things which pre-exist relations, so that one thing effects another thing (cause to effect), affect produces and is produced in *relations*. Relations between things – affect – might therefore be non-linear, coincidental, resonant, rather than straight-forward consistency or predictable correlation.

Brian Massumi (2002a) explores this understanding of affect as the potentially non-predictable and non-constrained relations between things through a psychological study with children and three versions of a short film. After watching the film the children's memory was tested and they were asked to 'rate the version they saw on a scale of "pleasantness"' (2002a: 23). Briefly, the study found that the children were aroused by, or most happy with, the saddest film; there was no logical or rational connection between a cause (the film) and an effect (the children's reaction). Instead, as Massumi argues, 'the primacy of the affective is marked by a gap between *content* and *effect*: it would appear that the strength or duration of an image's effect is not logical or connected to the content in any straightforward way' (2002a: 24).[10] Instead, affect is the relations of possibility between two apparently unconnected things, between a content and an effect. Sadness can be happy. Affect is attached to but also free from two, or more, points. It is a relation between points but a relation which is not determined by, or known in advance to, these points. In an interview about hope, Massumi (2002b) describes the uncertainty and vagueness of affect not as states of pessimism or paralysis but as 'empowering'; 'It gives you the feeling that there is always an opening to experiment, to try and see. This brings a sense of potential to the situation' (2002b: 212).

The sense of potential, openness, experimentation is a consequence of how affect is not directed or determined towards a goal but is unbounded as the present, as *this* moment. Affect is the 'margin of manoeuvrability, the "where we might be able to go and what we might be able to do" in every present situation. . . . It's . . . like being right where you are – more *intensely*' (Massumi 2002b: 212). Massumi highlights the unknown quality of the present and its potential disconnection from other, past and future, temporalities and spatialities:

> Intensity would seem to be associated with nonlinear processes: resonation and feedback that momentarily suspend the linear progress of the narrative present from past to future. Intensity is qualifiable as an emotional state, and that state is static – temporal and narrative noise. It is a state of suspense, potentially of disruption. It is like a temporal sink, a hole in time, as we conceive of it and narrativise it. It is not exactly passivity because it is filled with motion, resonation. And yet it is not yet activity, because the emotion is not the kind that can be directed (if only symbolically) toward practical ends in a world of constituted objects and aims (if only on screen). Of course, the qualification of an emotion is quite often, in other contexts, itself a narrative element that moves the action ahead, taking its place in socially recognised lines of action and reaction. But to the extent that it is, it is not in resonance with intensity. It resonates to the exact degree to which it is in excess of any narrative or functional line. (Massumi 2002a: 26)

Massumi makes links between affect as intensity and narratives but argues that affect as intensity *exceeds* narrative. Narratives organise intensity into 'socially recognised' temporalities and spatialities that constrict nonlinear resonance, motion, excess, into lines of action and reaction, cause or content and effect. I return to the concept of intensity in Chapter 2.

Affect as intensity also exceeds emotion, partly because of how emotion is organised as narrative, but also because of how emotion 'is a subjective content, the sociolinguistic fixing of the quality of an experience which is from that point onward defined as personal. Emotion is qualified intensity. . . . It is intensity owned and recognised' (Massumi 2002a: 28). Affect cannot be qualified, owned or recognised, it is not a possession. Affect is not a subject or object, nor does it belong to a subject or object but is the relations of possibility, the affective capacities between different things. Affect is not *not* emotion but affect is not *just* emotion. Massumi writes:

> Affect is autonomous to the degree to which it escapes confinement in the particular body whose vitality, or potential for interaction, it is. Formed, qualified, situated perceptions and cognitions fulfilling functions of actual connection or blockage are the capture or closure of affect. Emotion is the most intense (most contracted) expression of that *capture* – and of the fact that something has always and again escaped. Something remains unactualised, inseparable from but unassimilable to any *particular*, functionally anchored perspective. That is why all emotion is more or less disorientating, and why it is classically described as being outside of oneself, at the very point at which one is most intimately and unshareably in contact with oneself and one's vitality. (2002a: 35)

Affect is, or can be, emotion but affect exceeds and escapes emotion; according to Massumi, '[a]n emotion or feeling is a *recognised* affect, an identified intensity as reinjected into stimulus-response paths, into action-reaction circuits of infolding and externalisation – in short, into subject-object relations. Emotion is a contamination of empirical space by affect' (2002a: 61, my emphasis).

Massumi's argument is that emotions are the (socially) organised recognition of affect; what remains ambiguous or cannot be ordered as emotion – what exceeds emotion as recognisable – is affect. In redefining emotions in terms of what they do rather than what they are, Sara Ahmed (2001; 2004) explores *how* emotions become to be recognised. Ahmed begins from a similar position as Massumi in being interested not in subjects and objects but in the relations and movements between them. She defines emotions as 'not simply "within" or "without"' (2001: 10) but as emerging, or 'surfacing' interiorities and exteriorities:

> Emotions [...] do not simply reside positively in the body of the individual or in the social. It is through emotions, that bodies come to surface or appear in the first place. Indeed, I would argue that what characterises emotionality is precisely this lack of positive residence; the way emotions circulate without inhabiting any particular object, body or sign, although one effect of the circulation might be that certain objects, bodies or signs are endowed with emotional meaning and value. Another way of putting this is to think of emotionality as an affective economy: emotions involve relations of displacement and difference, whereby what is 'moved' and what 'moves' is precisely the rippling effect of intensification. (Ahmed 2001: 13)[11]

Emotionality understood as an 'affective economy' is concerned with how emotions circulate and create distinctions, surfaces and borders. Ahmed argues that emotions, which are free in the sense that they move and do not reside or belong in any body, object or sign, become 'stuck' or 'attached to' – recognisable as – particular bodies, objects and signs. Ahmed does not conceive emotions as automatically or inevitably recognised but as socially organised and attached through relations of power. Asking the question 'what sticks?' (2004: 11), Ahmed is interested in how emotions are at once movement and freedom and attachment and sticking:

> what attaches us, what connects us to this or that place, is also what moves us, or what affects us such that we are no longer in the same place. Hence movement does not cut the body off from the 'where' of its inhabitance, but connects bodies to other bodies – indeed, attachment takes place through movement, through being moved by the proximity of others. The relationship between movement and attachment is contingent, and this suggests that movement may affect different others differently: indeed ... emotions may involve 'being moved' for some precisely by 'fixing' others as 'having' certain characteristics. (2001: 11–12)

In understanding emotion as both movement and attachment, circulation and sticking, Ahmed points to how bodies, despite their differences, are intimately connected – bodies affect and are affected by other bodies. Emotions circulate not freely or straightforwardly but through affect by making recognisable certain bodies through emotion. Movement for some bodies is fixing for other bodies (see Chapter 5). Conceiving emotions as affective economies means for Ahmed that the excess of emotion is not necessarily affect. Ahmed does not understand emotion as just the recognisable aspect of affect, as Massumi's argument implies. Emotion is for Ahmed not just *part of* affect but *is* affect. Emotion itself can exceed its recognisability, for example the possibility of an emotion not sticking and surfacing a body or object might be its excess, its un-recognisability.[12] According to this understanding, there is no clearcut distinction between emotion and affect; emotion is affect but affect does not exceed emotion.

Although Massumi and Ahmed have different conceptions of affect and emotion, both are interested in the ways in which the vagueness of relations between things might be made meaningful or recognisable. However, their projects are not to define 'what' emotions are but instead to explore 'how' emotions work. This is what Vinciane Despret (2004) aims to do in her analysis of relations of affect between human and animal bodies. Discussing William James' theory of emotions, Despret understands James' theory not in terms of a definition of emotions but as an exploration of what emotions do. James' aim 'was not to define what is felt but what makes us feel, it was not to define a passive affected being, but rather a being that both produces emotions and is produced by them. *An emotion is not what is felt but what makes us feel*' (Despret 2004: 127, my emphasis). Accordingly, what makes us feel – an emotion – changes and, as noted above, cannot be defined in terms of cause-and-effect. As Sedgwick argues, affects can be attached to and produced through any thing so, as Massumi suggests, sadness can be happy. Despret writes,

> Emotional experience, in other words, is an experience that makes us hesitate. Each of the events that composes it may not be firmly divided up, may hardly be defined as unequivocal cause or unequivocal effect, may not be definitively said to belong to the world, the body or the mind. Each of the emotional experiences can remain equivocal: they appear ambiguous. (2004: 126)

Bodies (things) affect other bodies through ambiguous, vague, and perhaps illogical relations where it is not clear what affects what; 'should we say that the wine made us happy or that we made the wine joyous?' (Despret 2004: 127).

An ontology of becoming

In introducing and discussing these concepts, it is clear that 'becoming' is both a concept itself *and* a framework in which these concepts make sense and connect. That is, becoming in this book is both a concept and an *ontology*. Understanding bodies as becomings is not only conceptual but also ontological; bodies *are* becomings. In this sense, the ontology of being, upon which the subject(ivity)/object(ivity) distinction rests is replaced, or exploded, with the ontology of becoming; bodies and images, for instance, are not independent, bounded beings but are, and are constituted through, their transformative relationality. So far, in exploring the concepts of assemblage and BwOs, the fold, the actual and the virtual, relationality, affect and intensity, my discussion has been abstract. In the rest of the chapter I want to outline some of the important shifts that are made in moving feminist empirical research on the relations between bodies and images from a model of subject(ivity)/object(ivity) to an ontology of becoming. Some of these have been hinted at above, but this section draws them together to consider the consequences for feminist empirical research on the relations between bodies and images in shifting to an ontology of becoming. What is at stake here, I suggest, is a move away from asking, 'what is a body?' to exploring what a body might *do*, that is what a body *might become*.

A first consequence to note in Deleuze's shift from a philosophy of being to becoming is that subjects and objects become replaced with *bodies*. In a Deleuzian sense, 'bodies' are not organic entities that are made of a distinctive stuff but rather are molecular processes of becoming. In conceiving the world in terms of molecular becomings, one of Deleuze's aims is to debunk the subject from its privileged position and therefore to discard the binary of subject/object. Deleuzian bodies are assemblages of connections of different things. Their molecular nature means that these 'things' can be, potentially, any things. That is, 'bodies' do not necessarily mean, or take the form of, *human* bodies.[13] Instead bodies are capacities, are transforming and transformational, are becoming. Multiplicity and difference are key to Deleuze's concept of becoming and it is through the connections between multiple and different things that bodies must be understood. For example, a Deleuzian account would understand bodies not as a bounded subject that is separate from images but rather would see the connections between humans and images as *constituting* a body. Models which map fluid and dynamic becomings on to static and closed systems of being (subject/object for example) risk ignoring the ways in which bodies are constituted and, crucially, could be constituted differently. This notion not of what a body is but of what a body becomes implies that bodies and images are not inherently distinctive nor in need of distinction. As such, according to a Deleuzian approach, bodies and images cannot be mapped onto a pre-existing distinction between subjects and objects; a body is not a subject and an image is not an object. Instead, bodies and images can assemble and become through each other. In terms of the discussion here and in the Introduction, for Deleuze then, the 'gap' between things becomes displaced (capable of being) infilled, outcontexualised, disappeared. If subjects and objects become as and through the molecularity of each other, models of spectatorship which work outwards from a subject to an object and notions of narcissism which operate through a gap are difficult to sustain.

In highlighting how a body becomes through its inter-connections with multiple and diverse things, Deleuze is arguing that a body is a relational becoming, is 'never separable from its relations with the world' (Deleuze 1992: 628). Bodies are processes which become through their relations and, as such, there are not relations between pre-existent entities (bodies and images, subjects and objects) but rather entities are constituted through their relations. A body is not a human subject who has relations *with* images, then, but rather a body *is* the relation between what philosophy has conventionally called a human subject and images. A second shift introduced by a Deleuzian perspective on the relations between bodies and images is that it is the *relations*, rather than the bodies and images themselves, that are brought into focus. A Deleuzian account of bodies must attend to how that body becomes through its relations. This would suggest that what is at stake in such research is the ways in which relations constitute bodies and images and the ways in which it is through relations that bodies and images become. This might mean that instead of focusing on what are "good" and "bad" images, or what are dissatisfying or unhealthy bodies, research would focus on what the relations between bodies and images limit or extend. For example, what knowledges, understandings and experiences of bodies are produced through images? How do relations constitute particular kinds of bodies and images?

Shifting to examine relations as extending and limiting particular becomings of bodies raises a third implication for feminist research on bodies and images. Deleuze argues that relations create certain *affects*: 'a body affects other bodies, and is affected by other bodies' (1992: 625). According to this Deleuzian perspective, it is not that images have negative *effects on* the vulnerable bodies of girls as there are no clear lines of division between them. Instead, the relations between bodies and images produce particular affects, some of which – like 'feeling bad' – might be particularly intense and limiting to the becoming of bodies. This is, I would suggest, a radically different understanding of the relations between bodies and images from the model of 'media effects', not only because of how bodies and images are understood as in constitutive relations but also because studying affective relations involves new questions for feminist research. Considering what these new questions might be, and how feminist research might study them, is a concern of the rest of the book, which is addressed most explicitly in terms of methodology in Chapter 2.

The concept of the fold, which for Deleuze in part refers to the actualisation of the virtual, constitutes a fourth shift for feminist empirical research. 'The fold' designates a relation between the world and things, between 'the entire series' and an intense expression of it. As such, attention is drawn both to specificity and generality. Drawing on the discussions above, relations are specific to a particular assemblage; relations emerge in and through a specific encounter. Such relationality can be understood as the actualisation of the virtual, where the virtual refers to the wider series of relations which become actualised as the specific relations of an assemblage. Deleuze's notion of the virtual is of a finite wider series; that is, while the possible refers to an infinite series which is realised – everything is possible and can be made real – the virtual refers to a series which is, in some way, structured and determined. Not everything constitutes the virtual and not everything can be actualised, 'there exists an actual that remains possible, and that is not forcibly real' (Deleuze 2003: 104). Deleuze's distinction between the possible/real and the virtual/actual raises a problem for a consideration of the bodies of the girls involved in this research. The possible is for Deleuze what may be realised through bodies, while the virtual is what may be actualised in monads (or souls). However, in Chapters 3–6, I hope to demonstrate that in relation to the girls' bodies, all possibilities are not realisable but rather the possibilities of becoming are limited and fixed in particular ways, for example, in Chapter 6, through past experiences. In this sense, the girls' bodies might better be understood as actualisations of the virtual, where the virtual is a finite set of possibilities. This is why in following chapters I discuss the actualisation of the virtual, rather than the realisation of the possible. In other words, here Deleuze's concepts, in relation to empirical material, are put to work and re-invented.

Examining questions of specificity and generality of the becoming of bodies through the concept of the fold designates a shift from a framework of structure/agency to the virtual and actual. While the 'coupling' of the virtual and actual cannot be mapped directly onto the dichotomy of structure/agency, as a field of finite possibilities the virtual accounts for the limitations or restrictions of what becomes actual. In this sense, the virtual is a limit of what a body might become, it structures the possibilities of actualisation. The virtual/actual coupling therefore engages with but pushes the key sociological dichotomy of structure/agency; it considers the relationship between generality and specificity but does this through an ontology of process and becoming. This shift for feminist empirical research is explored in more detail in Chapters 5 and 6, but what it is important to note here is that, as outlined above, the focus is on bodies, rather than on individual subjects. Whereas the structure/agency dichotomy attends to the freedom, or not, of individual subjects to act, and accounts for this relative freedom in terms of social and cultural structures, the virtual/actual coupling conceives bodies as processual assemblages of multiple and diverse relations which complicates the linearity of the determination of agency by structure. According to an ontology of becoming, where bodies are actualisations of the virtual, bodies do not 'have' agency which is determined by social and cultural structures, but rather bodies *are* the becomings of the actualisation of the virtual. As such, the relations between the specific (the actual) and the general (the virtual) are explored in a non-deterministic way: the virtual does not *determine* the actual (see Chapter 6 and Conclusion) but rather the virtual is actualised through relations of affect. In Chapter 2, the relations between the specific and general are examined in methodological terms, and especially through Deleuze's concept of 'transcendental empiricism' (2001a, 2001b, Deleuze and Parnet 2002), in Chapter 5 the relations of affect between different bodies are examined in terms of the structure/agency debate and the Conclusion takes up this debate to consider issues of construction and constructivism.

The ontology of becoming, and the concepts of enfolding, the virtual, the actual, assemblage, relationality, affect and intensity examined here and in the previous chapter are key to the analyses of the empirical material in the following chapters. The shifts involved for feminist empirical research are 'fleshed' through the empirical material and I argue that they open up a way of exploring the relations between bodies and images which differ from the models discussed in the Introduction. In particular, I suggest, what emerges as central through the exploration of the relationship between the empirical material and Deleuzian concepts are issues of *intensity* and *temporality*. These two issues thread their way through the chapters of the book and are differently actualised through the empirical material. In this chapter I have focused discussion on the becoming of bodies, in order to outline the notion of bodies which underpins this book. In the next chapter I turn to consider more closely the relations between bodies and images and experience. I explore the relationship between becoming and experience and argue that thinking about bodies and images differently involves understanding bodies as experienced through images; how do bodies become through experiences of bodies? How are bodies experienced through images, and what do these experiences make possible, and impossible, for the becoming of bodies? At stake then, are not only the relations between bodies and experience but also between experience and images, and Chapter 2 examines these relations in methodological terms.

Notes

1 Deleuze and Guattari give the hypochondriac body, the paranoid body, the schizo body, the drugged body and the masochist body as examples of BwOs that 'want . . . to slough . . . off' their organised organs (1987: 150).
2 Here Deleuze inserts a diagram of the world as a circle which monads erupt out of at a particular point. See Deleuze (2003: 26).
3 The distinction that Deleuze makes between monads or souls that actualise the virtual and matter or bodies which realise the possible is returned to towards the end of the chapter where I indicate my intention to think through the virtual/actual coupling.
4 Deleuze uses architecture here to express the concept of the fold because the fold is worked through in terms of the Baroque, of which one aspect is architecture. Note here the class terms in which the two floors are described; on the lower the moving 'Commoners' who act on each other and on the upper the private rooms decorated by interior designers.
5 Here Deleuze inserts a diagram expressing the lines of the virtual and possible on one side and of actualisation and realisation on the other. See Deleuze (2003: 105).
6 Note here that phenomenology is concerned with being-in-the world whereas Deleuze describes Leibniz's philosophy as concerned with being-for-the world (see above).
7 This 'oneness of the two', or the common world of the simultaneous multiple, can be examined with regards to Merleau-Ponty's understanding of the senses which he argues have been unhelpfully segregated into discrete types with vision designated as the primary and most perceptually significant sense. See Martin Jay (1994) for an interesting discussion of Merleau-Ponty's notion of the visual.
8 Indeed, for feminist phenomenologists, in conceiving the body and the world as the folding of the same flesh, the question of sexual and gender difference emerges for phenomenology. Iris Marion Young's classic essay 'Throwing Like a Girl' (1990/1998), for example, draws on de Beauvoir (1949/1997), to suggest that the 'pure' movement between the body and the object that Merleau-Ponty conceives is not possible for feminine movement because the 'free subject who participates in transcendence' (Young 1998: 262) on which phenomenology rests, is denied for feminine movement which, through her situation, limits or ties her to immanence. For Young, flesh does not guarantee a smooth fluidity for feminine movement; there is a gap that exists between the body and the world. See Gail Weiss (1999) for an interesting discussion of Young's essay, and in particular Young's reliance on the transcendence/immanence split.
9 Deleuze also defines ethology as the study of, secondly, 'the way in which these relations of speed and slowness are realised according to circumstances, and the way in which these capacities for being affected are filled'

and lastly 'the compositions of relations or capacities between different things' (1992: 628). While these definitions refer to the longitude and latitude of a body, here I am interested in introducing and moving with Deleuze's interest in affective capacities so as to take them up in relation to bodies, images and experience in Chapters 2 and 5.
10 Massumi's 'gap' here is not the gap that has been critiqued above for it refers not so much to the 'differentness' of different things as the relations between different things.
11 See also Ahmed (2004) for a development of this argument.
12 This argument could be framed within a critique of language and the notion that materiality is constituted through discourse. Thinking about emotions as embodied rather than as produced and knowable through language challenges the idea that we cannot know anything outside of language. Emotions escape and evade language; there is something about emotions that we cannot know and express through language. As Deborah Lupton says, 'language can frequently sadly fail our needs when we try to articulate our feelings to another person, and facial expressions or bodily movements can often be far better indicators of a person's emotional state than words' (1998: 83). See also, Bendelow and Williams (1998); Burkitt (1999); Csordas (1994).
13 See, for example, Chapter 4 which examines bodies as 'images' and Chapter 5 which examines bodies as both 'conventional' human bodies and as bodies of comments.

2

Immanent experience

So far, I have been concerned with mapping out the theoretical underpinnings of the book in terms of bodies and images. In this chapter, I develop the concept of experience in methodological terms. I outline what I mean by a concept of experience, where it 'fits' in the study of the relations between bodies and images, and how experience might be a methodological 'tool'. The understanding of experience as a methodology is pivotal to this book because it takes up and sets up questions, issues and problems that are explored, and not always resolved, in the rest of the chapters. This is where the theories of the Introduction and Chapter 1 are opened up to the bodies of the girls who participated in this research, not in an attempt to impose the theory on the bodies but to consider the different possibilities of the theoretical and empirical *through* their bodies. How can bodies as becomings be studied through experience? Or, more accurately, how can the becoming of the girls' bodies through images be understood in terms of experience? This chapter is an attempt to think of experience as at once theory and practice. As Deleuze argues, 'theory is an inquiry, which is to say, a practice: a practice of the seemingly fictive world that empiricism describes; a study of the conditions of legitimacy of practices that is in fact our own' (2001a: 36). Experience is the practice, the doing, of this book.

The chapter begins by outlining the importance of experience to feminist methodologies, focusing particularly on the links made between embodiment and experience. One of the reasons that feminist work has made this link is to highlight issues of multiplicity and, moving with this emphasis, I turn to examine how the becoming of bodies might be understood through experience. Taking up the Deleuzian concepts of relationality, affect and assemblage discussed in Chapter 1, I introduce Deleuze's notions of 'immanence' (2001a) and 'intensity' (1986/2005) to re-work a methodology of experience. I explain this in terms of a shift Deleuze proposes from a philosophical model in which the starting point is an abstraction into which practice is fitted to what he terms 'transcendental empiricism' (2001a, 1968/2001b, Deleuze and Parnet 1977/2002), a creative practice whereby concepts are produced through the multiplicity of states of things.

Embodied experience as a methodology

'Experience' is one of the few terms that crosses the lines of the 'academic' and 'popular' and has a currency, a significance, in both. Partly, of course, the meaningfulness of experience across different areas is because of feminism's insistence on the importance of women's experience, on taking seriously the lives of those who have usually been excluded from producing knowledge. As such, it is perhaps unsurprising that a feminist research project should focus its discussion of methodology on experience; arguments concerning experience as a methodology are a mainstay of feminist research (see classic arguments on methodology such as Alcoff and Potter 1993; Maynard and Purvis 1994; Stanley 1990; Stanley and Wise 1983; and on experience, Scott 1992). Such feminist arguments concerning methodology and experience often focus on interviewing and, more specifically, on the ways in which interviews produce 'data' which seeks to 'get at' and explore women's experience (for example, Glucksmann 1994; Gray 1992; Holland and Ramazanoglu 1994; Letherby 2003; McRobbie 2000a; see also my discussion in the Introduction on work in psychology and media and cultural studies).[1] Joan Acker, Kate Barry and Johanna Esseweld (1991) argue that the method of women interviewing women also serves to highlight and dislodge the conventional subject/object binary between researcher(s) and researched as women researchers, never purely 'subject' (see Introduction), are able to empathise with and theorise from the position of their women interviewees. A methodology of experience is therefore another way for this project to think outside of a framework of subject(ivity)/object(ivity).

One of the key ways in which feminist research has explored experience is through its link with issues of bodies and embodiment (see, as just a few examples, Black 2004; Davies 1995; Gimlin 2002; Puwar 2004; Skeggs 1995, 1997).[2] In so doing, an understanding of experience as coherent and unitary is disrupted and attention is instead drawn to how women's embodiment of experience is necessarily contradictory, multiple and partial. It is the diverse work in sociology and cultural studies which theorises and takes up feminist methodologies of experience that has inspired and informed the research explored in this book. For example, to take just one approach, Donna Haraway's work (1990, 1992, 1997) has examined the embodiment of experience through particular figures or figurations. In 'A manifesto for cyborgs', Haraway (1990) conceptualises the cyborg as 'a matter of fiction and lived experience that changes what counts as women's experience' (1990: 191). The cyborg is a 'condensed image of both imagination and material reality' (1990: 191), at once real and unreal, physical and imaginary, fact and fiction, subject and object, natural and artificial so that the boundaries that demarcate these distinctions become confused and can potentially be re-constructed. Haraway's cyborg is, therefore, not a subject, individual or human who 'has' experience and, through their agency, organises this experience into coherent or rational narratives. Rather, 'the cyborg [i]s a fiction mapping our social and bodily reality and [i]s an imaginative resource suggesting some very fruitful couplings' (1990: 191).

The cyborg is a *figure* or *figuration*. Haraway describes figuration as 'about resetting the stage for possible pasts and futures' as part of her attempt to shape a feminist world which, in contrast to modernist, generic, male humanity, 'must, somehow, both resist representation, resist literal figuration, and still erupt in powerful new tropes, new figures of speech, new turns of historical possibility' (Haraway 1992: 86). The cyborg (1990), the trickster (1992), FemaleMan© and OncoMouse™ (1997) are figures through which she wants to 'trouble identifications and certainties' (1997: 11) and make possible new understandings of spatial and temporal identities and bodies. Haraway's figures are attempts to live with chaos and confusion through difference, diversity and multiplicity, indeed, they are figures that do not, and are not made to, fit into a grand story but are purposefully chosen for the ways in which their suffering, dismemberment and disarticulation might produce 'possible connection and accountability' (Haraway 1992: 86; see also 1997: 8–14).[3] One such figure is 'the trickster', a figure that engages in story-telling that does not claim to be authoritative, detached or truthful but rather is embodied and partial, real and imaginary, situated and multiple. Haraway takes up the figure of Sojourner Truth as a trickster to think through how 'dismembered' and 'disarticulated bodies of history' (1992: 86) might be bodies of multiplicity, connectivity and accountability. In discussing Truth's 'Ain't I a woman?' speech (see Haraway 1992: 91) in which Truth uses her body as a way of exposing racist patriarchy, Haraway argues that the 'speech was out of place, dubious doubly; she was female and black; no that's wrong – she was a black female, a black woman not a coherent substance with two or more attributes, but an oxymoronic singularity who stood for an entire excluded and dangerously promising humanity' (1992: 92).

In examining the intersection of the embodiment of race and gender in and as the figure of Truth, Haraway argues that Truth is not a coherently organised body with assorted features ('two or more attributes') but is 'an oxymoronic singularity': difference. Truth (the 'singularity') *embodies* many things, many differences (race/gender for example), at once. A body, then, is not so much the incorporation of difference into a coherent narrative as it is the ability to live as situated partiality, accountable multiplicity. The trickster is both constituted through fictions but also constitutes these fictions through her storytelling. Haraway conceives figures as *singularities* where experience is constitutive (rather than owned, for example) and is embodied as many fictions and possibilities (rather than organised into a coherent narrative, for example). The trickster is a figure who embodies and lives difference. In terms of experience, Sojourner Truth reworks her experiences of race and gender and class into a partial and located understanding of identity which challenges universalised assumptions of what it is to be 'a woman'. 'Trickster experience' produces a sense of potential multiplicity, 'oxymoronic singularity'. Sojourner Truth's experiences expose and challenge racist patriarchy and help construct an alternative feminist world, because of their ability to move and become articulated as different moments, the moment of the meeting where Truth makes her speech, for example.

Haraway's notion of trickster experience highlights matters of the multiplicity and difference of bodies – Sojourner Truth's experience is unavoidably embodied so that her body is the spatial and temporal multiplicity of oxymoronic experiences. Bodies of experience are the partial locations of differences, intersections, imagination, reality, fact and fiction. Bodies are changing and changeable but are also limited or fixed in particular ways; Truth's body is fixed through race, gender and class. Haraway's understanding of a body has resonances with how Felly Nkweto Simmonds (1997) considers how her body has become fixed and inescapable through race, disease and medical intervention. Simmonds thinks this through the impossibility for her of writing a disembodied sociology; she can make no distinction between being an 'academic' and a 'person'. She writes,

> talking about the body, my body, becomes both a strategy and a technique, to deconstruct my positioning as a woman, an African woman (a 'third world' woman) and an academic in a western institution. It is neither essentialist nor narcissistic. I want to explore the relationship between my body as a social construct and my experience of it. I want to examine the relationship I have with my body and how I negotiate, daily, with 'embodied social situations'. (1997: 227, references omitted)

Simmonds develops this impossibility of disembodiment into an embodied sociology which examines the links between her body and the world.

Through these relations, Simmonds pays attention to how theory and practice, construct and reality intersect through and as her body: she is a woman, an African woman and an academic in a western institution; her body is socially constructed (a fiction) but experienced and lived nonetheless (is real). Simmonds argues that an embodied sociology such as the one she describes is 'neither essentialist nor narcissistic' but a means, a methodology, through which different knowledges and experiences of her body can be explored. Simmonds' body is thus not a contained entity but is different relations, situations, constructions and experiences.

According to Simmonds' argument and Haraway's figuration of Sojourner Truth, a body is a multiplicity – of constructs, knowledges, experiences. A body is many things at once whilst never being reducible to them. Is Truth just a black woman? Is Simmonds only a woman, an African woman, an academic in a Western institution, a survivor of cancer? Their arguments suggest not. The point of arguing that experience is embodied is not to reduce or summarise what a body *is*. Simmonds is not trying to define her body nor Haraway Truth's. Instead, what their arguments demonstrate is the capacity to embody and live difference, multiplicity, diversity. Simmonds' and Haraway's interests in the multiplicity of a body lie in the embodiment, or figuration, of natural and cultural constructs; how are gender, race, age, illness, profession, suffering, disarticulation embodied? In this book, I am interested in exploring *bodies as multiplicities of experience*. I ask, how do bodies become through experience? Drawing on the feminist work discussed, briefly, above, this is an interest in a body as process, where experience is not that which a body has gone through and that is in the past but where *experience is the past, present and future possibilities of a body*. Experience therefore becomes a way to think about bodies not just as what they are (a black woman, a white girl, for example), but as how bodies do and might become. In this sense, bodies are not understood in terms of gender, race and age, for instance, but are always in the process of, the becoming of, gendering, racing, ageing. These processes are not straightforward lines of progression but involve movements in and from different directions. A body, for example, understood as becoming through experience, may be 'young' and 'old', 'girl' and 'woman' at once.[4]

Thinking of a body as experience becomes a methodology for exploring the ways in which bodies become without assuming that there are prior ways of knowing what it is to be a particular body. By concentrating on bodies as not necessarily linear, narrative, processes of space and time, it becomes possible to examine how, for example, a body is known and lived, at once, in a multiplicity of ways without reducing it to that particular set of multiplicities. It becomes possible to explore how the girls experience their bodies as gender, race, age, and more without claiming to know what it is to be a white, 13 or 14 year old girl. The methodology of embodying experience developed here, then, leaves these multiplicities open as virtualities. Questions do not deliberately inquire about race, gender, age, sexuality but examine how these possibilities and impossibilities emerge, are, or are not, actualised. Experiences might, and most often do, involve gendering, sexing, racing, ageing, but also involve other complexities and surprises. My focus, then, is on what experience might make possible or impossible for the becoming of a body. This is an understanding of experience as the diversity of spatial and temporal moments that move and become assembled and re-experienced as other spatial and temporal moments.

Immanence, empiricism and experience

Feminist theory and methodology, then, has pointed to the ways in which experience is both multiple and embodied. In this sense, experience is not owned by a subject but is constitutive of bodies. In the terms of this book, bodies become through experience. Turning to Deleuze's work at this point offers a productive way of developing such an understanding of the relations between bodies, multiplicity and experience. In this section I explore the concepts of immanence and (transcendental) empiricism (Deleuze 2001a, 2001b) to consider further how the becoming of bodies can be researched through a methodology of experience. In so doing, I pull through a number of the concerns of the previous chapters and demonstrate their relevance to a feminist empirical study of the relations between bodies and images.

In his essay, 'Immanence: A Life' (2001a), Deleuze suggests, '[a]bsolute immanence is in itself, it is not in something, to something; it does not depend on an object nor belong to a subject' (2001a: 26). Pure immanence is 'A LIFE, and nothing else. It is not immanence to life, but the immanent that is in nothing is itself a life. A life is the immanence of immanence' (2001a: 27). Immanence is, for Deleuze (a) life itself. It is what it is in itself and therefore cannot be known, understood – experienced – in or to or depending on something else. In the Introduction, I outlined Deleuze's concept of the plane of immanence, 'on which all bodies, all minds and all individuals are situated' (1992: 625). I explained that the plane of immanence is a non-hierarchical, geographical plane through which the relations between multiple, diverse and infinitely connected things can be mapped. The plane of immanence is thus an attempt to consider the 'in itself', that is an attempt to understand things not depending on a supplementary or representational framework but as a thing in itself, and as becoming through its relations with other things. I return to Deleuze's critique of an understanding of things through a supplementary model below, but an important point to note here is that while immanence refers to the 'in itself', this does not suggest that the 'in itself' is an isolated moment. As I discuss in terms of affect, Deleuze argues that immanence 'does not depend on an object nor belong to a subject' but is 'in between'.

Indeed, it is this 'in between' which for Deleuze and Parnet defines multiplicity: 'In a multiplicity what counts are not the terms or the elements, but what there is "between", the between, a set of relations which are not separable from each other' (Deleuze and Parnet 2002: viii). I have explored in previous chapters how this book understands bodies and images not as separate and separable entities (subjects and objects, for example) but as becomings. As such, I suggest, what is brought into focus is not so much the bodies and images themselves but the relations between them, the relations of becoming through which bodies and images are produced. In order to study the relations which constitute a multiplicity, Deleuze and Parnet argue that a particular style of empiricism is required.[5] This is an empiricism developed through Whitehead where 'the abstract does not explain but must itself be explained; and the aim is not to rediscover the eternal or the universal, but to find the conditions under which something new is produced (*creativeness*)' (Deleuze and Parnet 2002: vii). Deleuze and Parnet explain this style of empiricism in contrast to rationalist philosophies in which 'the abstract is given the task of explaining, and it is the abstract that is realised in the concrete. One starts with abstractions such as the One, the Whole, the Subject, and one looks for the process by which they are embodied in a world which they make conform to their requirements' (Deleuze and Parnet 2002: vii). Empiricism, on the other hand, 'starts with . . . extracting the states of things, in such a way that non-pre-existent concepts can be extracted from them' (Deleuze and Parnet 2002: vii).

Deleuze's argument that, in beginning with the 'states of things', empiricism produces 'non-pre-existent', creative concepts can be developed in methodological terms through the discussion of affect in Chapter 1. 'States of things are neither unities or totalities, but *multiplicities*' (Deleuze and Parnet 2002: vii) and, in the terms in which I have explored multiplicity so far, are therefore relational things. In his essay on ethology, Deleuze (1992), Deleuze defines a body as the capacities of affecting and being affecting that are produced through its relations with other bodies. Bodies are involved in and become through their affective relations with other bodies; *relations which cannot be known in advance*. To repeat a quotation from Deleuze, 'you do not know beforehand what a body or a mind can do, in a given encounter, a given arrangement, a given combination' (1992: 627). We do not know, in advance of the relations specific to a particular encounter, what the capacities of a body might be(come). We therefore do not know in advance what concepts can be extracted from that body, that is what concepts are appropriate to know and understand that body. Accordingly, rather than begin with 'pre-existent' concepts, empiricism 'treats the concept as object of an encounter, as a here-and-now, or rather as an *Erewhon* from which emerge ever new, differently distributed "heres" and "nows"' (Deleuze 2001b: xx).

In arguing for an empiricism through which 'non-pre-existent', creative concepts are produced from the 'states of things', Deleuze is pointing to an empiricism which becomes through immanence. That is, empiricism is a way to study the multiplicity of a thing – its relationality – through beginning from and extracting the immanence of that thing. Immanence here, then, refers to the specificity or singularity of a thing; not to what of a thing can be made to fit into a pre-existent abstraction (Subject(ivity), for example), but to the 'something new [that] is produced' through the becoming of the thing. In this sense, whereas abstractions refer to a supplementary plan through which a thing can be understood, immanence refers to the in-itself of the thing. However, as I indicated above, a focus on the 'in-itself' is not a model of isolating particular things, or particular aspects of things, from their relations. Deleuze's empiricism does not 'stop' with the 'in-itself' but rather traces it through its constitutive relations. Such a project of tracing the lines between immanence and 'a wider series' is what Deleuze (2001a) explains as 'transcendental empiricism'.

The 'transcendental' referred to in Deleuze's transcendental empiricism is not, as should be clear, an abstract, supplementary framework into which immanent 'in itselfs' can be fitted, it is not 'the transcendent' (Deleuze 2001a: 26). For example, Deleuze states that 'transcendental empiricism is in contrast to everything that makes up the world of the subject and the object' (Deleuze 2001a: 25). By this, Deleuze draws attention to how Western philosophy conventionally operates to organise the flow of life – becoming – into discrete, recognisable entities; subjects and objects, for instance. As discussed in previous chapters, subjects are then seen to possess and act out particular attributes and capacities (consciousness, rationality, logic, for example). For Deleuze: 'Immanence is not related to Some Thing as a unity superior to all things or to a Subject as an act that brings about a synthesis of things' (Deleuze

2001a: 27). Instead, Deleuze describes how there 'is something wild and powerful in this transcendental empiricism' (2001a: 25):

> The life of an individual gives way to an impersonal and yet singular life that releases a pure event freed from the accidents of internal and external life, that is from the subjectivity and objectivity of what happens . . . It is a haeccity no longer of individuation but of singularisation: a life of pure immanence. (Deleuze 2001a: 28–29)

The notion of singularisation that Deleuze refers to here is an attempt to 'capture' the 'impersonal yet singular' nature of life, that is, the relationship between the actual and the virtual. In my discussion of the fold (Chapter 1), the virtual and actual were explained as a 'coupling' through which Deleuze accounts for both specificity and generality; for the particular expression of the world in a fold. The notion of singularity points to how the virtual and actual might be explored in methodological terms, that is, in Massumi's (2002a) terms, through understanding a thing or an example as 'neither general . . . nor particular' but 'singular' (2002a: 17–18).[6] Singularity is a means to account for the ways in which a wider series is folded into a specific body. This body is, therefore, neither general nor particular, but a singularity in and through which is folded generality and particularity.[7] With his notion of immanence, Deleuze is attending to the connection between the actual and the virtual. He argues that immanence 'contains only virtuals. It is made up of virtualities, events, singularities' (Deleuze 2001a: 31). Immanence is actualised in states of things but 'the plane of immanence is itself virtual' (Deleuze 2001a: 31). The virtual is that 'impersonal and yet singular life' through which particular bodily capacities are actualised. Bodies are actual, and yet also exceed their actualisation; bodies are both actual and virtual. Transcendental empiricism must trace this multiplicity of bodies, that is, must explore the becoming of bodies through the actualisation of the virtual.

Claire Colebrook explains the project of Deleuze's empiricism to trace the ways in which the virtual is actualised as 'a commitment to beginning from singular, partial or "molecular" experiences, which are then organised and extended into "molar" formations' (Colebrook 2002: 82). In the following section, I discuss in more detail the relations between the molecular and molar in terms of intensity and extensity. Here, though, I want to develop the discussion of immanence and transcendental empiricism in relation to experience. How, in this book, is experience a methodology which attends to the connections between the specific becomings of the girls' bodies and more general social and cultural processes? At the beginning of this chapter, I outlined, briefly, the centrality of experience to feminist theory and methodology. One extremely influential account of experience is from Joan W. Scott (1992) who argued, 'it is not individuals who *have* experiences, but subjects who are *constituted through* experience' (1992: 25–26). Scott's argument is important because it shifts the emphasis of feminist theory away from the masculine notion of bounded, rational, logical 'possessive individuals' (see Lury 1998) to the ways in which subjects are constantly being constituted, through experience and the relationships between the past, present and future for example. Drawing on this idea of the constitutive nature of experience, the discussion so far pushes Scott's argument in a consideration of how experience exceeds subjectivity (and objectivity), that is to consider how *experience is virtual*.

As outlined above, the immanence of transcendental empiricism is 'impersonal yet singular'; it takes as its starting point the force of life 'before' its organisation, as subjects and objects for example. In Colebrook's terms, immanence is 'molecular experiences', where '[e]xperience is not confined to human experience' but 'include[s] all the different events of response and impression that characterise life. This includes the body's affects – before being ordered and represented by ideas – and affects beyond the human. There are molecular perceptions and non-organic lines of difference' (Colebrook 2002: 81). What this suggests is that '[w]e do not begin as subjects who then have to know a world; there is experience and from this experience we form an image of ourselves as distinct subjects' (Colebrook 2002: 74). It is in this way that experience is molecular, or virtual, and is then organised into molar, or actual, forms. As a methodology, then, experience can be understood as becoming; as a process of becoming through which the virtual possibilities of bodies are actualised. Indeed, as I pointed to at the beginning of the chapter, experience has the capacity to cross differences (between the abstract and concrete, the virtual and actual, the academic and 'everyday', for example) and 'mean' in both. In this book, experience as a methodology is an attempt to connect the concrete (or actual) experiences of bodies that the girls involved in this research explain with the conceptual work of Deleuze. Experience 'means something' to the girls involved in the research – and I was therefore able to ask them about how they experience their bodies through images – and it means something in the feminist Deleuzian perspective that I take up.[8] Experience as a methodology is also an attempt to engage in transcendental empiricism, to connect the actual experiences the girls explain with 'wider' social and cultural virtualities. The experiences of their bodies that the girls describe in this research are understood as immanent – as multiplicity, in-themselves, not knowable in advance – and the task of transcendental empiricism is to examine the actualisation of the virtual; 'to find the conditions under which something new is produced (*creativeness*)'.

Experience, intensity and images

The understanding of experience as immanent, and the methodological practice of immanent experience, can be developed through Deleuze's concept of intensity. Intensity is an important concept in this book, as it works in a dual sense. First, intensity expands the conception of bodies as multiplicity, that is, in Deleuze's terms, how a body is an assemblage of multiple aspects or organs which, crucially, is always changing and transforming. This builds on the concept of the BwO (Deleuze and Guattari 1987, see Chapter 1), where a body is an assemblage of different organs, organised not in terms of being an articulate or interpretable signifier but as an immanent becoming. A BwO is not necessarily a human body but 'include[s] all the different events of response and impression that characterise life' (Colebrook 2002: 81). The organs of a BwO are assembled not according to a pre-existent or hierarchical system, but are situated on a plane of immanence. Drawing through the discussion of immanence and experience, one way in which the organs of a BwO can be conceived is as different moments of spatial and temporal experience, organised not in terms of when they happened (as a linear progression from past to present to future, for example) but arranged and connected to each other through their intensity. As moments of intensity, experiences are in affective relations, that is, in relations through which intensity is produced and which cannot be known in advance of the given arrangement. As such, the intensity of moments of experience is capable of changing. Organs become; they are experienced more or less intensely. The first sense of the concept of intensity therefore refers to what of a body is experienced intensely. This is both a methodological and analytical concern with intensity; methodological because asking the girls how they experience their bodies through images is a question which involves the prioritisation of some relations between bodies and images over others, and analytical because the organs explained to be most intense are the basis of my discussions in later chapters. Chapter 4, for example, explores the relations between 'looks' and 'selves' as particularly intense organs through which the girls' experience their bodies, and Chapter 6 examines the temporality of moments of experience by focusing on how particularly intense moments in 'the past' endure.

The second sense of the concept of intensity develops the emphasis on the affective relationality of bodies and accounts for the immanence of becoming. As discussed above and in previous chapters, Deleuze's work is an attempt to consider what a body might do and might become other than its organisation into a recognisable, and therefore subjectifiable, organism. Intensity might be likened to immanence in that, as Colebrook puts it, 'before signs are representative and extensive, they are *intensive*. Before there is a system of language that allows us to refer to a world stretched out before us, there are investments in intensities' (2002: 108). Deleuze's concept of intensity is therefore a critique of the dominant mode of understanding the world as 'extensive', as the conscious, spatial organisation of the world into discrete entities (subjects and objects, bodies and images, for example). As extensive, experience would be the possession of an individual; as intensive, experience is that which produces the individual, is the virtual through which a body is actualised. Deleuze's focus on the immanent force of (a) life is also a focus on the affectivity of intensity: 'affect is intensive because it happens to us, across us; it is not objectifiable and quantifiable as a thing that we then perceive or of which we are conscious' (Colebrook 2002: 39). The relations between immanence, intensity and affect, then, suggest that experience is 'resonant' (Massumi 2002a: 26), 'before' representation and signification, activity and passivity, subject(ivity) and object(ivity).

So far, I have suggested that experience is immanent ('in-itself'), affective (in relations of affect which are not knowable in advance) and intensive ('before' signifying systems and organisational dichotomies). The introduction of the dual sense of the concept of intensity here is significant in its opening up of the way in which images, and the relations between bodies, images and experience, are understood in the book. The central research question that this book explores is, how do the girls' bodies become through images? Or, put another way in methodological terms, how do the girls experience their bodies through images? For me here, then, experience is the methodology through which I attempt to research the becoming of bodies. That is, and as I have outlined above, experience is the actualisation of the virtual; not the actual of the virtual but the *actualisation* of the virtual, the process of becoming. However, in suggesting this as the way in which to understand the methodology of experience, I am not implying that bodies and images are separate entities between which experience traverses. Rather, the ontology of becoming is an attempt to examine the relations through which entities are produced. Bodies and images are therefore not separate but are experienced through each other. Images therefore do not reflect or represent bodies but produce the ways in which it is possible for bodies to become. As such, there are no neat distinctions between bodies, images and experience.

One way to consider this point further is to argue that experiences are intense *images* of bodies through which these bodies become. This is to take up Colebrook's suggestion above, 'there is experience and from this experience we form an image of ourselves as distinct subjects' (Colebrook 2002: 74), and to pull through the discussion of immanence. As intense moments of experience, images are not representations or significations of something else (a real, or actual, world, for example), but are 'in themselves':

> There are images, things are themselves images, because images aren't in our head, in our brain. The brain's just one image among others. Images are constantly acting and reacting on each other, producing and consuming. There's no difference at all between *images*, *things*, and *motion*'. (Deleuze 1995: 42)

Deleuze develops the immanence of images, things and motion in *Cinema 1* (1986/2005), where he explains the shift from ancient philosophy to modern philosophy in terms of a movement from understanding life and the world through 'privileged instants' (the eternal, the immobile, for example) to a potential attention to 'any-instant-whatever' (Deleuze 2005: 4).[9] This, he suggests, is a shift from the transcendent to the immanent. 'If', he argues, particular instants of the any-whatever 'are privileged instants, it is as remarkable or singular points which belong to movement, and not as the moments of actualisation of a transcendental form' (Deleuze 2005: 5). The singular 'is taken from the any-whatever, and is itself an any-whatever which is simply non-ordinary and non-regular' (Deleuze 2005: 5). The singular any-instant-whatever is, for Deleuze, a moment capable of movement which emerges from a more expansive series, or 'whole': 'movement is a mobile section of duration, that is, of the Whole, or of a whole. Which implies that movement expresses something more profound, which is the change in duration or in the whole' (Deleuze 2005: 8). The singular instant is a particular movement of a whole. It is a 'mobile section' of the whole which, through its movement, indicates and expresses a change in the whole. Thought through in terms of the actualisation of the virtual, not only is the actual body changed through what is actualised, but the virtual is also changed through actualisation. The possibilities of the virtual become changed through actualisation. As such, as Colebrook suggests:

> This means that there is not a world (actual) that is *then* represented in images (virtual) by the privileged mind of man (the subject). Life is just this actual-virtual interaction of imaging: each flow of life becomes other in response to what it is not. The anticipation goes beyond what is actual, but also produces a new actual. **The image is neither actual nor virtual**

but the interval that brings actuality out of the virtual. (Colebrook 2002: 87–88, italics in original, bold my emphasis)

This understanding of the image as 'neither actual nor virtual but the interval that brings actuality out of the virtual' is, in methodological terms, important. As the interval through which the virtual is actualised, the image is that which can be studied; it is what of experience that can be studied. In terms of my focus, images are understood as the interval, or screen, or frame, though which bodies become. Images make possible and impossible the becoming of bodies. In order to study this becoming, as I explain in more detail below, the research was concerned with asking the girls, in different ways, how they experience their bodies through images. What experiences of bodies do images produce? And how do these experiences limit or expand the becoming of bodies? Experience is here, then, the process of actualisation – the process which accounts for how and what a body becomes, and which makes it possible to conceive the virtual, the conditions under which something new is produced.

Immanent experience as a methodology

To recap: my argument so far has been that the becoming of bodies can be studied through the ways in which a virtual experience is imaged and actualised. The imaging of experience is the process of actualisation. However, this remains – in methodological terms – vague. How is experience a way of researching the image as an interval through which a body becomes? Furthermore, how do we do research if what is at stake are affective (changing and not knowable in advance) relations? Before outlining how I did my research, a discussion of the status of the research data is helpful. In arguing for a methodology of immanent experience, I am suggesting that data produced through the relations of research be explored as it is in itself. To examine what such an endeavour practically involves, thinking through the concerns that some of the girls expressed to me about participating in the research is suggestive. Before I began interviewing, I met with the girls in their schools and explained to them that I was interested in talking to them about how they know, understand and experience their bodies through images. I told them that I did not have a list of questions to ask but that I was interested in hearing the different things that they thought were important to experiences of their bodies, even if they thought they were transgressing from the subject. Apart from one girl,[10] all of those who attended that first meeting were happy to continue participating in the research but some were concerned or unsure about what the research might be used for and how I might use what they told me. Their concerns seemed to settle around an anxiety that I would 'go beneath' what they were saying and would interpret them according to ideas that they might not be aware of, that they might not understand and that they might not be comfortable with; that I would 'psychologise', 'psychoanalyse' and 'sociologise', them. Of course, it could be argued that this is what this project is doing, that I am using difficult concepts through which to understand bodies, images and experience. However, as an attempt to practice transcendental empiricism, I argue that what I am not doing is trying to understand *the girls* through these concepts. I am interested in the experiences of bodies through images not as things that say something about someone but as immanent in themselves.

One way of explaining this further is through a comparison of the aims and interests of this book with some, now classic, work on the relationship between girls and popular culture by Valerie Walkerdine (see, for example, Walkerdine 1997; Walkerdine *et al.* 2001[11]). Among other methods including analyses of popular cultural texts such as television adverts, films and pop songs, Walkerdine's work has involved interviews with and observations of young girls and their families. Indeed, Walkerdine interweaves analysis of different kinds of data in order to 'ask some questions about the relation of little girls to the popular by interrogating both media presentations of little girls and little girls' own engagement with popular culture' (Walkerdine 1997: 3). Walkerdine's methodology is rooted in psychoanalytic concepts, where reflecting on and interrogating her own responses, feelings and fantasies towards the texts and people involved in her research constitutes a means of 'deal[ing] with the complex issues of power and interpretation' (Walkerdine 1997: 54) with which she was confronted. In a chapter where she analyses working class girls watching the film *Annie* at home, for example, Walkerdine's novel methodology allows her to critique audience research for its failure to explore subjectivity and focus instead on the ways in which the subjectivity of the girls and their families who participated in her research is constituted through the viewing of the film (Walkerdine 1997: 108). In this sense, then, and in light of the discussion in the Introduction, images in popular culture are not separate from the girls but rather help to produce the possibilities of subjectivity for the girls (and their families). For example, Walkerdine argues that:

> The video of *Annie* does indeed give the participants a way of dealing with extremely difficult aspects of their lives. While it does not shape an overt discussion of the middle-class kind, sitting round the television, it

allows them to dream, understand and face conflicts over what is happening to them. The video is a relay point in producing ways of engaging with what is going on – and so am I, because my presence permits other people to address remarks to me that can be heard by other members of the household and therefore be attended to. (1997: 119)

Walkerdine's work has clearly been important in directing attention to the ways in which the subject/object distinction is difficult to maintain from the position of working class girls and their families. For Walkerdine, images in popular culture do not 'effect' girls in any linear way but rather produce the very possibilities of what it means to be a girl. For example, Walkerdine suggests that *Annie* produces the narratives through which some of the girls who participated in her research forged relationships of trust with their fathers and through which mothers can be understood as drunken, nasty and cruel (Walkerdine 1997: 125). As such, Walkerdine's psychosocial approach contends that the relations between girls and images are certainly more complex than a cause-and-effect model would suggest.

At stake in Walkerdine's work, then, is what it means to be, or to grow up as, a girl. Furthermore, Walkerdine's work is concerned with 'the making of female *subjectivity*' (Walkerdine 1997: 3, my emphasis). That is, her aim is to examine the relations between images in popular culture and girls in terms of how popular culture is involved in the making of the subjectivity of little girls. This is a different interest than the one that underpins this book. What I am interested in exploring here, and as I have indicated above, are the *relations between bodies and images*. Rather than my starting point being the category 'girl', or the concept of subjectivity, my focus is the *becoming* of *bodies* through images, where bodies and images are not separate entities but entangled processes. This book takes a category of bodies which has been important to feminist research, and asks different questions about them. I ask, 'how are the bodies of the girls who participated in my experienced through images?', which is a different question to focusing on subjectivity and asking, 'how are bodies girled through their relations with images?' The detachment of bodies and images from subjects and objects and the ontology of becoming, rather than, for example, a psychoanalytic approach to subjectivity or a phenomenological approach to the body, requires questions to be asked of how to understand and research bodies. As I discussed in Chapter 1, my focus is on *relationality*; becoming is a concept concerned with the relations between things. Furthermore, and also picking up on the discussion in Chapter 1, shifting to a focus on bodies, for me here, involves putting to work concepts other than that of subjectivity.

For example, for Walkerdine, research on girls' subjectivity necessarily involves a consideration of the psyche and the psychological (1997: 8). For my Deleuzian exploration of the becoming of bodies through images, the concepts of affect, assemblage, enfolding, the virtual/actual, intensity, immanence, are necessary. There is, I suggest, a different set of interests, aims and concepts at stake here.

In methodological terms then, and as discussed above, my interest is in attempting to understand the interview 'data' as immanent. This is not to isolate it from its relations of production but rather it is to trace the lines of becoming between the actual (the actual experiences produced in the research) and the virtual (the interviews, social and cultural conditions, for example). This means that what the girls say and do are taken not as symptoms or signs of something else ('the girls' or their psyches, for example) but as knowledges, understandings, experiences that can be thought through in-themselves. The experiences that are produced within the research are inevitably relational and it is these relations, rather than the bodies or images, that are at stake. That is, it is the relations of the *becoming* of a body through images that is central to this book. In Deleuze's sense, such a focus on relations is ethical. It is, to draw on his discussion of Spinoza and ethology (1992), an understanding of bodies as constituted through affective relations which cannot be known in advance of a given arrangement. As Colebrook succinctly puts it: 'For Deleuze, empiricism is an ethics precisely because it takes any social formation, even one as general as "humanism" and shows its emergence. We do not begin *from* an idea, such as human culture, and then use that idea to explain life. We chart the emergence of the idea from particular bodies and connections' (Colebrook 2002: 82). In focusing on the becoming of bodies, we are not beginning with an abstract idea but are tracing the actualisation of a particular body through its relations with the virtual.

To argue that experience is immanent and to highlight relationality has important methodological implications, not least because it is to refuse an approach to research as 'truth finding' or 'exposure'. The notion of immanent experience as methodology being developed here takes experience to be necessarily partial, non-essential and constantly changing and moving. This does not mean that experience is false or made up but rather that experience can never be complete, absolute truth. In terms of my position as researcher, to understand experience as intense, immanent moments is to try and know the experiences told to me in this research as always incomplete and constituted through its relations. Those involved in this research are not fabricating stories or telling lies and I am not entering into duplicitous relations with them.

Instead, I accept and explore the experience told or shown to me in the interviews as an experience in itself. That 'the same' experience will be told differently in another set of relations does not mean that one 'version' of this experience is any more 'true' or 'complete' than the one I record. It is instead to acknowledge the relational nature of research, to acknowledge my role in the research without becoming involved in a debate about how to find 'better' versions of experience, as if experience can be known outside of its constitution as different moments.[12] It is to recognise and explore the partial and located experiences I am told in the research without searching for what these experiences might 'really' mean but also without neglecting to consider the conditions under which these experiences are produced.

It is an attempt to endorse the partiality of the experiences that my research thinks through and enter into relations with these experiences as crucial knowledges of bodies. It is an attempt to engage in 'feminist research' concerned with experiences of bodies without presupposing an already existing body, image or experience from which to begin. A body, an image, an experience cannot be known prior to the relations that they might be involved in. Bodies and the experiences through which they become are on a plane of immanence. Elspeth Probyn (1993) argues something similar when she reconceives a feminist notion of experience as a means of making connections between different women without subsuming one experience with another. Her aim is to:

> stretch my experiences beyond the merely personal, not as a way of transcendence but as a way of reaching her experiences, the experiences and the selves of women. In other words, I want to put forward a mode of theorising that encourage lines of analysis that move from her experiences to mine, and mine to hers. (1993: 4)

Probyn's rejection of experience as transcendence suggests an impulse to stay with experience as immanent, as lines that maintain difference but where difference does not mean that one experience cannot be connected with another, different experience.

To think through a notion of immanence rather than transcendence is, as I have suggested above, to ask questions of 'interpretation'. Research is generally understood as the interpretation of data. If I argue that experience (and bodies and images) is 'immanent', what does this mean of and for interpretation? To argue that experience is immanent and produced through spatio-temporal relations is not so much to see my role as researcher as the interpreter of experience but rather as constituting this experience in my relations with those who are telling it to me. Thinking through experience in this way emphasises those relations that constitute experience and argues for research which does not claim experience as a way of necessarily or inevitably separating or connecting myself with those involved.[13] It is to understand experience as immanent in the research relations and not to make, in Probyn's words, transcendental links between these relations. A commitment to feminist research which does not presuppose any already existing gendered connections is what Angela McRobbie (2000b) points to in her critique of the notion of research as the search for the 'oneness' of women. She writes,

> Feminism forces us to locate our own autobiographies and our experiences inside the questions we might want to ask, so that we continually do *feel* with the women we are studying. So our own self-respect is caught up in our research relations with women and girls and also with other women field-workers. That said, feminism should not be taken as a password misleading us into a false notion of 'oneness' with all women purely on the grounds of gender. No matter how much our personal experience figures and feeds into the research programme, we cannot possibly assume that it necessarily corresponds in any way to that of the research 'subjects'. (2000b: 127)

To search for the oneness of women is, according to a conception of experience developed through notions of immanence, empiricism and becoming, to imply some sort of transcendental grounding to the experience of being a woman that can be identified and interpreted to include all women. For McRobbie to dispute a search for a oneness of experience is to critique a notion of experience as lying latent, ready to be tapped into and interpreted.

Drawing on this understanding of immanent experience as methodology, the research was designed with a number of approaches to allow for the girls participating to discuss the different ways in which they experienced their bodies through images. Partly this was to enable the production of different kinds of experiences (focus groups might facilitate different experiences to individual interviews) and partly this was to open up the ways in which images could be considered. In one sense, this opening up of an understanding of images was designed to expand the focus of feminist research from, for example, photographs, mirrors, film and magazine images. Examining these types of images has, as discussed in the Introduction, been especially significant to feminist theory and empirical research and, drawing on this work, my interest was in exploring other types of images that the girls involved in my research might deem important. In asking them generally about 'images', the girls talked about images in terms of how they saw themselves and thought others saw them and many different physical and imaginary experiences of bodies were produced within the interviews involving clothes, make-up, friends, boys, comments, school, looks, selves and more. In another sense, the opening up of the conception of images was to develop a methodology of studying the becoming of bodies. As I outlined above, images in this project can be understood as intense experiences through which bodies become. As that which actualises the virtual, images are an 'interval' through which becoming can be identified and explored. As such, and as detailed in the following section, the research was designed around thinking through images in different ways.

A note should also be made on the status of the empirical categories of gender, race, class and age. This book is not an empirical study of class or race, or indeed gender, although issues concerning 'classing' and 'racing' and 'gendering' do emerge at various points. This is, of course, an obvious limitation of the study, not only in that the research only involves a small number of what might be called working and middle class white girls who are interested in talking about experiences of their bodies, but also because of the apparent non-reflection on regular empirical categories. I explain this through arguing that in exploring the *relations between things*, rather than focusing on subjects and objects for example, this research is interested in processes which cannot be assumed in advance. It therefore does not *begin with* the objective of investigating the girls' bodies in terms of gender, race, class and age, but rather it traces the actualisation of the virtual. As virtualities, social and cultural categories might be, and most probably will be, actualised, but this is not to be presumed in advance. This is also research which is, in Deleuze's terms, 'practice' – theoretical *and* empirical. Bodies, images and experiences are processes of becoming which involve settling and sticking, but which also involve change, movement, excess. By paying attention both to process and stoppage, movement and sticking, the bodies of the girls participating are understood not as a set thing but as always becoming through images. Some images 'stay', and gender, class, race, sexuality, age might be images that stick and is stuck to some bodies.

Indeed, Beverley Skeggs (2004) makes a similar point concerning the 'sticking' of race to some bodies in an exploration of how contemporary class is known and experienced. Skeggs discusses Manthia Diawara's (1998) notion of how black working class masculinity in popular culture is a 'mobile cultural style available to different characters in film, be they black or white' (2004: 1). Diawara understands black working class masculinity as a mobile identity that can be embodied by white actors. In the film *Pulp Fiction*, for example, Diawara argues that the characters played by John Travolta and Bruce Willis embody a certain 'coolness' which usually only belongs to black actors. Diawara argues that 'Tarantino's discovery was that white characters can play Blaxploitation roles, and that black maleness, as embodied in *esthétique du cool*, can be transported through white bodies' (Diawara 1998: 52). However, the mobility accessible to white actors, and white people (men[14]) more generally,[15] is not necessarily equally available to black people; the mobility for black bodies to embody whiteness is restricted. Here Diawara provides the example of Marsellus, a black character in the film who cannot escape his blackness. He is a black character who must be vilified before he is raped to demonstrate that he is black, but not cool. In this sense, 'coolness' is a raced cultural style which is assumed to be black and must be demonstrated to be otherwise. Because they are not black, Travolta and Willis must be shown to be cool and because he is black the character of Marsellus must be shown to be uncool; blackness *is* cool. Skeggs describes this as such:

> Diawara uses the example of *Pulp Fiction* in which John Travolta acts 'black cool' (remember the walk?) whilst Samuel Jackson *is* cool. A particular version of racial inscription thus becomes a mobile resource for some whilst being fixed and read onto some bodies as a limitation. The black male character appears not to be acting; he just *is*. (2004: 1)

Skeggs goes on to consider this white acting/black being distinction as part of a 'symbolic economy where the inscription and marking of characteristics onto certain bodies condenses a whole complex cultural history. Some bodies can be expanded rather than condensed. At the same time they become a resource for others' (2004: 1). What Skeggs is pointing to is the way in which some bodies become stuck with certain cultural assumptions and limitations – black coolness sticks more easily to black bodies (hence the need for Marsellus to be *shown* as not-cool) but not to white bodies – whereas other bodies are more mobile – white bodies can play or not play black cool.[16] What this book explores is the ways in which bodies both become extended and become stuck at certain points through processes which might involve gendering, racing, classing, aging, sexing and more, how some bodies can be expanded and others are condensed.[17] What I try to do is think through immanence not only as where things become stuck or trapped but also as that which cannot be escaped or transcended; immanence cannot be transcended (there is no thing other than immanence as Deleuze says) and so immanence is at once movement and stoppage, mobility and trapping, multiplicity and sticking.

Outline of research

The girls who participated in the research came from two UK schools, one in south-east London and one in rural Oxfordshire. I had one contact in each school, a white male teacher in the London school and a white female counsellor in the Oxfordshire school. I had explained the kinds of things the research was interested in to these contacts and asked for six girls from each school to participate.[18] The girls were self-selecting rather than sampled in any way; the contacts in both schools explained the research to a class of year nine students, aged 13 and 14, and asked for any girls interested.[19] Between them, the contacts and the girls negotiated six participants in the London school and seven girls in the Oxfordshire school. All the girls were white. This is not particularly surprising in the Oxfordshire school as records show a predominantly white student population with 1.8 per cent coming from ethnic minorities. Records of the London school, however, showed that 40 per cent of students came from ethnic minorities. It is difficult to offer reasons for why only white girls volunteered to take part in the research as I was not involved in the process of explaining the research to any students or in negotiating who would be involved. The majority of students in the Oxfordshire school came from what is described in their Ofsted report as 'a comparatively favourable area although with some pockets of deprivation' with a well-below-average number claiming free school meals. The London school is in a deprived area and records show that 30 per cent of students were eligible for free school meals, a figure high nationally but not unusual for London, and 37 per cent of students have special educational needs. Both schools are comprehensives and have no selection policy for students.[20]

The research was organised into focus group and individual interviews in the two schools. Schools were decided upon as because this was an accessible way to do research,[21] I could meet with the girls over a set amount of weeks and could be more or less guaranteed that they would be present (not least because some of them saw it as a legitimate way to avoid classes). The schools also meant I had a certain support structure. I was aware that the interviews could produce experiences that I might not be able to deal with in the way that the schools, the girls, and their parents (who had to give permission for their daughters to participate), might want. I therefore had the systems that the schools had in place, for example counselling services, to refer the girls to if necessary. The interviews took place in both of the schools.[22] I met with the girls once before the interviews to introduce myself and the research. The interviews were: (i) a focus group interview; (ii) individual interviews[23] and;

(iii) a group workshop session involving images. These were all recorded and transcribed. The interviews were carried out over a six week period and I spent approximately one half-day a week in both schools. The first focus group interviews were general discussions about experiences of bodies through images which lasted approximately ninety minutes. Taking up methodologies developed in feminist social and cultural research and in visual sociology where images are used at the beginning of an interview to stimulate discussion around something concrete, and to ensure images become part of the research process, the focus groups began by asking the girls to comment on photographs of themselves that they had brought with them and moved to other images through which knowledges of their bodies might be produced. Images that the girls discussed included mirror images, popular media images, images of how they imagined themselves and how they thought other people saw them through their comments about their looks and personalities. Within these two groups, the girls all knew each other through their school classes. However, there were clearly different friendships between the girls and some knew and liked each other more than others. These relations between the girls were extremely interesting and important in the experiences that were discussed in the interview, particularly in terms of trust (see Chapter 5).

Given these relations of trust, the second set of individual interviews sometimes produced very different experiences. There were clearly different relations between each girl and myself than there were when we were a group. For some girls, the relations of the individual interview meant that they discussed experiences that they would not have done within the group interviews. Anna and Katie, for example, said that they felt more able to discuss certain bodily experiences in their individual interviews because they did not know or trust the other girls enough. Some girls also 'bitched' about other participants in their individual interviews (see Chapter 5). Other girls experienced the relations of the individual interview as more constraining than the group interview. Fay, for example, found it more comfortable to produce experiences with the other girls, some of whom were her close friends, than she did with just me. The relations of the group and individual interviews produced in some cases very different experiences. The way in which experience is conceived in this project, as explored above, does not understand some experiences are more true or complete than others but emphasises how experiences are produced, are re-made, re-worked and re-experienced through their relations; what Katie said in her individual interview is not truer or more comprehensive than what she said in the group interview but rather both sets of experiences are specific to certain spatial and temporal moments. The semi-structured individual interviews were intended not so much to follow up what the girls had said in the first group interview but as an opportunity to develop, or not, things that they might have found interesting. In the individual interview, temporality was also focused on and I asked the girls if they imagined themselves in the future and what they might be doing (see Chapter 6).

The last interview was an image-making workshop session which was designed to make images not only the subject of the project, what the interviews were about, but also an integral part of it. For this interview, I provided the girls with materials to produce images of experiences of their bodies. The 'brief' was kept as open as possible so that the girls could decide what images to create. Although this is not a comparative study and I would not like to speculate on the reasons why, I had also piloted this interview with a group of five women sociology PhD students. Interestingly, this group found this open brief difficult. In particular, most of the PhD students asked for clarification on what the images should be about, what materials they should use and what I was looking for. In contrast, the majority of the girls who participated had no problems with what this interview was about and asked no questions concerning what materials, experiences or images they should involve. The materials that I provided for this interview included teen and fashion magazines, a Polaroid camera, cling film and tin foil, make-up, petals, stickers, sweet wrappers, pipe cleaners, glitter, coloured sand, wrapping paper and various pens, pencils, papers, scissors and glue. The girls were also told that they could use personal photographs. (The images the girls produced are explored in more detail in Chapter 4.)

These materials, that is the relations of the interviews and the image-materials, form what could be called an archive, which obviously sets possibilities, limits and selections, which is extremely evident in the images they produced. However, the evidence of a selective archive is not necessarily problematic, or, better, is not necessarily more problematic than any other kind of research. Rather, I would argue that in this method of the research, the selective dimension of the archive is more evident. There is something about the visual images that the girls created that demonstrate the range of materials through which they could communicate experiences of their bodies which was not so apparent in the interviews. Indeed, when presenting papers on different themes and ideas of this research, I have only been questioned specifically about the limits of the research methods in relation to the visual images where it is clear what materials were provided and what were not; I have not been asked to justify the questions I asked or discussions I had with the girls in the same way. But to think of an archive only in relation to visual images is a mistake because the 'tools' or materials through which experience can be expressed, and thus (re)constituted, are always partial, limited and selected (see, for example, the special edition of the journal *History of the Human Sciences*, 1998, on 'The Archive'). Moreover, the archive is not something that can be taken apart or avoided but is a necessary set of (research) relations which produce experiences. By thinking through different methods, group and individual interviews using discussions and visual images, then, different archives are available and therefore different experiences and knowledges can be made and re-made.[24]

Inventive methodology

The term 'inventive' or 'innovative' is often used to describe research methodologies which in some way develop or push the ways in which topics can be studied. However, I would also like to point to a further understanding of what it means to do inventive research, an understanding which is closely tied to the notion of creativeness mentioned a few times above. Towards the beginning of the chapter, I explained Deleuze's empiricism in terms of a challenge to abstraction and an attempt instead to 'find the conditions under which something new is produced (*creativeness*)' (Deleuze and Parnet 2002: vii). Creativeness in this sense refers to the necessity both of understanding becoming as inherently 'new'[25] and to the invention of 'new' concepts. For Deleuze, concepts are not representative, reflective or descriptive but are *creative*. Concepts are 'no longer "concepts of", understood by reference to their external object' (Tomlinson and Habberjam 2005: xv) but are inventive; concepts *invent*. Deleuze and Parnet's understanding of concepts emerges through the ontology of becoming where '[t]o become is never to imitate, nor to "do like", nor to conform to a model' (Deleuze and Parnet 2002: 2). As such, concepts cannot 'capture' becoming if they seek to imitate or 'do like' it. That is, in a Deleuzian sense, a concept is neither a pre-existing theoretical framework into which empirical material is fitted and interpreted nor a notion which springs from empirical research (although it is probably closer to the latter). Rather, *concepts do things*. As 'doing things', concepts both do and are done to, both affect and are affected. Understanding concepts as doing is, fundamentally, an understanding of concepts as becoming; as always in process and, moreover, as always in processes of enfolding. Deleuze and Parnet argue concepts must be inventive and, in the process, concepts invent:

> Let us create extraordinary words, on condition that they be put to the most ordinary use and that the entity they designate be made to exist in the same way as the most common object. (Deleuze and Parnet 2002: 3)

Indeed, Massumi (2002a) argues that the invention of concepts are an essential project to ensure that ways of knowing, engaging and perhaps changing the world are made possible. He writes,

> Invention requires experimentation. The wager is that there are methods of writing from an institutional base in the humanities disciplines that can be considered experimental practices. What they would invent (or reinvent) would be concepts and connections between concepts. The first rule of thumb if you want to invent or reinvent concepts is simple: don't apply them. If you apply a concept or system of connection between concepts, it is the material you apply it to that undergoes change, much more markedly than do the concepts. The change is imposed upon the material by the concepts' systematicity and constitutes a becoming homologous of the material to the system. This is all very grim. It has less to do with 'more to the world' than 'more of the same'. It has less to do with invention than mastery and control. (2002a: 17)

Drawing on the discussion above, concepts are inventive in their capturing of 'a simply non-ordinary and non-regular' instant of the any-whatever. The concept is extraordinary in its capture of the becoming of the ordinary. Invention in this sense does not only refer to the remarkable but to how the ordinary, the mundane, the repetitive, is becoming (see Chapter 6 and Conclusion). 'When one relates movement to any-movement-whatevers, one must be capable of thinking the production of the new, that is, of the remarkable and the singular, at any one of these moments' (Deleuze 2005: 8).[26] Moreover, in terms of my explanation of moments of experience as intensive images, Deleuze and Parnet suggest that 'concepts are exactly like sounds, colours or images, they are intensities which suit you or not, which are acceptable or aren't acceptable' (Deleuze and Parnet 2002: 4). Concepts, then, are images, intensities which make sense in their grasping of an entity, or not. In the rest of the book, I develop this notion of concepts in order to try to explore the bodies of the girls' who participated in the research as becomings. That is, in exploring these bodies as becoming through intensive images, rather than according to a subject(ivity)/object(ivity) framework, this book tries to 'invent' ways of understanding the relations between bodies and images.

Notes

1. Of course, this is not to suggest that interviews are the only way of exploring embodiment and experience; rather it is to situate my research within a feminist methodological tradition.
2. Another important way in which experience has been dealt with is in narrative theory which has pointed to how individuals construct and have

constructed narratives or stories of their life. These theories consider experience not necessarily as that which has happened and that remains in the past but as dynamic and moving, as capable of being re-experienced and therefore as constitutive of an individual's present, and perhaps future. These theories are extremely wide-ranging and have a number of different focuses; narrative identity (Ricoeur 1992), biographical projects (Giddens 1991), autobiography (Cosslett, Lury and Summerfield 2000), auto/biography (Stanley 1995), for example. In addition to these theories of narrative are those that seek to account for the *fictive* and *figurational* nature of experience and of life such as the work of Donna Haraway (1990, 1992, 1997), see below.

3 Indeed, interestingly for this methodology chapter, Rosi Braidotti discusses Haraway's figurations as a methodology. The term 'figuration' 'refers to ways of expressing feminist forms of knowledge that are not caught in a mimetic relationship to dominant scientific discourse' (Braidotti 1994: 75) but rather 'produce affirmative representations' (Braidotti 1994: 3). 'Representation', then, is not so much a reflection of what is but rather is, as Haraway argues, a way of producing what might be possible.

4 Indeed, this is what was apparent in the interviews when the girls knew and explained themselves as at once a 'young woman', a 'young lady', a 'girl', a 'child', a 'teenager', an 'adolescent' without ever settling on which one they were. Fay, for example, describes herself and her friends as such; 'now we're still children, like older children, young adults and at secondary school'.

5 For Deleuze, 'style' is 'not a signifying structure, nor a reflected organisation, nor a spontaneous inspiration, nor an orchestration, nor a little piece of music. It is an assemblage, an assemblage of enunciation. A style is managing to stutter in one's own language' (Deleuze and Parnet 2002: 4). I discuss what 'one's own language' might refer to below in terms of empiricism.

6 Massumi (2002a) explains singularity in the context of a discussion of method, application and exemplification: 'It holds for all cases of the same type', Giorgio Agamben writes, 'and, at the same time, is included in these. It is one singularity among others, which, however, stands for each of them and serves for all.' An example is neither general (as a system of concepts) nor particular (as is the material to which a system is applied). It is 'singular'. It is defined by a disjunctive self-inclusion; a belonging to itself that is simultaneously an extendibility to everything else with which it might be connected (one for all, and all for itself). In short, exemplification is the logical category corresponding to self-relation' (2002a: 17–18).

7 Through a focus on the mutations of a body-sex, Luciana Parisi discusses singularity in terms of '*abstract materialism* (a symbiotic and mutlifacted matter)' which 'does not involve the analogy between the general (ideal) and the particular (individual) body or between pluralistic (many) and specific (one) categories of the body defined by the principles of identity (analogy between inert nature and body). Quite the contrary, this method produces

a map of the non-liear movements of conection between causes and effects unfolding the poential (force) of a body to mutate through an ecosystem of indefinite mixtures' (Parisi 2004: 28–29).

8 Indeed, in the context of her development of a feminist corporeal cinematographic philosophy, Theresa L. Geller argues that feminism is 'invite[d] . . . to return to experience, a foundational principle in the history of gender studies, but in order to recognise it as an affect' (Geller 2005/2006: paragraph 11). She continues: 'In this way, experience is no longer something that is meaningful, representing something for the subject, as it is more commonly understood. Feminist cinematographic theory, on the other hand, molecularises experience, breaking it into even smaller segments, for Deleuzian thinking holds that "we can only radicalise politics by deforming experience away from 'meanings' (or ordered wholes) to its effective components (those singularities which produce meanings)"' (Geller 2005/2006: paragraph 11, references omitted). Moreover, Geller suggests 'cinema affords feminism access to the time-relations otherwise unseen in experience. The alternate temporality of cinema provides a fulcrum to expose gender/sexuality as temporal phenomena, since so many slices of lived experience are made to cohere in space and time but are in fact ontologically incoherent' (Geller 2005/2006: paragraph 12). I return to the question of temporality in Chapter 6 and in the Conclusion.

9 This explanation is in the context of Deleuze's argument about the emergence of cinema as a modern phenomenon which, he argues, produces new ways of seeing and knowing movement and time.

10 One girl from the school in Oxfordshire decided not to participate in the research after the initial meeting. She did not give me any reasons but other members of the group gave me reasons that she was not particularly interested, that she did not want to miss art classes during which the interviews were scheduled and that she did not like, or had fallen out with, some of the other girls in the group.

11 Walkerdine's work on girls is extensive and it is beyond the scope of this discussion to refer to it all. In this discussion I focus primarily on *Daddy's Girl: Young Girls and Popular Culture* (1997) because this book is explicitly concerned to examine the relations between girls and wider cultural images and ideas, a concern which I pick up in the following chapters dealing with the empirical material. However, as well as the work that I discuss here, see also Walkerdine 1989; 1991; 1993.

12 This is in keeping with what Skeggs describes, albeit with a different research focus, when she writes, 'it was me who made decisions about what I thought was worth knowing about. I made interpretations and selections from their and my experiences within the research context which best illustrated the research inquiry . . .. Also, their accounts are just as partial as my selections. In the process of representing their experiences, encountered as they were lived, I reduce them to written utterances' (Skeggs 1997: 28–29).

13 Of course, for some research it might be productive to either separate from or connect with those participated, for example Probyn's notion of connection without subsumation (see above).
14 Skeggs points out that Diawara's analysis is based on a reading of black male bodies. In addition to this, I would also argue Diawara's analysis is also based on the masculine distinction between transcendence and immanence that is critiqued by Deleuze (see above). Diawara distinguishes between immanence as 'the trapping of a cultural role in a character' and 'transtextuality' which is 'the movement of cultural styles from character to character in film: hybridity, multiple subject positions' (1998: 51). Diawara's notion of immanence has similarities with Young's de Beauvoirian argument discussed in Chapter 1 concerning how feminine bodily existence is 'overlaid' with immanence.
15 Diawara also gives the example of Bill Clinton's mobility in black culture.
16 See Adkins for a discussion of the 'expanding' and 'condensing' of bodies through what sticks and what is mobile in relation to gender (2001) and sexuality (2002) at work and Ahmed (2004) for how emotions in contemporary media culture 'stick' to some bodies more than others.
17 To argue that race sticks, or not, to some bodies is not, then, to understand race as essential but rather as mobile for some. For how this mobility of race might be understood in terms of passing, or being passed by others, see Ali (2003) and Ahmed (2000).
18 I decided on this number because much writing on successful focus groups argue that six is an appropriate number, see, for example, Morgan (1997).
19 This age group was decided upon because I was interested in doing research with young women who are often seen as in vulnerable relationships with images. For practical reasons, year 9 was thought to be most accessible to me because the students were understood by the contacts as having less educational commitments; I interviewed in June and July and year 9 had no exams to prepare for.
20 Information about the schools is from online Ofsted reports and from details provided by the contacts.
21 This is not to say that was easy or quick; my details had to be checked by the police to ensure I was fit to enter schools, for example.
22 There is an immense amount of literature and research concerned with the relations between girls and school, some of which pays attention to some of the experiences explored here – bodies, friends, boys. I do not reflect on how schools produce experiences of bodies or the relations of the school. For sociological commentaries on girls, bodies and schools see Cockburn and Clarke 2002; Edwards 2002; Hey 1997; Holland and Blair with Sheldon 1995; Prendergast 1995; Renold 2001; Susan Williams 2002; and from a psychoanalytic perspective, Brown and Gilligan 1992.
23 The exception to this is the joint interview I did with Catherine and Tina because Catherine had not been in school when her individual interview was scheduled.

24 See for example Ali (2003: 33–37) for her use of both verbal and visual research methods with mixed-race children to provide them with different tools for thinking about their experiences and to 'illuminate . . . different ways of seeing the children' (2003: 34).
25 'New' in this sense is does not disregard the old, the past, or what is repeated but rather sees becoming as always creative. I return to this issue in Chapter 6 and the Conclusion. See also Coleman (2008a).
26 Deleuze's notion of a concept is developed through Bergson's method of intuition where an object is 'grasped' 'as it is in itself'. For Bergson, such a method involves the creation of new concepts, precisely because the world is a becoming of the new. See Bergson (1903/1999) and Deleuze (1988). For a discussion of how Bergson's method of intuition might be a way of understanding the empirical material of this book, see Coleman (2008c).

3

What can images do?

BECKIE: So when I say images, what do you think are the most important or significant to you?
CHLOE: I dunno, like what you look like and what others look like

[The] in-itself of the image is matter: not something hidden behind the image, but on the contrary the absolute identity of the image and movement. (Deleuze 2005: 61)

The purpose of this chapter is to begin to develop the theoretical and methodological arguments made in previous chapters through the empirical material produced in the interviews with the girls. What I am particularly concerned with here is what the shift from a model of subject(ivity)/object(ivity) to an ontology of becoming does to a conception of images. The quotation from Deleuze above, taken from his work on cinema and 'the movement-image', indicates that matter and images are necessarily entwined; matter is not that 'hidden behind the image' but is the 'in-itself of the image'. As such, the immanent becoming of bodies can be – and should be – explored in terms of images. What I explore further in this chapter is the proposition made in Chapter 2: if moments of experience are images through which bodies become, what are these images? And, moreover, what do these images do to the becoming of bodies? In focusing on the girls' understandings of images, I begin to pay attention to the specifics of this research. What do images make possible and impossible for the becoming of these girls' bodies?

The starting point is that for the girls who participated in this research, 'images' are difficult to define and to 'pin down'. As such, one of the aims of this chapter is to engage with the girls' understandings of images and to open up the ways in which the relations between bodies and images might be conceived. Underpinning the model of subject(ivity)/object(ivity) is a recognition of what images are; images are separate to bodies and can be studied as specific 'types' (photographic, mirror or popular media images, for example). In contrast, this chapter suggests that images are multiple and diverse and cannot be precisely delineated from bodies, nor from each other. Consider, for example, Chloe's comment above and the different ways in which images are understood in the following extracts from individual interviews with Sarah, Hannah, Fay and Emily when I asked them what they think of when I talk about images:

> SARAH: erm
> BECKIE: it's not a trick question, I'm just interested
> SARAH: yeah, I'm just thinking of pictures of myself and people I care about
>
> HANNAH: . . . I think of other people's images, like celebrities and then I think of myself and what I look like
> BECKIE: ok, so is that in comparison with media images?
> HANNAH: sometimes but I mean I'm, obviously I'm not going to be like them so I'm like myself but I don't know, my image, if I walk down the street in like a bright pink outfit then what would I look like compared if I went in just normal clothes, sort of what people think I look like if that makes sense
>
> FAY: a lot of the stars and stuff, like the celebrities and all pictures in magazines and stuff, you just think that's the image of what I'm suppose to be, I think
>
> EMILY: how you see yourself in the mirror, or sort of how you think other people see you, and you're always like see the bad side of you when everyone else is always saying 'oh no you're really nice, you're really pretty' and everything and then you're always thinking 'well no I know I'm not'

These extracts demonstrate the diverse and multiple ways that 'images' are understood and experienced by the girls; 'pictures', 'my image', 'what you look like and what others look like'. Images in this sense are not 'objects' which are separate from bodies but rather it is *through* images that (the possibilities of) bodies can be known, understood and lived. Hannah, for example, discusses 'celebrities' as images and notes how 'stars and . . . celebrities and all pictures in magazines and stuff' are a way for her to 'compare' (in my words), imagine and examine the possibilities of her 'own'[1] body. This is also the point that Fay makes; 'you just think that's the image of what I'm supposed to be'. Emily draws attention to how in mirrors she 'sees' her bodily possibilities as different to the possibilities that other people tell her about; 'you always like see the bad side of you when everyone else is always saying "oh no you're really nice, you're really pretty" and everything and then you're always thinking "well no I know I'm not"'. Emily experiences her body through 'how you think other people see you'; her body is not separate from either other bodies or images but rather is known and understood through images that are produced through her relations with other bodies.

Images are vague, they are not that which settle or can be settled on. As I have argued of bodies, images are not things that are knowable in advance but rather are processes that are never fully finalised. As these relations cannot be known in advance to that which they constitute, images are that which is, potentially, always moving, changing and becoming different (and the same). Central to this chapter, then, is the aim not to define 'what is an image?' but to examine 'what might an image be(come)?' For the girls in the extracts above, the matter of images makes possible particular knowledges and understandings of and ways of living a body. *It is through these knowledges, understandings and lives that bodies become.* The aims of this chapter are to begin to think through how images are understood by the girls, and what knowledges and experiences of bodies these understandings of images make possible and impossible for the becoming of bodies. There are particular issues raised which pick up the theoretical propositions made so far and are developed further in later chapters. These include: *temporality* as a central organising principle for the becoming of bodies through images (photographic, mirror and popular media images are understood by the girls to involve different temporalities which produce specific knowledges of bodies); *accuracy, actuality and virtuality* (different images produce different knowledges of bodies, 'accurately' showing what they 'actually' look like, or what they 'could' possibly look like); *movement* (images involve different possibilities of movement which produce particular becomings) and; the *extension or limitation* of the possibilities of becoming (different images make possible and impossible the becoming of bodies).

The chapter begins with an exploration of what 'images' mean to the girls and then moves to discuss the girls' experiences of their bodies through (i) photographic images; (ii) mirror images and (iii) popular media images.[2] The focus on these three kinds of images has a dual purpose. First, during the interviews, photographic, mirror and popular media images emerged as particular 'types' of images that the girls identified and that made possible particular experiences of bodies. This identification of photographic, mirror and popular media images by the girls is interesting because, as indicated by Chloe's comment above, 'images' were often discussed in vague and ambiguous terms. This chapter considers these particular kinds of images in order to open up an exploration of the ambiguity and multiplicity of images in the rest of the book; what (else) might images be(come) and do?

The second and related purpose of exploring these kinds of images is to develop the focus of the Introduction, where relationships between women's bodies and images are concentrated around popular media (Duke 2000, Grogan and Wainwright 1996), art (Betterton 1987, 1996, Pollock 1987), mirror images (de Beauvoir 1949/1997), film (Doane 1992) and photographs (Lury 1998). In picking up the girls' identification of photographic, mirror and popular media images, my intention is to develop, through an ontology of becoming, three of the primary ways in which women's bodies have been conceived by feminist theory in relation to images. From the analysis of photographic, mirror and popular media images, the chapter moves to consider how the girls found it difficult to ultimately determine the boundaries of images. Following the proposal that relations cannot be planned for in advance but rather are produced through the research, the chapter concludes by exploring what other types of image might be involved in the becoming of bodies.

The relations between bodies and images

Photographic images

In both the group and individual interviews, photographs emerged as important images through which bodily knowledges and understandings were produced. In particular, the girls discussed photographs as images of their bodies *in the past*. Photographs showed the girls what they *had* looked like. For example:

> EMILY: yeah, well, I've got quite a few pictures of where I was a bit younger where I thought I looked really nice but I actually didn't, I looked a lot bigger than what I actually was and that put me down quite a lot

> BECKIE: so in relation to kind of how you think about and feel about your body, how are photos part of that? Or are photos part of that?
> DIONNE: well, yeah, cos if you take a really bad picture you're like, you hide it, don't you? Cos like
> SAMMY: cos you don't want other people to see it
> FAY: yeah to see what you actually look like
> KATIE: but it's funny then when you look back and like it's only even a year ago and you think 'God I was really fat then' or something and I've really changed a lot
> FAY: yeah I've got this picture of me playing badminton and I was like, 'look at my belly!' And you just think, oh, I don't know
> DIONNE: what was it, a centimetre? Don't worry
> ANNA: or you think you like that clothes and then you look back in a photo and yeah

KATIE: oh, I don't like that now
FAY: yeah pink and purple and stuff and it's just nasty

In these extracts, Emily and Dionne, Fay, Sammy, Katie and Anna discuss their bodies in terms of different spatial and temporal moments. Photographs are understood as (in Tina's words, see below), 'capturing' what a body looked like in the past. This past body that is captured within a photograph can then be compared to what a body looks like in the present. In the cases above, the past body is understood as distinct from the present body; the girls' comparison between their past and present body understands their past body as different to, and worse than, their present body.

The comparison between what their bodies were and what their bodies are is made possible for the girls through an understanding of photographs as capturing what their bodies 'really' or 'actually' looked like. Such an understanding was discussed at many points by the girls but is most eloquently expressed in this extract:

BECKIE: ok, so if a photo makes you feel bad, why does it make you feel bad?
TASHA: cos you don't like the way you look
SAMMY: yeah
BECKIE: ok
SAMMY: because you just look bad, and it makes you think 'is that, is that what I actually look like?'
FAY: yeah and,
ANNA: yeah, 'is that what I actually look like?'
SAMMY: yeah, yeah
DIONNE: when you took it at the time, like taking pictures on a film and you think, you know, 'I want to look nice in those' and you get them developed and then you see what you really look like it's a bit depressing
FAY: yeah, cos when you walk around you don't see your own face, yeah, like you might sometimes catch it in a mirror or in a window or something
ANNA: but then that's a reflection!
DIONNE: on purpose!
FAY: yeah, but in a photo
TASHA: it's like, 'that is what I actually look like?'
SAMMY: and you're like, 'errrg, I'm gonna cry'
BECKIE: so that's why you don't like them? Because you think that's what you actually look like?
FAY: yeah because it's gonna show you how you actually look

According to this discussion, a photograph is a productive way of comparing how a body looked in the past to how a body looks now because it is understood, in particular ways, as *accurate*. A photograph shows what a body 'actually' looks like. As Sarah says in her individual interview, '[it's] my view that the camera doesn't lie, cos you can look in the mirror and you can see something completely different and you can take a picture of yourself and think "oh, do I really look like that?"' This is also worked through by the girls in terms of the difference between a photograph and a reflection in a mirror or a window. Anna and Dionne discuss how reflections show a body 'on purpose' whereas photographs catch a body. According to this understanding of it, because a photograph does not show a body on purpose but rather 'captures' it, a photograph involves a surprise; 'it's like "is that what I actually look like?", "ergh, I'm gonna cry"'.[3]

However, the surprise involved in the 'capture' of a body in a photograph can also involve the deliberate display of that body, that is, the surprise does not necessarily come from a photograph being taken without the girls' knowledge. Earlier in the extract above, for example, Dionne describes how before having her photograph taken she thinks, 'you know "I want to look nice in those"'. The surprise of seeing what her body actually looks like is produced through it not matching her anticipation of it looking nice: 'you get them developed and then you see what you really look like it's a bit depressing'. Trying to 'look nice' in photographs was also discussed by some of the other girls in terms of specific bodily practices. 'Actually' looking nice did not just happen but had to be worked at; it did not just happen that a body was 'caught' looking nice. If the girls thought there was no possibility of looking nice, they avoided having their photograph taken. Anna, for example, said 'since year 7[4] I hardly have any photos of me . . . I always dodge the camera' and Catherine described how when she goes out 'that's why I always take my camera, people are like "I'll take it" and I'm like "no, I'll take it, it's my camera" and it's just an excuse to get out of the picture'.

If the girls thought there was a possibility of looking nice in a photograph, they engaged in specific bodily practices and techniques to increase their chances:

> BECKIE: so what makes a nice photo then?
> EMILY: just when you're looking nice
> FAY: and when you look natural and you don't look like you're posing
> SAMMY: yeah yeah
> DIONNE: I can't, I can't be natural, I always pose
> SAMMY: like when us two, like when your dad took a photo of us two
> FAY: yeah,
> SAMMY: kind of nice but natural as well weren't we?
> FAY: yeah, we did her hair all nice so she was like really pleased with that

BECKIE: so like, you've made an effort but you look, you don't look posed
FAY: no, no you don't look false, it's just kind of snapshots of you all through your life

Looking nice in a photograph for these girls involved looking 'natural'. In the sense that they discuss it here, looking 'natural' is in opposition to looking 'posed' and 'false'. Looking natural, then, is not appearing in a photograph as you actually are but instead involves *looking* natural. There is here a distinction between how a body looks natural and how it actually is which involves a difference between what a body is and what a body might be.

In the previous extract, actuality refers to what a body 'is'; is that what I actually look like? In this extract, looking natural refers to what a body might become; how can I look nice (when I actually do not look nice)? Looking nice in photographs is not looking how I 'actually' look but involves the *production* (or becoming) of a body that looks nice.[5] In this sense, the body of a photograph – or better, the body that is produced through its specific relations with photographic images – is according to the girls a complex assemblage of what a body was, is and might become. The body of a photograph is shown and understood through multiple temporalities. Looking nice through looking natural, for example, involves knowledges (or moments of experience) of what a body has looked like in 'the past', what a body looks like in 'the present' and what a body might look like in the becoming of a photograph. The multiple temporalities through which a photograph is experienced by the girls is an understanding of a photographic image not as an entity separate from a body; a photograph is not the straightforward 'capture' of a body but rather involves the assemblage of different (temporal) possibilities of a body. The girls, then, begin from the assumption that their bodies cannot be known in advance to how they know, understand and experience it through, in this case, the temporal possibilities of photographs. *Their bodies do not exist externally to their experience of it through images,* there is nothing prior to or behind their knowledges and experiences of their bodies.[6]

The notion of a photograph showing a body as it 'actually was' in 'the past' is therefore more complex than a reflection of that body. The 'past' body of a photograph is a knowledge of a body that becomes assembled and known through other (temporal and spatial) knowledges. Indeed, the notion of the 'actuality' of a photograph comes not so much from the understanding that this was what a body actually looked like as it does from the understanding that the body has in some way been spatially and temporally captured or caught. A body might not 'actually' have looked like that in the past but that body did actually look like that at that specific captured temporal and spatial moment. There is no knowledge of how a body 'actually' looked behind the knowledge of how it looked at the precise moment of the photograph. The girls' understanding of the relations between their bodies and its capture in a photograph is interesting in terms of the model of cause-and-effect that has been critiqued in previous chapters. For the girls, their body is not the *cause* of the photograph; there is no straightforward causal link between what their body was and the body that is produced in the photograph. Instead, the relations between the body that was and the body of the photograph are more ambiguous, vague, affective; indeed, *the 'actual' body of the photograph can be understood as the actualisation of the virtual.*

Because a photograph does not necessarily show a body as it actually was outside its imaging, a photograph does not 'capture' a body entirely. Instead, only a particular spatial and temporal moment has been captured, or actualised. For example, Tina discusses her body in photographs as the 'capture' of a body's movement:

> TINA: yeah cos like in a picture you capture like . . . say I did something with my lips or something, like pushed them right out, it would make me look worse so people might think I look like that whereas normally if I just do that then I can put it back and you can see it's just like that

For Tina here, the movement of a body that is caught in a photograph is only a partial image of her body. A photograph has caught only one movement (her lips 'pushed . . . right out') which her body cannot be reduced to ('whereas normally if I just do that then I can put it back and you can see it's just like that'). The pose that has been caught is not the entirety of her body but rather her body escapes and exceeds its capture as the photograph. There is a virtual that has not been actualised in the body of the photograph. The 'past' body of a photograph does not, for example, depict 'accurately' the body as it 'actually' was. Nor does the body of a photograph remain in or as 'the past' that has been captured. Rather, the body of the photograph encompasses the multiple possibilities of that specific temporal and spatial moment of the past (looking nice through looking natural, for example) and makes possible present and future experiences of that body (and indeed other bodies[7]). In making possible particular knowledges of a 'past' body that is 'caught' but not contained within its frame, a photographic image produces for the girls specific bodily becomings which involve the assemblage of different temporal moments of experience; what a body 'actually' was (in the past) and what it might become (in the possible present and future). The notion of a body as an assemblage of different temporal moments is explored in the next section on mirror images in terms of how 'the present' involves multiple temporalities.

Mirror images

When discussing photographic images, the girls describe the capture of a specific spatial and temporal moment. While a body's movement and becoming cannot be reduced or restricted to this moment, a photograph does capture one particular image of what a body was, it actualises a virtual. Through this capture of movement, photographic images produce specific possibilities for knowing, understanding and becoming a body including the capacity to compare different spatial and temporal moments (was this what I actually looked like in the past?) and to attempt, both physically and imaginatively, to become different (looking nice through the natural pose, for example). With photographs, then, the becoming of bodies is through a virtual moment in the past which has been captured. In contrast, relations between their bodies and mirror images were discussed by the girls in terms of the movement of the present. According to the girls, mirrors show bodies not as a captured past but as a *changing and changeable present*. Katie, for example, explains mirrors as 'it's kind of, *there and now, there and now*, isn't it, it's like what you look like at that point' (my emphasis) and Sammy says, 'I mean if I look in the mirror I just see myself now, like *how I'm looking now*' (my emphasis). Hannah and Tina also discuss the differences between photographic images and mirror images in temporal terms:

BECKIE: so in relation to kind of how you feel about yourselves and your body and stuff, how important are photos in that? . . .
HANNAH: they are important cos like say I'm wearing a bikini and I'm standing in front of the mirror and I would just see myself from my perspective, in the mirror, but say someone took a picture of me and then I looked at it then I'd think, 'ok, maybe I don't look like that', you just see it from different
BECKIE: ok
TINA: it's like a picture, is like one movement so like you can make yourself look nice in like the way you stand and that and you've got like, in a mirror, say you stood that way and like you didn't like it, you could stand that way so you could like it better, but say in a picture it's just that picture and you think 'ergh'. And you could change your facial expressions and that
BECKIE: ok, so it's something about it being still?
TINA: yeah

In this extract, photographic and mirror images are compared through the capacity of a body to move and be moved. In Tina's terms, photographic images 'capture' a body as 'one movement'. With photographs, a body's movement can only be experienced through how movement has been captured (the movement involved in looking nice, for example, is caught as one moment); a body is, in my words, 'still'. However, mirror images show a body *as it is and as it might be in the present*. A body in the present can be moved, as Tina says, 'you could stand that way so you could like it better'.

As with photographic images, the girls discussed mirror images in terms of *accuracy*. With photographic images, accuracy was understood through the capturing of a past body's movement (as it might have been). In the extract above, Hannah points to how a mirror only shows her body from her own 'perspective' whereas a photograph shows her something 'different' and makes her question or 'think' about her own understandings of her body; 'ok, maybe I don't look like that'. For Hannah here, in showing her someone else's perspective of her body, the photograph produces knowledges and understandings of her body that, through only her 'own' relations with mirrors, are not possible. However, for other girls, the capacity to move their 'own' body in the present of the mirror image showed them a more 'accurate' image of their bodies than photographs. Here, for example, Catherine and Tina discuss how being able to change a body in a mirror image provides, in my words, a 'better' knowledge and understanding of their bodies:

> BECKIE: ok, so what about like looking in the mirror? Is that better than looking at photos of yourself?
> CATHERINE/TINA: yeah
> BECKIE: why?
> CATHERINE: cos you change yourself
> TINA: yeah like you can turn to different angles and stuff and think, well if I turn to this angle I look better
> CATHERINE: yeah like this is my best side
> TINA: yeah

As with the comments from Sammy and Katie above, Catherine and Tina describe mirror images as a more accurate image of their bodies than photographs because of the movement that is involved in mirrors; 'you change yourself', 'you can turn to different angles and stuff'.

In discussions of photographic images the girls described 'accuracy' in terms of 'actuality' (a photograph is 'accurate' because it shows a body as it 'actually' might have been) whereas in discussions of mirror images 'accuracy' is understood in terms of the change and movement made possible through the present; 'if I turn to this angle I look better', 'yeah like this is my best side'. Accuracy in a mirror image, then, is not what a body 'actually' might have looked like but is rather what a body might look like in the present, in the here and now. Moreover, rather than being a temporality that is caught, the present involves not just one here-and-now but many. For example, the 'pose' that is involved in the mirror image (turning to different angles) is different to the pose involved in having a photograph taken. While with photography the pose is understood as culminating in the capture of a spatial and temporal moment, with mirrors the pose is understood as constantly moving, changing and, importantly, changeable. The body in the mirror changes as *this* time, not *over* time as with photographs (for example, 'I was really fat then', 'look at my belly").[8] *The image of the present of the mirror, then, involves the possibility of multiple presents.* A mirror shows what a body *does* look like here-and-now and what a body *could* look like here-and-now, if the body is moved to a different angle.

This capacity of the mirror to show an image of a body as it is and as it could be now was discussed by the girls in terms of make-up. For example, some of the girls discussed how during school they would look in mirrors to check their appearance and re-apply make-up if necessary. Casey talked about checking her make-up before break-times to ensure she looked her best in case she bumped into a boy she fancied. The girls who talked about checking their appearance in mirrors all said that they carried their own mirror (or mirrors in Emily's case) with them so that they could, potentially, check whenever and wherever they felt they needed to. In the focus group interview at one of the schools, the room was very hot and the interview discussion had involved talking about appearance. The girls, as Emily says, were concerned with how they looked. Emily produced two mirrors from her bag and the group passed these round, checking and commenting on their own and the other girls' appearance. The following, lengthy, extract is taken from this point of the interview and is interesting in terms of the kinds of bodily activities that are happening (and also how, trying to be a good 'embodied researcher', my questions are attempting to 'get at' these body-image relations).

> BECKIE: so what, are you just checking, now you're looking in the mirror?
> EMILY: yeah, cos you've all been talking about it so I just I'd check and see if I looked ok
> FAY: [inaudible]
> BECKIE: but what, what?
> TASHA: can I borrow a, that mirror?
> EMILY: yeah
> SAMMY: just so that, no, when you're in the mirror, I don't know you just like check if you need any more make-up and like

EMILY: yeah
DIONNE: can I borrow that after?
SAMMY: oh, I don't know
BECKIE: so does it help? Looking?
SAMMY: I don't think it helps I think it makes it worse cos if I . . . [inaudible]
BECKIE: so does it make you feel better, just looking at that, so do you think, 'oh I need to check in a mirror'?
TASHA: yeah I always 'oh I've got to look'
FAY: what makes me feel bad is like when these two say, oh, they've said something like erm, it's the end of the day and my hair just does not stay in the same place or it just doesn't, it just goes, and by the end of the day and like these two will say something and like that really puts me down
DIONNE: no we don't!
SAMMY: no
FAY: you've said stuff before that's really put me down, like you haven't meant to be tight but
DIONNE: I don't remember saying anything at the end of the day!
FAY: you've said stuff like that to me that's put me down
DIONNE: oh my god! That big mirror is really horrible!
BECKIE: so what, so do you kind of, do you look forward or do you plan to look in a mirror?
SAMMY: first of all you think, 'oh I've got to look in a mirror to make sure you look ok'
FAY: no, she means like at lunchtime do you have to look in a mirror?
SAMMY: oh ok
EMILY: yes!
ANNA: there's two mirrors
EMILY: I always carry two mirrors around with me!
DIONNE: this is making me feel worse!
BECKIE: so do you?
FAY: you look fine
SAMMY: yeah but I just look in the mirror when I think that something has rubbed off or something
FAY: yeah but we're all hot and sweaty in here
DIONNE: no but I thought I looked better than I do now, but then when you look in the mirror and realise what you really do look like, it's making me feel really upset now. There you go . . . [inaudible]
ANNA: there's 2 different mirrors! Look in that mirror!
EMILY: I always have two different mirrors
BECKIE: so what were you trying to say?
SAMMY: I was going to say if you think like you need to or like maybe you think something's rubbed off or like you need to you look in it but it doesn't actually make you feel better
BECKIE: ok

SAMMY: cos like you've looked in it and you think 'oh my god, that's actually how I look'
ANNA: but mirrors lie
FAY: but then it depends on who you are cos I don't have as a big thing about my make-up
EMILY: oh I do
DIONNE: I do
FAY: because I think, so yeah, like Sammy you like to have your make up, you like to check your make-up

This extract suggests, amongst many other things, that the girls use mirrors to know what they do and what they could look like here-and-now. This can be understood as a *checking* on bodies. 'Checking' as discussed here is about *reassurance* – not a narcissistic self-admiration, but, on the contrary, an inspection of how a body looks that often begins from the assumption that the body does not look nice ('I just look in the mirror when I think something has rubbed off or something') or ends in an understanding that the body does not look nice ('I thought I looked better than I do now').

In this extract, checking a body in a mirror involves different understandings of what images of a body in a mirror makes possible. For example, in one sense, mirrors are understood as the capacity to show a body as it 'actually' is. Emily and Sammy describe how they look in a mirror at lunch or break times to check their body looks 'ok'. For these girls, how a body 'actually' or 'really' looks in a mirror image is worse than how a body was imagined to look; a body 'actually' looks not nice ('"oh my god, that's actually how I look"'). In another sense, though, Anna argues that 'mirrors lie'; mirrors do not have the capacity to show a body as it 'actually' is, perhaps because bodies can be changed and moved to a 'better' angle. Fay's understanding of the bodies that are shown in mirrors is that they are dependent on what assumptions are involved in looking in the mirror. She says 'it depends on who you are cos I don't have as big a thing [as Sammy] about my make-up'. Fay and Anna understand their bodies as not (accurately) knowable through mirror images and therefore do not have the same need to check. Fay and Anna's bodies are known and understood through how they exceed mirror images. In contrast to Anna and Fay who cannot know their bodies 'accurately' through mirrors, for Emily and Sammy, their bodies become known through the accuracy of mirror images; their bodies 'actually' look a certain way. Checking in a mirror for them therefore involves the production of an image that makes possible a knowledge of how they actually look. That is, their bodies are known, understood and experienced as accurate through the image that is produced through checking.[9] For Emily and Sammy, checking in a mirror *makes possible* the very knowledges and understandings of and ways of living a body in the present. A body does not exist prior to or outside of mirror images and therefore cannot be *confirmed* by mirror images. Instead, a body is experienced *through* images; mirror images make bodies possible.

According to this argument that checking is for 'reassurance', looking in a mirror involves the capacity to see what could be made(-up) different here-and-now. Casey, for example, says that she checks her hair in a mirror at school not because she's 'vain' but because 'I'm just making sure I look alright instead of people at school going like "ergh she's got something on her" and stuff like that'. Similarly, Tina and Catherine describe how they look at available reflections of their body to check that they 'look alright':

> BECKIE: and what about sort of like if you're walking down the street and you're like catching your reflection in like windows or cars...?
> TINA: oh I always do that!
> BECKIE: what on purpose?
> TINA: yeah! And I always like walk past a car and like [bends backwards and looks to the side] [laughter] and then carry on walking, I always like have to look at each car I walk past, like in it, I can't just walk down the road
> CATHERINE: yeah make sure you ain't got no bird shit on ya, that's my worse fear, getting bird shit on me and I don't even know and everyone's laughing at me
> TINA: yeah like in school or something
> CATHERINE: yeah I'd probably start crying and walk out
> BECKIE: oh! So why do you check yourself? Is it to like-?
> TINA: to see like if I have a leaf on my head or something, cos they all might laugh if the wind had blown one on and I didn't notice, or to check that my mascara hadn't run, to check that I haven't got something, like say if I'd been sitting down to see if I didn't have no stuff on my bum

As with Sammy and Emily above, in this extract 'checking' for Catherine and Tina is not so much to admire what they like about their bodies as it is to check on what might possibly be not right with them. Indeed, rather than beginning from an assumption that they look 'alright', Catherine and Tina here begin from the very different assumption that they do not look alright. In this sense, through checking, mirror images (including reflections in car windows) make possible mundane and necessary ways of living that otherwise would be for the girls difficult if not impossible. For example, Catherine's 'worse fear' of 'getting bird shit on me and I don't even know' and Tina's worry that 'the wind might have blown [a leaf] on [me] and I didn't notice' are bodily insecurities that are, presumably, repeatedly encountered. Checking a body's mirror image in the here-and-now makes it possible to live with and through these concerns.

That mirrors can accurately show a body as it is here-and-now and as it might be here-and-now does not necessarily involve the production of liberating or affirmative possibilities of how a body might become. That is, the capacity of movement of a body in the multiple presents of a mirror image does not necessarily produce positive, or even 'better', images of a body. As with the extract above for example, in Butler's (2004) terms, sometimes mirror images just make lives 'liveable'. Indeed, the view that mirror images do not involve self-admiration was discussed by Fay, Dionne and Sammy who suggest that looking in a mirror for them involves a focus on what of their body they do not like:

> FAY: well, when you look in the mirror, all you see is the faults, so
> BECKIE: ok,
> FAY: I find it really hard to say something good about the way you look, someone could tell you thousands of time a day that you look good but you won't believe it cos all you see is what's wrong with you, well, I do anyway
> SAMMY: yeah, same here,
> FAY: 'oh I've got another spot, another' and you just, it's just like
> DIONNE: [laughs]
> FAY: whenever you look in the mirror, you just see what's wrong with you and all that double the worse, the bad, it is

Here, Fay and Sammy discuss how looking in a mirror involves seeing only 'the faults'; 'whenever you look in the mirror, you just see what's wrong with you'. Mirror images, despite involving the movement of the present, do not mean that 'what's wrong with you' can be changed. Sometimes, looking in the mirror 'doubles the wors[t]' of a body. The accuracy of a mirror image, then, does not always involve the capacity for changing the multiple presents that it makes possible. A mirror image is not necessarily accurate in either its rendering of a body nor in the possibilities that it produces. As Anna says above, 'mirrors lie'; they 'double' what is bad about a body and they show an image that is different to how a body has been said to look. Indeed, in spite of frequent checking, mirrors can also not be guaranteed to protect a body from not looking alright (bluntly, a mirror does not ensure that a bird does not shit on nor that a leaf does not blow on a body, but instead may confirm that they do).

Popular media images

The notion of the becoming of images suggests that images are not separate from bodies and therefore do not work on them in any straightforward causal way. In this sense, then, thinking in terms of the becoming of images offers an alternative way of understanding the relations between bodies and images than the 'cause-and-effect' model which relies on their separation and opposition into subjects and objects. It is particularly important to note this alternative way of thinking for a discussion of the girls' experiences of popular media images as these kinds of images are often the subject of cause-and-effect modes of analysis (see Introduction). Central to such media effects theories is the notion that media images are 'impossible' or 'unobtainable'. Such images were also discussed by the girls in terms of impossible relations. However, rather than conceive 'impossibilities' as stops or blockages to how a body might be experienced and lived, as media effects models often imply, what a notion of the becoming of images does is understand bodily impossibilities not as the 'end' of a body's becoming but as a body's becoming *through* limits and fixity. All of the girls said that popular media images had the capacity to make them feel 'down' and 'depressed' about their bodies. For the girls, popular media images were understood as comparisons to the girls' 'own' bodies. However, it is not so much that popular media images exist as images that are *separate* to the images of the girls' bodies as that it is *through* popular media images that the girls experience their 'own' body as limited or fixed in particular ways.

For example, in the following extract, Chloe can be understood as talking about experiencing popular media images as impossible ways of becoming:

> BECKIE: so how important are like media images and things like that to you?
>
> CHLOE: erm, I think they are quite important cos when you're looking through magazines and stuff you're like, 'well, I wanna look like that' and stuff but I can't cos of the things they might put themselves through in order to look like it so they are important when you're looking through magazines with like bare, like, tans and make-up and stuff and when you look in the magazine and you think 'that looks nice' and you try and do it yourself and it never goes right but it is quite important, it's depressing in a way
>
> BECKIE: why?
>
> CHLOE: cos like the things that run through your head when you're looking at them and you're like 'I wanna look like that', 'I wanna be her' and then you look at them and you just sit there and think 'well I can't' so it's just like depressing

Here Chloe draws attention to how her body is unable to become like the bodies in magazine images. This impossibility of becoming like these bodies is experienced both in terms of what her body *is* and what her body *cannot* become. As she says, 'you're like "I wanna look like that", "I wanna be her" and then you look at them and you just sit there and think "well I can't" so it's just like depressing'. The impossibility of becoming through popular media images is for Chloe two-fold. First, Chloe points to the impossibility of becoming *like* the bodies in magazines; 'I wanna look like that'. For example, Chloe attempts to make her body like the bodies in magazines through bodily practices such as tanning and make-up but she says 'it never goes right'. Second, and relatedly, Chloe points to the impossibility of *being* the body in the magazine; 'I wanna be her'. Chloe cannot make herself *like* the body in the magazine and cannot *be(come)* the body in the magazine.

The bodily practices that are involved in becoming-like and be(com)ing the body of a popular media image are therefore different to the bodily practices involved in the pose of the photograph. Whereas those involved in the pose of the photograph are understood in relation to the girls' 'own' body (albeit a body that temporally and spatially changes its relations), the bodily practices involved in becoming (like) the body of popular media images are understood in relation to the body of the popular media images. In the pose of the photograph, looking nice, through looking 'natural', is understood and attempted by the girls in relation to what their body can look like, that is in relation to the possibilities and impossibilities (limitations) of the girl's own body. Hence, a girl's hair can be styled in the 'nicest' way for her particular body. However, the attempts to become (like) the body of the popular media image are understood not in terms of the girl's 'own' body but in relation to the body of the popular media image. The girl's body must become not through her 'own' possibilities and impossibilities but rather through the possibilities and impossibilities that are decided *in advance and in relation to* the body of the popular media image. It is the body of the popular media image that sets the standard as to what the girl's body must become (like). In this sense, whereas with photographic and mirror images there is an openness to how a body might become (a body can be changed and altered), with popular media images there is a 'destination' for a body's becoming.

In their discussion of molecular becoming, Deleuze and Guattari (1987) argue, 'a line of becoming has neither beginning nor end, departure nor arrival, origin nor destination . . . A line of becoming has only a middle' (1987: 231). They go on to suggest,

> becoming is not to imitate or identify with something or someone. Nor is it to proportion formal relations. Neither of these two figures of analogy is applicable to becoming... Starting from the forms one has, the subject one is, the organs one has, or the functions one fulfils, becoming is to extract particles between which one establishes the relations of movement and rest, speed and slowness that are *closest* to what one is becoming, and through which one becomes. (1987: 272)

In the sense that the girls discuss them, popular media images are understood as a standard or a destination to become *like*. In Deleuze and Guattari's terms, this is imitation or identification; 'I wanna look like that', 'I wanna be her'. Whereas relations between photographic and mirror images in different ways expand the possibilities of knowing and experiencing a body, as this is not a becoming which has 'only a middle', popular media images can be conceived as limiting or making impossible particular becomings of bodies.

Part of how the body of a popular media image sets the standard is through the body's 'capture'. However, while with photographic images the capture of a body is understood in terms of catching *one* particular temporal and spatial moment of a body's movement, with popular media images the movement of a body is eliminated by its capture. Consider for example Chloe's comment that 'the things they [the bodies of popular media images] might have put themselves through in order to look like that' are not included in the popular media image. While with photographic images a body can move differently (Tina can move her lips back to normal), what Chloe suggests is that with popular media images a body cannot and does not move. The body of the popular media image is caught within the image and exists only as *that* image. On the one hand, then, according to Chloe, popular media images are understood as the reduction of a body to one particular image that cannot be changed. This results in the impossibility of a body becoming through popular media images; Chloe's body cannot become (like) the body of a popular media image. This suggestion evokes the assumption of a media effects model where media images offer 'impossible' and 'unobtainable' standards for the bodies of girls.

However, on the other hand, Chloe's comment also suggests that the body of the popular media image is *irreducible* to one particular image; bodies of the popular media image *exceed* the images in which they are caught through 'the things they might have put themselves through in order to look like that'. According to this second notion of the popular media image, the body of the popular media image is a process of becoming (like) that is caught at a particular moment. As such, as with photographic images, the bodies of popular media images are understood to involve movement. While the first understanding of the popular media image that is present in Chloe's comment has been the primary focus of research and debates on the relations between girls' bodies and images, it is the aim of this section to examine the relations between the first and the second understanding of popular media images. That is, rather than stop with the point that popular media images are 'impossible' and 'unobtainable', this section takes seriously how the girls discuss the impossibilities of becoming (like) the bodies of popular media images but also explores how their bodies become known, understood and lived *through* these limits and impossibilities.

In the extract above, the ways in which Chloe experiences her body does not 'stop' because she cannot become (like) the body of the popular media image. Rather, her body becomes through what she cannot become (like).[10] On a number of occasions, for example, Chloe pointed to how she was not able to afford what went in to producing a body that looked like a body of a popular media image (clothes, shoes, make-up for example). However, her body – her knowledges, understandings, experiences of her body – becomes through these limitations and impossibilities. In the following extract, Tasha, Fay and Dionne discuss the inaccessibility of other kinds of technologies that produce bodies of popular media images:

TASHA: yeah, but everyone always says, 'yeah I'd like to look like that person in a magazine' but they've been made up, and must have so much make-up and stuff on to look

FAY: yeah and photos, you can have them all airbrushed so they can look

TASHA: yeah, cos if they were us, if they had just a little bit of make-up on like we do then, they'd look so different

FAY: yeah when I look at them and I try when I look at them to think 'oh they must have their insecurities like everyone else' and you think they're this perfect image because everyone loves them don't you and you think 'I wanna be like them' but they must have their own insecurities as well

DIONNE: mind you, Victoria Beckham doesn't wear that much make-up and she's got a really nice face

FAY: yeah, but she's not talking about everyone is she? Like

DIONNE: no

TASHA: no I'm talking like about celebrities and like you look at magazines and they've all been made-up

FAY: and airbrushed

DIONNE: yeah

FAY: so they're probably like, like Cameron Diaz, like she has really really really bad skin,

DIONNE: oh yeah
FAY: but you'd never see it cos in films and stuff she has loads of make-up and like it's all covered up and stuff

According to the girls in this extract, there are specific technologies that produce popular media images that they are not able to access; the right make-up, the right amount of make-up, airbrushing, 'stuff'. Through what is inaccessible to them, the girls experience the limits and possibilities of their bodies; their bodies cannot become (like) the celebrities in the popular media images they discuss but become different and differently. The girls did not only discuss such technical technologies (airbrushing for example) as inaccessible and impossible but also more mundane technologies which were understood as, potentially, more accessible. Casey, for example, discussed how dieting and money were two technologies that were, for her, differently achievable:

BECKIE: ok, erm so how important do you think that media images and things like that are? Do you find them, I mean how do you feel looking through magazines and looking at all the models and celebrities?
CASEY: I dunno, I feel like 'oh I wanna be as slim as them' or I feel like I want what they've got, I like it so I want it, so I dunno, I'd just rather have money and want the things that they've got then just dream about it cos it just gives me the hump
BECKIE: and is that because like, because they need money to look like that, is that the sort of thing that annoys you? You think 'oh I want the money so I can do that' or do you think 'I need to diet or to exercise' or whatever to look like that?
CASEY: well both really
BECKIE: so do you ever try to diet or to exercise?
CASEY: I try to diet but it just don't work [laughs]
BECKIE: [laughs] ok why not?
CASEY: I dunno cos I always think, 'oh like I really like that' and I always wanna eat it so I do
BECKIE: ok, so like motivation lasts for a bit and then it just sort of goes
CASEY: yeah cos I think to myself, 'oh I wanna look like a model' or something and then I think, 'oh no', cos I want it!

Here, Casey discusses and compares the technologies of money and dieting. While money *should* be accessible to her but is not, dieting is a technology that *is* accessible to her but that cannot be maintained. These technologies are therefore impossible in different ways. Casey describes that she gets 'the hump' about money but not about dieting; dieting is something that she *can* do to her body but does not always do while the changes to her body that she understands money as making possible is something that she cannot do.

Models of media effects have traditionally understood 'the hump' that Casey gets from looking at popular media images as the effect that 'impossible' and 'unobtainable' popular media images have on girls' bodies. However, as suggested above, Casey's experiences of the relations between her body and the bodies of popular media images is not so clear-cut. In some ways, 'the hump' is not something that Casey understands as capable of correction through simply changing the popular media image. It is not so much 'the body' of the media image that Casey understands as impossible as it is *the processes through which that body is caught as that particular temporal and spatial image*. As such, the impossibilities involved in becoming through the relations between the girls' bodies and popular media images are not (only) the impossibilities of becoming (like) the bodies of popular media images but are the impossibilities of becoming 'caught' as the body of a popular media image. The impossibilities of becoming caught are the impossibilities of becoming through *the particular processes and technologies through which a body is 'caught'*, that is, of going through 'the things that they might have put themselves through in order to look like that'.

It is not, then, that Casey's body is separate from the bodies of popular media images; they are not mutually incompatible. Dionne, Fay, Anna and Tasha discuss this point in the following extract:

DIONNE: what makes me feel better is like when you look in magazines at like the rough pages where the photographers have just caught them when like they've just walked out of the house to get some bread from the corner shop
FAY: and you're like 'ha ha ha ha'
DIONNE: yeah
BECKIE: so does that make you feel better then?
FAY: yeah, but in a really bitchy way it makes you feel,
[laughter]
ANNA: or like those 'before and afters' when they were younger
FAY: yeah
ANNA: and you think they look like that now and
DIONNE: and I think there's stuff that puts you down, like when you see them looking nice or like when they're going to awards and they're wearing dresses and they're saying that's good or bad and you think 'oh god if they look bad in that imagine what we look like in the clothes we wear' cos they're not half as nice. Yeah
BECKIE: so why do those type of things make you feel better?
TASHA: cos it makes you think they're just the same as us cos but they're made up and when they're in magazines and stuff it's not their true face

FAY: and they have bad hair days too and they don't look very good, cos all you generally see are good pictures of them whereas of yourself you see good and bad pictures, so when you see them not looking good
TASHA: it's amazing how they can cover it though, cos like some people must have loads of spots of whatever, and it's all covered up and it's just like, like, pure skin and you think 'oh my god'
DIONNE: but the reason their nails and their skin and stuff is so nice is because they can afford the stuff and like they walk into a room and like it sprays fake tan on you and it just like dries straight and and sort of that's why their skin always looks so
FAY: brown all the time
DIONNE: brown all the time

In this discussion, the girls understand the impossibility of becoming (like) these bodies in terms of the processes and technologies involved in popular media images. It is not that their bodies cannot be like the bodies of popular media images as *'they're just the same as us'*, 'they have their bad hair days too and they don't look very good'. Through bitching and through exposing that specific bodily practices are involved in becoming a body of popular media images, the girls can and do live with and through popular media images. To draw on the discussion in Chapter 2, there is, then, a different kind of ethics involved in this way of understanding the relations the girls have with popular media images than those involved in the cause-and-effect model. Popular media images are not understood in advance as negative causes that make girls feel bad about their bodies but rather are explored through their immanent relations with these girls' bodies. As such, what becomes apparent through these extracts is not just how popular media images make the girls feel depressed or down about their bodies but how the relations between bodies and popular media images involve relations between other bodies and images. Popular media images, and bodies of popular media images, cannot in this sense be understood in isolation as also involved are relations of make-up, clothes, money, tanning and bitching (to name a few).

What can images do?

The sections above have aimed to demonstrate and explore how the girls experience their bodies through relations with different types of images – photographic, mirror and media. Each section has attempted to examine the *specific* bodily becomings that these different types of image make possible through the knowledges and understandings of and ways of living that they produce. However, it is inappropriate to argue here that these three types of images are exhaustive of 'images' or that these are the only possibilities of a body becoming through images. While I have so far distinguished between different 'kinds' of images, as the extract below demonstrates, ultimately these distinctions are extremely difficult to make. The notion that images exist 'only' as photographic, mirror or media images and that bodies are only experienced through these images is made redundant by the girls through their difficulty and ambiguity of speaking about 'images' and of answering my questions about which images were most 'important' to experiencing their bodies. Instead of 'images' being confined to one 'type' or ranked in a hierarchy of importance, the girls talked about experiencing their bodies through diverse and multiple images. Consider as an example Hannah and Chloe's comments in the following extract:

BECKIE: so if photos aren't kind of really important, what kind of images are important to what you think and feel about your bodies?
HANNAH: photos are important but
CHLOE: but like magazines will always make you think about it, so like if you see someone in a magazine you'll think like, 'oh, I wanna be skinny like that' or, oh, 'I want hair like that' and then you just start getting too obsessed by it and like go the hairdressers and try and get it cut like it and then you don't like it and then stuff like that
HANNAH: that's what's really annoying cos say like someone took a picture of me or like I had a picture of me, like in year 7 when I think we went to Canada, I can't remember, but like I was in a bikini and I thought it looked quite good and like I thought, 'oh it's a nice picture' and like, 'I like my bikini' you know, I was like quite happy with myself and then I was like looking in magazines and like I compared myself to them and they were so skinny, like all the people and they were all really brown and tanned and like had really nice hair and that and then I was like 'ok, well, maybe not' and that like puts you down,
[. . .]
BECKIE: so that's like comparing yourself to like media images and
HANNAH: yeah cos say, I looked at the picture of me in my bikini, and like that was in my head and then say I went and looked at magazines, and then went back to the picture and then maybe I'd think, 'ok, maybe I didn't look so good'
CHLOE: and in magazines, I'd love to be a model, I don't know why but like I wouldn't cos I'm too big and like that's what gets on my nerves cos of like when you're looking at the telly and they're got like adverts for like Next and like they've always got super-skinny girls and like that's what gets on my nerves about it cos like it completely puts me out of it and I don't know why but that's what really gets on my nerves

BECKIE: so in that way, is like looking at photos of yourself better than looking at magazines?
CHLOE: yeah, I'd rather look at magazines of myself, of like other big girls than all these super-skinny girls in like little bikinis and super-perfect tans and stuff

Hannah and Chloe discuss how they know, understand and live their bodies through multiple images; photographs of their bodies, popular media images of 'super-skinny girls', their imagination ('in my head', 'I thought I looked ok'). Bodies, according to this extract, are experienced through specific relations with images (for example, between the photograph of Hannah in a bikini and the popular media images of models and celebrities in bikinis) but also through more ambiguous relations, relations that cannot be pinned down to any particular image. The girls have images of their bodies that do not seem to 'fit' with any one (type of) image but are instead produced through and in excess of these multiple images. 'One' image cannot be settled on with any stability or guarantee. Where, for example, do the boundaries of a photographic image lie if it is known and understood through popular media images?

In arguing that knowledges, understandings and experiences of bodies are not produced through only one kind of image, nor only through a certain set of images, the suggestion is that the specificities of relations between particular bodies and particular images are crucial but not comprehensive. Indeed, consider the extract with which the chapter opened where Chloe answers my question by pointing to 'what you look like and what other look like'. While this chapter has tried to examine how photographic, mirror and media images produce certain knowledges and understandings of bodies, it is clear that 'what you look like and what others look like' cannot be covered only by these types. In the following extract, Hannah also discusses ways of experiencing her body that cannot be reduced to the focus of this chapter.

BECKIE: ok, so if you think you look nice in something and someone else hasn't told you that, then where does that come from? From like looking in a mirror and, like, seeing?
HANNAH: yeah, cos I mean, I normally go shopping with like my friends or I go with my mum as well but sometimes I take friends with me cos parents' decisions aren't always the best [laughs] but say I look in the mirror in the changing room and think my opinion of this is I think I look ok but it's got its downsides kind of thing and then I go and ask my friend and if she said the same thing then I'd either buy it or I wouldn't so, I establish my opinion first then see what other people say cos it's from different points of view when you look at yourself

Here, Hannah describes images of her body which exceed her relations with photographs, mirrors and media images and which are produced through the matter of her multiple and diverse relations with friends, her mum, parents, shopping, clothes, changing rooms, for example.

In opening up the possible ways in which 'images' might be understood, and in asking not 'what is an image?' but 'what can images do?', the aim of this chapter has been to explore, as Deleuze writes, 'the matter' of images; 'the absolute identity of the image and movement' (2005: 61). In conceiving images in terms of matter and movement, any clear distinction between bodies and images is made redundant. As matter and movement, bodies are experienced through images. Here, I have begun to consider how this matter and movement involves the relations between bodies and images that might be considered 'still' or 'caught'; photographs of 'the past', or popular media images which 'infill ... the distance between cause and effect, object and subject' (Lury 1998: 3, see Introduction), for example. In this sense, becoming is not restricted to any specific temporality or spatiality. The past body of a photograph, for example, does not remain in 'the past' but moves to produce present and future experiences of a body. The 'present' body of mirror image can be impossible. The 'impossibility' of a media image does not signal the end to a body's becoming. Instead, understood as becoming, the relations between the girls' bodies and images are involved in different rhythms, different affects, of motion and stillness and therefore make possible and impossible particular becomings. It is the aim of the following three chapters to explore these becomings through the ways in which the girls' bodies are known, understood, lived – experienced – through their relations with images.

Notes

1 Putting 'own' in inverted commas here draws attention to the impossibility of designating Hannah's 'own' body when Hannah experiences her body through other bodies, the bodies of celebrities. See Chapter 4 for a more detailed discussion of this point.
2 Popular media images refers to what the girls describe these in their interviews as media images; images in popular culture, for example magazines, advertisements, films, music videos etc.
3 In this sense, the girls' surprise might be compared to Barthes' (1980/2000) notion of the photographic *punctum*. The *punctum* is 'that accident which pricks me (but also bruises me, is poignant to me)' (Barthes 2000: 27) and refers to the ability of a photograph to wound its viewer, to generate emotion or interest through an attraction to a specific instant of what is captured. This is distinct from the 'photographic "shock" [which] consists

less in traumatising than in revealing what was so well hidden that the actor himself was unaware or unconscious of it' (Barthes 2000: 32). I am interested in the surprise in terms of the *punctum*; see following chapters for how other images 'wound'. Perhaps what attracts and wounds the girls to a photograph is the accuracy of its depiction of their bodies. What is also significant here in terms of the argument made in previous chapters for a geometrical model of immanent becoming rather than a hierarchical model of transcendence and being, is Barthes' description of the photograph as '*flat*, platitudinous in the true sense of the word' (Barthes 2000: 106).

4 Year 7 was the first year of secondary school for the girls. They were interviewed in Year 9.

5 The girls' discussion here that a photograph will produce an image of their body looking a particular way in some ways echoes the desire Barthes expresses that he will 'come out on paper' as a 'good sort' (2000: 11). For Barthes the desire is for photography to 'capture' a particular way of being, a personality for example, and render this as it (actually) is. However, for the girls, the desire is for photography not to capture *a personality as it is* but rather *a body as it might be*. The girls want their bodies to 'come out' not as they 'actually' are but as they might become.

6 Consider this point in relation to Deleuze's account of Foucault's notion of knowledge: 'there is nothing prior to knowledge, because knowledge, in Foucault's new conception of it, is defined by the combination of visible and articulable that are unique to each stratum or historical formation. Knowledge is a practical assemblage, a "mechanism" of statements and visibilities. There is therefore nothing behind knowledge' (1988: 51). Here Deleuze argues that for Foucault there is nothing prior to or behind knowledge: knowledge constitutes the thing that is known and experienced.

7 See, for example, some of the girls' discussion of photographs of their mothers in Chapter 6.

8 Consider here Ricoeur's use of photographs to illustrate his theory of a crisis in *idem* identity (identity as sameness). One of the ways in which sameness is identified is through resemblance. He argues that when a temporal dimension is introduced to *idem* identity, doubt emerges. For example, a temporal process of aging might make a reliance on resemblance impossible to distinguish a person *as the same* person. To deal with temporal doubt, Ricoeur proposes the requirement of 'the *uninterrupted continuity* between the first and the last stage in the development of what we consider to be the same individual' (1992: 117). This serves to frame the 'ordered series of small changes which, taken one by one, threaten resemblance without destroying it. This is how we see photos of ourselves at successive ages of our lives' (1992: 117).

9 In a study of American older women's beauty shop culture, Frida Kerner Furman (1997) discusses one of her participants checking and re-checking her appearance for reassurance. The participant, Marny,

says 'for reassurance let's check in the mirror'. Marny describes how 'at parties I'll get up and look in the mirror, but I don't know what I expected to see, but that I wanted to know if I looked OK. A lot of mirror business. . .A lot of mirroring' (Marny, quoted in Kerner Furman 1997: 61). In Marny's terms, looking in a mirror involves checking that she looks 'OK'. This is also how Emily and Sammy describe their checking; how does a body look?

10   This might be a mundane point but such an approach highlights that being unhappy, depressed or angry with a body are still kinds of becoming. That is, *a body does not stop becoming because it is unhappy, depressed or angry.* This is not to neutralise or overlook the unhappiness, depression or anger of these becomings but rather to open up alternative ethical ways of thinking about, and perhaps 'dealing' with, them which, for example, do not depend on certain assumption being made in advance.

4

Looks and selves

TASHA: well, yeah, what Dionne was saying was true... why we should have to be pressured to look the ways the boys want us to look and like it just makes you think that maybe that is true, like why don't boys go for your personality and like why do they have to go for what you look like?...

The strength or duration of the image's effect could be called its intensity. (Massumi 2002a: 24)

In examining what an image might do and in exploring the relations between bodies and images, I have argued in previous chapters that bodies become through the ways in which they are experienced through images. So far, the emphasis has been on the relations between bodies and particular types of identifiable images: photographic, mirror and popular media images. However, as I suggested at the end of Chapter 3, 'images' were also understood by the girls in more ambiguous and indefinable ways. Indeed, according to the extract above, Tasha knows her body through images of how she thinks other people, and here specifically boys, see her. In this context, Tasha makes a distinction between *how she looks* and *who she is* (her personality); 'why don't boys go for your personality and like why do they have to go for what you look like?' In making this distinction, Tasha draws attention to the ways in which she experiences her body through its multiplicity, in this case through her looks *and* personality. In beginning to open up the concept of the image by considering how the girls think other people see them, my focus in this chapter is again on what these images make possible and impossible for the becoming of bodies. What do knowledges and understandings of other people's views of their bodies do to the becoming of the girls' bodies?

This chapter pulls through and develop a number of Deleuzian concepts explored so far. For example, in opening up the notion of images and in understanding the 'in-itself of the image [as] matter' (Deleuze 2005: 61), in this chapter I examine the art-work that the girls produced in the research, not as illustrative of the points they make in their interviews but as 'data' which itself can be examined in terms of the becoming of bodies. This chapter focuses on the girls' bodies as *assemblages*, that is as the arrangement of a multiple and diverse set of experiences on a plane of immanence. I examine the process whereby 'looks' and 'selves' become particularly significant organs of their bodies. As indicated above, 'looks' and 'selves' refer to the girls' concern in their discussions and art-work with 'how I look' and 'who I am' or 'what my personality is'. I argue that these concerns emerge through the relations between the girls' bodies and other bodies. For example, Tasha's comments indicate that looks and selves emerge as important organs of her body through her relations with other bodies, in this extract through her relations with boys. In this sense, this chapter also draws through the importance of *relationality* to a Deleuzian understanding of bodies; assemblages are the relations between various organs. In understanding looks and selves through relations, I explore how they are prioritised in different ways and how the relations between looks and selves limit or extend the possibilities of becoming. In particular, I attend to how the becoming of the girls' bodies are limited through the reduction of their bodies to looks, that is through the reduction of the multiplicity of their bodies to one specific aspect of it.

The concept of intensity is also developed here and in later chapters. In this chapter, the concept is intended to draw attention to the ways in which not all organs of a body are equal or equivalent. As indicated in Chapter 2, intensity refers both to the multiplicity of a body and to an understanding of life 'before' its organisation into extensity. In one sense, intensity refers to the way in which certain organs – looks and selves for instance – become more intense than other organs. Looks and selves, then, might be understood in terms of Massumi's point above; as strong and/or durable images of a body. In another sense, this chapter understands the reduction of the multiplicity of a body to one specific aspect of it as the process whereby the molecular intensity of a body is organised according to extensive molar forms. To put this another way, this chapter takes up the project of transcendental empiricism (see Chapter 2) to trace the ways in which the virtual is actualised. For example, Tasha's comments above suggest that looks are produced as a particularly intense experience of her body through relations with boys because looks are extensively meaningful; they signify for boys – wrongly for Tasha – something about her body. As molecular, intensive, virtualities, the possibilities of bodies are multiple and diverse so in what ways do looks and selves emerge as the dominant ways in which the girls' experience their bodies? More especially, what do 'looks' and 'selves' make possible and impossible for the becoming of the girls' bodies?

Look good, feel good

There were many different relations between looks and selves that the girls explained in their art-work and interviews. As the discussion below demonstrate, these relations involved different prioritisations and different knowledges and understandings of their bodies. One of the ways in which the girls discussed looks and selves was in terms of feeling good through looking good. For example, in the following extract from Chloe's individual interview, we discussed how knowledges of her body as looking good were produced:

> BECKIE: so if you feel good when you've . . . like done your hair nice, how do you know you look good? Is it from looking in a mirror or is it what other people say or do you just feel good or –?
>
> CHLOE: well when I look in the mirror and I think I look good then I feel good so it basically is from a mirror cos if I think I look nice then I will wear it, I will wear my hair like it there could be some times when like I'm walking, like say I go into Casey's house and I say 'does my hair look nice?' and if she doesn't think so then she will tell me so I'll just try and do a little something to my hair or to my eyes or something to try and make it look nicer, so, yeah, it depends, mainly from mirror images, from what I see myself as, so if I think I look good then I feel good so mainly it is mirrors yeah

In this extract, Chloe attaches how she looks and how she feels through different images of her body. One of the ways in which she knows she looks good is through her mirror image. Looking in a mirror for Chloe provides an image of her body where she knows she looks good and therefore can feel good. Feeling good becomes experienced through how she looks. In this extract, Chloe discusses the relations between her 'own' body and a mirror image; Chloe's body is the 'only' body involved. However, Chloe also discusses her relations with Casey as involved in the production of looking good through feeling good. Chloe's mirror image does not necessarily guarantee that she looks good as Casey might disagree. The knowledge of looking good produced through a mirror image is therefore not secure but must be confirmed by Casey ('say I go into Casey's house and I say "does my hair look nice?" and if she doesn't think so then she will tell me so I'll just try and do a little something to my hair or to my eyes or something to try and make it look nicer'). Looks must be 'checked' (with Casey) in order to ensure that the looking good is an accurate knowledge.

According to Chloe, then, looking good is a knowledge that is confirmed by mirror images, and by Casey's support. While looking good and feeling good are in relation with each other, there is a distinction between them. In the context of this chapter, 'feeling' is not necessarily equitable with 'selfhood', that is 'how I feel' is not necessarily 'who I am'. However, of interest in the extract above is how 'feeling', as distinct from 'looks', is understood as an 'internal' aspect of a body. For example, while Chloe discusses 'looks' in relations with other 'external' things – people (Casey) and images (mirrors) – 'feeling' is understood through relations with Chloe's 'own' body; Chloe 'feels'. As is discussed below, although the difference between 'inside' and 'outside' a body is not simple or permanently achievable, the distinction that the girls make between 'how I look' and 'who I am' involves definitions of their bodies as insides and outsides. 'Looks' are the 'outside' of a body and 'selves', or 'feeling' in the cases above, are the 'inside' of a body. This distinction between the inside of a body as 'self' and the outside of a body as 'looks' can be explored through how Chloe continues the conversation above.

BECKIE: and what about photos and stuff? Do they ever come into it [looking and feeling good] or –?
CHLOE: I dunno, I mean if you don't look good in a photo then you just don't look good
BECKIE: it doesn't like mean anything so?
CHLOE: no, like if you're doing something so you don't look good, or you're doing it for a reason like to make yourself laugh or other people laugh then so, yeah I think, photos do come into it a lot but then you just think 'well, it's just a laugh at the end of the day' and if you keep all those photos from when you were older, you'll just think, you can all have a laugh at them, so yeah it does matter but not that much of a big a deal
BECKIE: ok, so like looking in a mirror is much more important
CHLOE: yeah cos if you're looking in a mirror then you're ready to go out so

In photographs, where Chloe thinks that she does not look good, looks and self can be detached. Self is detached from looks so looks do not stand for Chloe's self. Her self is distinguished from her looks and is not influenced, or known, through her looks; 'I mean if you don't look good then you just don't look good'. In detaching the outside of her body (looks) from the inside of her body (self), Chloe's body is not just experienced, by herself and by others, as 'not looking good'. There is something other than looks through which Chloe's body can be experienced. However, in photographs where Chloe thinks that she does not look good 'for a reason like to make yourself laugh or other people laugh', looks and self are both attached and detached. Not looking good in photographs 'for a reason' involves a detachment of looks from self – so Chloe's 'self' is not experienced through her 'looks' – but also involves

116   *The becoming of bodies: girls, images, experience*

an attachment of looks and self – by not looking good to make herself or other people laugh, Chloe's 'self' becomes knowable. That is, for Chloe, 'who I am' becomes known through 'how I look'; not looking good to make myself or other people laugh indicates something about who I am. The 'inside' and 'outside' of Chloe's body are therefore distinguished but are also blurred; if 'who I am' is known through 'how I look' (making people laugh by not looking good for a reason for example) where are the lines to be drawn between what is internal and external to a body? In the next section, this question is examined through the art-work that the girls created but it is important to note that this question emerges through an understanding of a body as the *relations* between different things.

Imaging looks and selves

In the art-work that Sarah, Sammy and Tasha created, it is difficult to distinguish between looks and selves. The art-work provides a particular example of the relations between looks and selves because the lines between them become blurred and they are experienced *through* each other, the 'inside' and 'outside' of a body become difficult to mark.[1] This section examines how looks and selves are attached and blurred through consumption in Sarah's art-work and performativity in Sammy's and Tasha's art-work. These modes of attachment are then compared with Anna's art-work which attempts to re-assert the distinction between looks as 'inside' and selves as 'outside' that the other girls' art-work disappear.

In Sarah's art-work (Figure 4.1),[2] looks and selves are attached so that selfhood is expressed through looks; 'how I look' is 'who I am'. Central to this relation between looks and selves that Sarah makes is *consumption*. One way to understand how Sarah's art-work is put together (or assembled) is through its repetition of certain techniques and conventions of teenage girls' magazines, both in terms of design and content. The art-work is neatly put together to fit within the size of the page and there is a careful balance of colour and size of the cut-out images. The images that Sarah mixes and collages are taken from girls' and women's magazines: 'boys' (male models, celebrities and sport stars), fashion (clothes, shoes), designer products (labels, cars, perfume) and sweet 'naughty' food (chocolate, cake, ice cream). Sarah produces an experience of her body through these visual materials as the attachment of looks and self through consumption, for example through the actual and imaginary consumption of designer products, as Sarah says when she (verbally) explained her art-work to me:

Looks and selves 117

Figure 4.1 Sarah's art-work

SARAH: Erm this sort of shows I like designer labels and it's just sort of things I like, like boys and shoes, clothes, and I do like cars as well
BECKIE: oh ok, . . . do you wear these labels now or is it stuff that you'd want to?
SARAH: erm, I'd like to, some of them I do, but not all of them

Sarah's art-work involves experiences of both what she actually consumes and what she would 'like to'. Designer labels, for example, are both 'actual' and 'virtual' and through what she likes and what she aspires to, looks and self are attached. In this sense, 'experience' is not contained within what *has* happened or what *does* happen but also exists as what *might* happen. Sarah's attachment of looks and self is produced through the 'future' possibilities of her looks and self. These possibilities evade and escape location within one experience and involve consumption as the potential to become. In her art-work, Sarah's body is therefore not complete or finished but through the attachment of looks and selves can become something else that she would like. Consumption is a process which Sarah understands as enabling the possibilities and potentials of

Figure 4.2 Sammy's art-work

her body; buying and wearing designer products or driving a sports car are modes through which the possibilities of her body's becoming might be expanded.

In her art-work (Figure 4.2), Sammy also attaches looks and selves to extend the possibilities of how her body might become. As with Sarah's art-work, Sammy's art-work attaches looks and selves through a magazine-style format in which a Polaroid photograph of Sammy, taken during the workshop, is labelled 'before' and pictures of three celebrities – two female and one male – and an image of a bikini top on a tanned model are labelled 'I wish'. This repeats the format of a magazine make-over where a 'member of the public' is given a 'new look', and consequently a 'new 'self'.[3] Sammy attaches looks and self through presenting her body as one thing ('me') and desiring to be something else, something better ('I wish'). Accordingly, Sammy understands her body as unfinished, as not right, and wants her body to become different; tanned, or a celebrity, for example. This desire that Sammy expresses through organising her art-work around the 'before' and 'I wish' of her (potential) body is not considered futile or unachievable. Sammy's attachment of looks and selves cannot be contained within this particular organisation but can also be understood through the Polaroid photograph. The group workshop lasted for eighty minutes, of which Sammy spent about half preparing to have her photograph taken. Sammy heated up hair straighteners that she had brought with her and Tasha straightened Sammy's hair and applied make-up. Sammy experimented with a number of poses before allowing Tasha to take her photograph. What this indicates is that Sammy wanted to present an image of her body in the photograph which attached her looks and self; my self is my looks.

How Sammy attaches her looks and selves, then, are not contained within the still of the Polaroid photograph, nor within the frame of the art-work. Indeed, neither the Polaroid photograph nor the art-work are 'still' but rather they contain within them movements and relations of becoming. Sammy's *performance* – or, better, *performativity* (Butler 1990, 1993), whereby the 'actor' is constituted through the performance rather than existing prior to it – of her body, held 'within' the Polaroid photograph, suggests that she thinks that the 'gap' expressed in the art-work between what she *is* and what she *wants to be* might be closed; Sammy can become what she wishes. The understanding of her body through the attachment of looks and self is an attachment which involves the potentiality of becoming what she wishes through performance, through performing her body in particular ways. The pose that Sammy settles on for her Polaroid photograph, for example, repeats, although probably not deliberately or self-consciously, the pose of the pop star Christina Aguilera[4] in one of the images in Sammy's art-work. The heads are both angled to one side, the faces have similar expressions and their bodies are held in corresponding fashions. The photographic portrait then, repeats certain poses in order to designate certain 'kinds' of people (Lury 1998), in this case, female celebrities.

The performativity of Sammy's body is also through the attachment of looks and selves in terms of the clothes she likes to wear. Through clothes, Sammy says, she can perform her body in certain ways:

BECKIE: ok, so at what moments now do you like your body?
SAMMY: erm, when I don't know, just when I can wear tight clothes cos I mean if you're wearing baggy you're not really showing it off if you know what I mean
BECKIE: ok
SAMMY: so, like 'if you've got it flaunt it' kinda thing so just really that's why really when I'm out of school I feel more confident as well

Wearing 'tight clothes' which 'show off' her body enables Sammy to become what she wishes. Sammy can perform her body as she wishes to extend the possibilities of what her body might become. Sammy's body is here experienced as possibility through the attachment of looks and selves. For example, Sammy attaches feeling 'more confident' and liking her body to her looks; how she 'feels' (the 'inside' of a body) is known and performed through how she 'looks' (the 'outside' of a body). This understanding of 'feeling', then, disrupts the boundaries between the inside and outside of a body as 'feeling' is dependent on 'looks'. Indeed, 'feel[ing] more confident' is 'looking' good. This is, I think, slightly different to the distinction that Chloe makes between 'feeling' and 'looking' as for Chloe 'feeling' can also be 'felt' separately from 'looking', as is the case when she wakes up and doesn't look her best. However, in Sammy's art-work and comments above, 'feeling' or 'self' is understood through looking, and not as a separate/separable aspect or 'organ' of her body.

Tasha's art-work (Figure 4.3) also involves a Polaroid photograph of herself in a similar pose to Sammy (and Christina) and is also constructed around a desire to be different to what she understood her body to be.[5] Around the Polaroid photograph, Tasha has spelt out 'why can't I be like that' and has written comments next to different images of women: 'absolutely gorgeous', and 'to die for' label images of women that Tasha wants to be like, 'do we eat to much' next to an image of a woman eating a burger and 'ooo I hate to be fat' next to the only image of an 'overweight' woman Tasha could find in all of the magazines. While Sammy's art-work is about who and how she might become through a successful performance which attaches looks and selves (a performance in which Tasha was involved), Tasha's might be understood as about how, through the attachment of looks and selves, she cannot perform what she would like to be. Sammy performs her body in certain ways to become who and how she wishes but Tasha, in both her art-work and interviews, understands the gap between what she is and what she would like to be as unable to be filled in or closed. Indeed, the attachment of looks and selves that Tasha experiences does not enable a successful performance of how her body might become but rather *stops* or *blocks*

Figure 4.3 Tasha's art-work

performance, her body becomes through an *unsuccessful performance*. Tasha understands her body not as future possibilities and potential but rather as restricted to what it is now. Her body becomes through what she *is* rather than through what she might be.

In the art-work by Sarah, Sammy and Tasha, looks and selves are attached so that selves, 'who I am', are known through looks, 'how I look'. For both Sarah and Sammy the attachment of looks and selves expand the possibilities of how their bodies might become; Sarah through the consumption of products that enable her to become what she aspires to and Sammy through the performance of her body in particular ways that close the gap between what her body is and what it might be(come). However, for Tasha the attachment of looks and self means that her body cannot become what it might be but rather is stuck with what she experiences it as.

The attaching of looks and selves within the art-work can be understood to, at least partly, emerge through the archive materials that were provided (see Chapter 2). These materials were primarily 'visual', or, the more 'tactile' materials that were also provided were not used by the girls as much. These 'visual' resources, then, might be understood to restrict the possible ways in which bodies might be expressed in the art-work. That is, by providing visual materials, the girls can be understood as

Figure 4.4 Anna's art-work, front

Looks and selves 123

Figure 4.5 Anna's art-work, back

limited in how they might express their bodies in non-visual ways. While I do not want to suggest a straightforward correlation between visual materials and looks – visual materials might also produce expressions of 'selves' separated from looks for example – most of the girls do seem to use the visual resources to produce images of their bodies which attach, and subsume, 'selves' with 'looks'; who I am is how I look. These processes of attachment are particularly evident in Anna's art-work which wants to *resist* or *detach* how looks and selves become attached through the visual materials provided in the art-work workshop. In other words, the limits of the visual materials are made explicit by Anna's art-work because Anna found it difficult to create a visual image of her body with the materials provided. In particular, she did not know how to express experiences of her body through the popular magazines that the other girls had requested and which formed major parts of their art-work.

Anna's collage (Figure 4.4 and 4.5) is very different to the other girls', both in her group and at the other school. It is very small in comparison and is the only one to present a coherent and recognisable body shape (head, torso, limbs) and is also the only one to use materials (moulding putty) to 'flesh out' 'her' body. In Anna's art-work there is a desire to *detach* how looks and selves are attached through the visual materials. Anna produces a visual experience of her body which is expressed through her looks but where the art-work also refuses to restrict her body to these looks. Anna writes on the art-work to undercut the way in which she has expressed her body by saying 'Doesn't matter what you look like! On the outside (even if they do look weird!)' at the top of the image and on the right hand side of the body has written 'it's what's inside what counts (meaning personality) no matter what they look like.' On the back of the image, Anna has also written 'U don't have to wear makeup to look pretty'. Anna therefore makes a clear distinction between the 'inside' or 'self' of a body and the 'outside' or 'looks' of a body. This both recognises the blurring that Sarah and Sammy experience but also resists the confusion of looks and selves and reasserts them as separate and separable aspects of how a body might be known and understood. As with Tasha's comments with which the chapter opens, not only is there a distinction between looks and selves but selves are argued to be more important to a body. Anna argues that selves should be more intense than looks as 'selves' define a body more than looks; 'it's what's inside what counts'. In the next section the ways in which the attachment of looks and selves is experienced by the girls in terms of the desire to detach them is explored through the notion of 'knowing' a body.

'They don't even know me'

Part of Anna's desire to detach how looks and selves are attached is to avoid being known only through her looks. In prioritising selves over looks, Anna argues that the 'outside' of her body, that is what other people see, does not give them the right kind of knowledges of what her body is and what it might be. This prioritisation of selves over looks is also evident in Tasha's comments about how people know her body through 'judging' how she looks. *Judging* is when the relations a body has with other things (be they bodies or other organs of that body) are reduced to only one aspect of that body. In the cases discussed so far, 'judging' a body refers to when a body is only known through how it looks. In her interviews, Chloe talked about how photographs are an important part of her experiences of her body. In particular she described a collage of photographs on her bedroom wall. She says that these are important to her because they are both experiences she remembers with her family and friends and because her family and friends are those who *see* the photographs. Chloe is in relations of *trust* with these people and so feels able to put up images of herself where she thinks that she does not look good. The people who see the photographs of Chloe not looking good are people that she trusts not to attach her looks and self and to subsume her self within her looks. Instead, those that see these photographs *know* Chloe and so are able to detach how she looks from who she is.

However, Chloe says that she often experiences her body through how relations with people she *does not know* involve 'judgement', that is the attachment of her looks and selves so that her body becomes understood only through her looks. For example:

> CHLOE: ... I mean I've had rows with people at school about them saying stuff about me and stuff but most of the time it's just people walking down the street and they don't even know me and it's like 'well why are you starting on me, you don't even know me, give me a chance and start to know me and still don't like me then fine but if not don't talk to me', know what I mean
> BECKIE: so do you think you're really judged on your looks?
> CHLOE: yeah, very much so

In this extract, Chloe points to how, through such encounters with people 'who don't even know me', her body is judged through her looks; the possibilities of Chloe's body, of what it might become, are restricted to how she looks. As with Tasha's explanation above, the attachment of 'looks' to 'selves' does not involve the expansion of the possibilities of becoming, but rather restricts how a body might become to what it is thought to be, here-and-now. Looks and selves become subsumed within a restricted spatial and temporal moment of non-possibility. Chloe, however, wants to re-assert the distinction between looks and self through separating their attachment in judgement; 'give me a chance and start to know me'. Through detaching looks from self, Chloe argues that her body cannot be reduced to her looks because there is something else, (an)other aspect(s), which cannot be known only through her looks.

Indeed, Chloe argues that she cannot be judged only through her looks by people who don't know her because they will always be missing what else she is. For example, to make a judgment of her looks from a photograph where she does not look good might be to miss the 'reason' for looking not good:

> BECKIE: ok, so you don't care if someone you don't know says something?
> CHLOE: no
> BECKIE: why? Because they don't know you?
> CHLOE: because they don't know me so
> BECKIE: ok, and so you think it's more important that people know you?
> CHLOE: yeah, if they know me then fair enough, but they don't but they're trying to call me a tramp when they don't know me, I might just be wearing those clothes on that specific day so they don't really know me, like the whole of my life but just for that one minute

To judge Chloe only through her looks is not 'fair' because it reduces her body to a discrete and isolated moment of space of time; 'that specific day', 'that one minute'. Chloe argues that her body cannot be reduced to 'that' moment and then abstracted and generalised to 'know' who she is because her body is a *process;* 'the whole of my life'.

This can be understood in terms of the actualisation of the virtual whereby what is made actual cannot stand for all of the virtual. The process of Chloe's body becoming in this case involves *knowing* her. Knowing Chloe involves the connections and assemblages of multiple and different moments of spatial and temporal experience so that 'one' moment cannot stand for 'the whole of my life' (what might be termed the virtual). *Judging* involves an immediacy where a moment is understood as self-contained or disconnected (as actualised perhaps). *Knowing* a body, however, involves both *immediacy* and *duration* as different spatialities and temporalities are involved. To return to Chloe's comments discussed in the section 'Look good, feel good' where she describes understanding her body through relations with mirrors, photographs and Casey, looking at a photograph, looking in a mirror before going out and asking Casey's advice on how she looks are all relations involving different spatialities and temporalities and therefore produce different – immediate and/or enduring – knowledges of a body. For Chloe, immediate knowledges, because they are disconnected from the process of her body, are less meaningful. Immediate knowledges involve the attachment of looks and selves so that looks subsume selves. In contrast, more enduring knowledges of her body involve the capacity of detaching looks and selves. This ability to detach looks and selves is perhaps why she trusts Casey's opinion more than her own.

Casey also discusses how her looks and selves are attached through relations with people she does not know:

> CASEY: ... like the other day I was walking past and she called me a slag and I said 'if you've got something to say come down here and say it' but she didn't but then she came out later and I was having a go at her and stuff but she doesn't even really know me, I don't like her, and for her to say that she doesn't even know me so how can she say that cos I'm not and it really gets on my nerves, and like if she says it then boys sometimes say it to me but I'm not, 'what part of it don't you understand?'

In this extract, Casey describes how it is her *behaviour*, rather than looks, that becomes the focus of judgement through its attachment to her self. Casey's behaviour is attached to self and subsumes self so that her body is only known through this.[6] Like Chloe, Casey argues that people who do not know her should not reduce her to one aspect of her body (behaviour) because this is to miss what else she is and might be:

> BECKIE: so is that like the worst thing someone can call you or is that just the worst thing someone can call *you*? Do you know what I mean, is that like something that just gets to you personally?
>
> CASEY: yeah it annoys me cos I'm not, I'd rather be one and let them say it instead of not being one and them saying it cos it's just annoying cos they don't even know who I am, and like they haven't even took the time out to get to know who I am and for them to just walk past and say it is just pathetic, like a little girl and I just don't see the point of it

'Who I am' is for Casey a body which cannot be contained within or reduced to one aspect. Calling Casey a 'slag' is to not know Casey. For people to know Casey, they must make sure they have 'took the time out to get to know who I am'; this cannot be known by 'just walk[ing] past' because 'who I am' involves an enduring temporality and not a immediate one. For both Chloe and Casey, knowing, as opposed to judging, involves the detachment of looks and selves so that looks do not subsume selves and restrict the ways in which that body might be experienced. Detaching looks and selves extends the possibilities in which their bodies might become. This is examined in the next section in terms of how 'personality' is discussed by the girls as preferable to 'looks' for a body to become known.

Personality versus looks

As indicated at the opening of the chapter, Tasha believes that boys will not go out with her because although they like her personality (they are her friends) they do not like her looks. On a number of occasions throughout the interviews, Tasha said how much she would like a boyfriend but cannot get one because boys judge her on looks rather than personality. For example, in the extract with which this chapter begins (taken from her individual interview), Tasha argues that not only do boys attach looks and selves but they also prioritise looks over selves. Tasha distinguishes looks from personality and says that she prefers her personality to her looks and would rather be 'known' (and not 'judged') through her personality. Although this is what Tasha wants, she does not necessarily think this is possible, that is she experiences her body through how boys judge her according to how she looks and does not think that boys could prioritise her personality over her looks. In this case, personality and looks are not so much organs or aspects of a body that can be experienced at once but rather Tasha experiences personality and looks as in competition with each other: personality versus looks. Looks and personality are separate organs that are attached in particular ways that Tasha wants to detach. Rather than looks being prioritised over selves, selves should be prioritised over looks; selves should be the more intense knowledge and experience of her body.

Talking about similar comments that Tasha made in the group interview, Emily also detaches looks and personality:

> EMILY: when Tasha said, like when she was saying that whenever she fancies someone they won't go out with her cos she's really fat and ugly and stuff and I said it wasn't, that's not what it should have been but no offence to my sister or anything but she isn't really that pretty but she's got a boyfriend and everything and so I don't really think it is how Tasha said it is
> BECKIE: ok, so how do you think it is?
> EMILY: well, I don't think you should go for looks, it's just like, if you're a nice person and you've got a really nice personality and stuff then, yeah, you should go out with them
> BECKIE: that's more important?
> EMILY: yeah
> BECKIE: do you think Tasha was saying that or do you think she was saying you shouldn't go out with someone?
> EMILY: well, I don't know cos, she was saying, cos I know she's got a really nice personality cos I know her, but she kept saying that no boy would want to go out with her cos she's really ugly and she's really fat and everything, but I don't think she is

In this extract, Emily argues that looks and personality should be detached so that personality is prioritised over looks; 'I don't think you should go for looks, [. . .] if you're a nice person and you've got a nice personality and stuff then, yeah, you should go out with them'. However, Emily's argument is, I think, slightly different to Tasha's. Tasha argues that looks should be *replaced* with personality so that her body is known not through how it looks but through who it is. This is the incorporation of looks into personality so that looks become in some sense redundant. Emily, though, is not arguing that looks can or should be replaced but rather is suggesting that personality should be *prioritised* over looks. Looks and personality, as aspects of a body, both exist but personality can and should be experienced more intensely. This is demonstrated through how Emily makes her argument by referring to her sister who she says 'isn't really that pretty'. By referring to how she thinks her sister looks and saying that 'she's got a boyfriend and everything', Emily refuses Tasha's understanding of why she does not have a boyfriend, 'so

I don't really think it is how Tasha said it is'. Selves or personality can be detached from each other so that one is prioritised, but one cannot replace the other; 'personality' does not replace 'looks'. According to Emily's argument, then, just as the aspect of 'looks' is not all there is to a body, neither is the aspect of 'personality'. That is, a body cannot be known only through 'personality'.

One starting point in Emily's analysis of Tasha's comments is that Emily *knows* Tasha; 'I know [Tasha]'s got a really nice personality cos I know her'. Emily's knowledge of Tasha is the basis of how she understands her. Through this knowledge, Emily's understanding of Tasha differs both from how Tasha describes boys' understandings of her body and how Tasha understands her body. Emily's knowledge of Tasha in this sense positions her 'outside' the relations between Tasha and boys and within Tasha's 'own' body. This position enables Emily to understand, or know, Tasha through a different spatiality and temporality that is not possible for either Tasha or 'boys'. As I suggested earlier, looks and personality are given different spatialities and temporalities through different relations. Tasha's relations with boys, Tasha's relation with her 'own' body and Emily's relation with Tasha's body all produce looks and personalities as different spatialities and temporalities. According to Tasha, the boys understand her body through looks because, despite being friends, they don't really know who she is. The boys therefore produce their understanding of Tasha through discrete, disconnected moments of experience, that is by only focusing on looks. Emily argues that Tasha's understanding of her 'own' body is also discrete and disconnected because it wants only to focus on the organ of personality. Emily's *knowledge* of Tasha, however, makes connections across and through these different spatial and temporal moments of experience by understanding her body through *both* looks and personality. Emily therefore draws attention to and dismantles how Tasha sets up an either/or dichotomy between 'looks' and 'personality' to understand her relations with boys and with her 'own' body.

Emily argues that Tasha's wish to detach looks from personality and replace looks with personality is not possible: a body cannot be understood and experienced through only one aspect. Anna also points to the fragility and ambiguity of attempts to replace looks with personality. In one sense, Anna's art-work suggests that personality and looks should be detached so that personality is not subsumed into looks; personality should be prioritised or experienced more intensely. However, in another sense, Anna recognises that this detachment of looks from selves cannot maintain the privileging of personality over looks. For example:

BECKIE: ok, so do you think fashion is really important? I mean even in school uniform?
ANNA: yeah I think it is, but I think again we just can't let it rule our lives but people do, I mean I do, but you've just got to stop it,
BECKIE: ok, and what does it mean for fashion to rule your life? I mean what sort of things does that involve?
ANNA: everyday, erm, you putting make-up on, you thinking 'oh do I look nice?', thinking about what your hair looks like, spending a long time, stuff like that
BECKIE: so do you find doing stuff like that is actually quite boring, and quite, or do you actually, do you ever get enjoyment out of it?
ANNA: I do get enjoyment out of it, but then sometimes I just can't be bothered cos I can't make myself look nice

Here, Anna argues that fashion and looks ('oh do I look nice?') should not 'rule our lives', partly because she 'sometimes . . . can't be bothered' and also because she suggests that it involves judgement; fashion and looks become the way in which a body is known. Although Anna wants to 'stop' fashion and looks ruling her life, she recognises herself as part of certain relations where such a stoppage is difficult. Anna says that she gets enjoyment out of doing fashion and looks (thinking about hair, putting on make-up) and also points to how fashion and looks are an integral part of how she experiences her body; 'we just can't let it rule our lives but people do, I mean I do'.

By placing her 'own' body in relations with fashion and looks, Anna's argument about how her body should not be judged through fashion and looks concerns what *should* happen rather than what does happen. The spatialities and temporalities of her body that Anna experiences are 'present', they are what happens. In arguing that looks and fashion should not rule our lives, though, Anna also indicates a different set of spatial and temporal experiences through which her body might become. These expand the possibilities through which Anna's body might become through enabling experiences of a body which do not necessarily involve 'mak[ing] myself look nice'. Through imagining how her body might be experienced differently – for example how a body might be enjoyed through practices of make-up and hair styles but also through the capacity to not 'bother' looking nice – Anna is not necessarily pointing to how her body might be experienced in the future, or was experienced in the past but rather is pointing to how her body might be experienced through multiple and different spatial and temporal moments. These are not so much 'past' or 'future' possibilities but more spatialities and temporalities that defy linear organisation by existing elsewhere and elsewhen to what the past, present and future might be.

Part of Anna's resistance to being judged only through looks is because of the time and effort that must be put into them if they are to be an intense organ of a body ('everyday, erm, you putting make-up on, you thinking "oh do I look nice?", thinking about what your hair looks like, spending a long time, stuff like that'). The temporality of looks that Anna discusses here is an enduring one; looks take time and effort and this time and effort must persist or make connections across different moments of experience. Looking nice is an experience of a body that endures. What Anna points to is that if a body looks nice at one particular spatial and temporal moment, there are connections made between that moment and other moments; a body is anticipated and expected to always look nice. Consider for example the following extract:

TASHA: cos if you don't wear eyeliner one day then you do notice a difference, because, when Dionne started wearing eyeliner once
FAY: we all noticed
TASHA: we all noticed and were all like Dionne you've got eyeliner on but then she
FAY: but then we're used to seeing you with and it would be a shock to see you without eyeliner
TASHA: exactly, so then if I didn't, if I came to school tomorrow with no make-up on then you'd all be like, 'oh, Tash what you doing?'
DIONNE: no, I wouldn't, it's up to you isn't it? and then like if we got used to seeing you without make-up on every day we'd probably wouldn't think anything of it but if you went from a sudden change
FAY: yeah, if now, I'd feel, even though, if you stopped wearing make-up you would probably feel, even though we say all this stuff, you'd probably feel kind of, 'don't want to leave the house without make-up on'

In this extract the girls point to how when they first saw Dionne wearing eyeliner, 'we all noticed'. However, now that 'we're used to seeing you with it . . . it would be a shock to see you without eyeliner'. Wearing eyeliner are moments of how Dionne's body is and can be experienced that connect different spatialities and temporalities.[7] This is what Anna is pointing to, but she is also emphasising the time and effort that goes into living up to these expectations; to look good in an enduring sense means 'bothering'.

In emphasising how looking good must endure, Anna is also arguing that a body cannot be known only through one particular spatial and temporal moment. Like Chloe's argument that experiencing a body on 'that specific day' or at 'one minute' produces judgement rather than knowledge of that body, Anna indicates how one moment of looking nice cannot be isolated from other moments of how a body looks. Looking nice at one moment cannot be disconnected from how else that body might look. As a body can look differently throughout 'the whole of [its] life', looks, by themselves, do not produce knowledge of a body. While Tasha argues that a body can be 'known' through its personality, that is through replacing looks with personality, Anna argues that neither looks nor personality guarantee knowledge of a body:

> ANNA: . . . I think year 8 was my worst year cos I used to fall out with my friends a lot and I used to get very down and stuff and I think it's important about fashion and stuff, cos fashion does put you down, and that you shouldn't always think about it and you should always think about other things and other people, not about what they look like
> BECKIE: so what things should you think about if you're thinking about fashion and looks? What things should you think about people?
> ANNA: if they're nice and if your personality, and if they do annoy you, you, it might not always be, it might just be a cover-up or something cos you just don't know, what really is going on

Through the previous extract from Anna I argued that 'looks' are given different – immediate and enduring – spatialities and temporalities and so looks as one aspect by itself cannot produce knowledge of a body. Here, Anna indicates that personality, as an organ by itself, cannot produce knowledge of a body; personality can be 'a cover-up'. In this sense, personality is also given different spatialities and temporalities so, for example, 'annoy[ing] you' is an immediate spatial and temporal moment and 'what really is going on' might be a more enduring spatial and temporal moment. Anna also discusses the potential multiplicity of personality in relation to the research interviews:

> BECKIE: . . . So from the group session, what did you kind of take away as most important to you?
> ANNA: erm, I found everyone was different from what I expected and what they thought about their views
> BECKIE: ok, in what ways?
> ANNA: that they weren't as bitchy as I thought they'd be

The focus group interview changed how Anna understands the rest of the girls in her group, 'everyone was different from what I expected', 'they weren't as bitchy as I thought they'd be'. The group interview enabled Anna to connect separate moments of experience to produce a more enduring knowledge of the other girls, 'what really is going on', rather than what she 'expected'. What is important here is how Anna complicates what 'personality' might be and refuses to prioritise personality over looks. Both aspects have different possibilities, that is spatialities and temporalities, and therefore neither organ can be solely understood to produce knowledge of a body. In the cases discussed above, the girls privilege *knowing as an enduring spatiality and temporality* over the *immediacy of judgement*. 'Knowing' is an understanding of a body produced through an enduring temporality which provides greater access to what that body might be(come), that is, in Anna's terms, knowing a body is the potential to understand 'what is really going on'. The next section discusses how this notion of 'knowing' works not only through relations between different bodies, as with Anna's and Emily's comments, but also through relations within 'one' particular body.

Looks and looks, selves and selves

The process of knowing that has been explored so far is the girls' understanding that a body cannot be reduced to, through judgement, one particular spatial and temporal moment of experience but rather is always becoming through the connection and assemblage of multiple and different moments. Knowing is therefore distinct from, and preferable to, judging. While Tasha says that bodies can be known through selves rather than looks, Emily and Anna complicate this by arguing that neither looks nor selves by themselves produce knowledge of a body. Indeed, Anna argues that looks and personalities, as organs of a body that is becoming, are themselves processes of becoming; 'personality', for example, might be a 'cover-up'. In arguing this, Anna suggests that 'organs' are not neatly bounded or coherent; a body does not 'have' or even 'become' through 'a' look or 'a' personality. Instead, looks and selves might differ as spatial and temporal moments of experience; a body can look nice *and* can not, a personality can be friendly *and* annoying.[8] In this sense, looks and selves can not only be attached to and detached from each other but also from themselves; looks can be attached to and detached from looks and selves can be attached to and detached from selves. In conceiving looks and selves in such a way, *knowledge* of a body cannot be contained to one organ as that organ is itself capable of becoming different, as Anna points out, one organ does not guarantee knowledge of a body.

Sammy discusses this through the 'gap' between what other people say she looks like and how she thinks she looks:

SAMMY: . . . I don't know I get compliments from people and stuff like that and I take them, I say thanks but I still don't believe it if you know what I mean

Here, Sammy describes not being able to 'believe' other people's 'compliments' about how they 'see' her. Sammy sees herself differently to how other people see her. This 'disjuncture' or 'non-coincidence' of how Sammy's body might be seen is the detachment of looks from looks; how Sammy thinks she looks is detachable from how other people think Sammy looks.[9] Katie also describes similar experiences of the detachment of looks from looks as different images of her body that she and her friends have:

> KATIE: cos I just don't like the way I look, like the way I see myself and other people are like, 'oh no, you're fine' and everything but, it's just not the way you think of yourself, I just don't like the way, like my body or anything like that
>
> [. . .]
>
> BECKIE: what about what friends say to you? why do you think that what they're saying to you is not as true as –?
>
> KATIE: cos they're my friends and, sort, a lot of them are actually quite up-front and say what they think, but they're not the sort of people that will turn round and say 'no you're ugly', they're sort of, 'oh no you're fine, you're fine, you're pretty' sort of, it's just, you don't know whether they're telling the truth really do you, it's not 100 per cent

Katie describes the detachment of looks from looks in terms of a disjuncture between what she thinks and what friends say to her. Friends' comments are 'just not the way you think of yourself'. Katie frames her understanding of this disjuncture in terms of 'truth', that is her friends cannot be trusted to be 'telling the truth'. However, rather than this involving her friends lying to her, for example telling her she looks nice if she doesn't, Katie explains it as 'not 100 per cent'. As with Sammy's comments, Katie's friends see her differently to how she sees herself. However, whereas in Sammy's comments there is an acknowledgment of this difference, in Katie's comments there is also a *privileging* of how she sees her body over how her friends see it. Both Katie and her friends 'know' Katie's body but, according to Katie, she 'knows' it better; 100 percent. Interestingly, in Katie's prioritisation of how she knows her body over how her friends know her body, there is a privileging of the immediate spatiality and temporality that a mirror image of her body produces. A mirror image is, in my terms, 'more accurate' because, in Katie's words, 'it's there and now isn't it, it's like what you look like at that point'. Katie's knowledge of her body, then, is preferable to how her friends know her body because she can see her body not only as the connection of different spatial and temporal moments but also as a specific spatial and temporal moment that her friends do not have access to. Katie detaches her knowledge of her 'own' body from her friends' knowledge of her body because her friends cannot know her body as completely (100 percent) as she can; they cannot 'know' her body through the immediate spatial and temporal moment of her mirror image.

Katie detaches looks from looks through distinguishing between how she thinks she looks and how her friends say she looks and by prioritising her 'own' knowledge of her body. However, in the following extract Fay discusses how she experiences and knows her body through different images of her body:

> BECKIE: ok, now, at what moments do you like your body now? Like at what times and places?
> FAY: well normally when someone pays you a compliment and sometimes just when you're at home and you look in the mirror and think 'oh I don't look, you know, that looks quite nice today', that just kind of lifts you up cos you think 'I don't look too bad today' or something like that
> BECKIE: and what would you be wearing?
> FAY: it's normally like when I'm in my own clothes and stuff and I'll just catch a glimpse of myself and think 'oh I don't look too bad'
> BECKIE: ok so where are these glimpses you catch of yourself?
> FAY: normally when you walk past a mirror, like we've got a big mirror in our bathroom and you kind of think 'alright', and just mirrors and you know, just sometimes, catch images like in the mirror or in a window or something, but yeah
> BECKIE: and what sort of moment don't you like your body?
> FAY: erm normally I'll be at home or something, when I'm in the shower and you look down and see your tummy sticking out or something and you think 'errgh', and you're looking in the mirror thinking 'is it that bad?' and stuff, again like you'll see something of yourself or you'll see a photo of yourself and you'll think 'ergh, is that what it's really like?' and then you'll start to worry about it, it brings you down, like makes you upset

In this extract, Fay discusses how she knows her body through different images which she experiences as 'glimpses'. Through these glimpses, looks and selves become attached and detached in complex ways which blur what they might be. For example, 'thinking' or being 'upset' might be conceived not as just 'looks' or 'selves' but rather as experiences of a body through *both* looks and selves where the distinction between them becomes difficult to maintain.

Moreover, to compare how Katie and Fay talk about knowledges of their body, Katie discusses the detachment of looks from looks in terms of how her friends' knowledges do not coincide with her own, better, knowledge of her looks. Katie has a knowledge – a mirror image – of her looks which her friends' knowledges can be detached from. In this sense, Katie's knowledge is that which other knowledges can either coincide with (attach to), or not. In contrast, Fay's comments do not set up her 'own' knowledge of her body which can be coincided with or not but instead points to how her body is known as *multiple and different images which might and might not attach or detach*. For example, rather than setting up a complete (100 per cent) or better image of her body, Fay describes 'glimpses' of her body ('compliments', 'a big mirror in our bathroom', 'the mirror or a window or something', 'in the shower', 'a photo of yourself') through which knowledges of her body become assembled. Fay does not prioritise any of these glimpses but rather explains them as producing different possibilities ('that just kind of lifts you up', 'you think "oh I don't look too bad"' or 'you think "alright"', 'start to worry', 'brings you down, like makes you upset'). These possibilities involve Fay knowing her body as an *assemblage* of different spatial and temporal images (glimpses). In describing how her body is known through assemblages of different spatial and temporal moments, Fay points to the different relations that her body is involved in. These are both relations between different bodies ('when someone pays you a compliment') and relations 'within' her own body ('when you're at home and you look in the mirror'). The concluding section of this chapter examines the implications of considering a body as *relations* through the notion of intensity.

Intensive experience

At the beginning of the chapter, I indicated that one of the aims of this chapter is to develop through the empirical material the Deleuzian concepts of assemblage, relationality and intensity. Looks and selves have been explored as organs of the girls' bodies which are experienced as intense through relations between the girls and boys, girls and girlfriends. As in previous chapters, I have here pulled attention away from the girls' themselves and towards the relations through which their bodies become. In focusing on these relations, I have also been concerned to think through the concept of intensity to trace the ways in which intensive experience becomes organised extensively. This is to engage with becoming as immanent, and as affective. To focus on intensive experience, then, is not to ignore or downplay the extensive organisation of bodies. That is, this chapter has attended to the ways in which the world is clearly organised so that gender, race, age, for example, represent and signify particular things, and to the girls' explanations that experiences of their bodies through their relations with boys are repeated so that looks are prioritised over selves. Indeed, one of my primary concerns in this book is to examine how the becoming of bodies is not endlessly open but is limited and fixed in certain ways, in this case through the organisation of intensive affects into looks, which represent or signify particular things. I want to consider the ways in which, as becomings, bodies are involved in processes which are restricted; bodies become through the actualisation of the virtual rather than the realisation of the possible (see Chapter 1). To return to the points made by Skeggs (see Chapter 2) and Ahmed (see Chapter 1), things stick. Or, as Massumi states in the quotation at the opening of the chapter, intensity is 'the strength or duration of the image's effect' (2001a: 24). In the case of this chapter, looks can be understood as things that stick, that is as the affective power of an image of a body produced through, and fixed and unfixed through, relations with other bodies. Looks are intensive experiences which become extensively organised to mean particular things. For the girls, looks limit whereas selves expand the becoming of bodies.

In this way, looks can be considered in terms of an affective intensity which is, socially and culturally, invested in. Colebrook explains how affect is 'both singular and collective' (2002: 107):

> Affect is singular because it has no reason or justification, no order or relation, outside itself. The Western investment in whiteness is singular – the investment in a specific intensity that is then made meaningful and justified after the event; it becomes a sign of reason and civilisation. Whiteness becomes the signifier for rationality and humanity; but the whole point of Deleuze's method is to say that these supposedly *signified* qualities that affects represent are the effects, not the grounds. It is not the case that there is the dominance of 'the West' which then leads to the elevation of white skin; it is the investments in the affects of white skin, in a style of thought, in certain bodies and gestures and so on that produces the West. We begin with an investment, say, in the white, phallic, powerful, active body and *then* elevate it as a 'signifier' of law or 'man' in general. (Colebrook 2002: 107)

Affects are 'the becoming of intensities'; 'not just qualities – such as redness' but 'say, the burning and wavering infrared light we see *as* red' (Colebrook 2002: 39). Affects are intensities which 'operate on us in divergent ways, differing in kind – the light that causes our eye to flinch, the sound that makes us start, the image of violence which raises our body temperature' (Colebrook 2002: 39). As a particular intensity which is invested in, looks can be understood as an *affect* (rather than *e*ffect), which 'is then made meaningful and justified after the event', that is becomes an extensity. The prioritisation of looks that the girls discuss are an investment in a particular kind of affect which is then elevated to a signifier. To focus on looks and selves through affect and intensity, then, is to examine the processes of investment through which particular aspects of the girls' bodies become organised according to a restricted extensity.

It is also to develop Deleuze's concept of the fold (Chapter 1), which attends to the relations between the specific (the actual) and the general (the virtual). For example, in examining looks and selves as attached and detached, it should be noted that attachment and detachment are understood here as neither done by the girls voluntarily nor imposed on them through some kind of structure. That is, the attachment and detachment of looks and selves are not understood in terms of structure and agency; attachment and detachment are not performed by the girls as a kind of 'strategy' for coping with different situations that they find themselves in (at this moment I'll prioritise my looks over myself, for example) but neither are the ways in which looks and selves are attached and detached always-already decided for the girls (at this moment my self is inevitably prioritised over my looks). While it is fair to say that the extracts and artwork I discuss could be interpreted and analysed in terms of structure and agency, here I am suggesting that looks and selves are understood as intensive affects. As such, looks and selves cannot (only) be understood as conscious, signifying extensities, for example, but must also be explored in terms of their investments; investments which are both singular and collective in that they 'happen... across us' (Colebrook 2002: 39) rather than as imposed on us or done by us. According to a model of structure/agency, the specificities of the girls' bodies are understood as the result either of the girls' active agency or of their enforced passivity against social and cultural structure. Understanding the becoming of the girls' bodies through the concept of the fold instead, sees the social and cultural as folded into the specificity of the girls' bodies. As such, the social and cultural acts not as a determining structure but as a virtual through which bodies become.

In this sense, the process through which particular intensities are invested in can be understood as the process whereby the girls' bodies are folded into the social and cultural and the social and cultural is folded into the girls' bodies. The girls' bodies express, more or less intensely, the wider series. Indeed, as the virtual, the social and cultural can be understood as the finite possibilities through which bodies can become. That is, as the virtual, the social and cultural involve limits and restrictions; bodies cannot become what they want but rather are actualised through the virtual. Drawing on my discussion in this chapter, I suggest that, for the becoming of these girls' bodies, the actualisation of the social and cultural is a process which involves the organisation of intensity into extensity. As is clear from the girls' experiences of their bodies, becoming is intensive in its affective relationality, but it is also extensive in its organisation; looks and selves, in Colebrook's (2002) terms, are 'elevated' as particularly meaningful. The social and cultural, is both intensive in its capacity to be folded into and expressed as the girls' bodies, and extensive in its organisation into clear, objectifiable and quantifiable meanings, representations, significations. Looks and selves, then, are intensively experienced, are actualised as the becoming of bodies, because they are, socially and culturally, invested in. In the following chapter I take up these inter-connected concepts of relationality, affect, intensity and the fold – and the challenge to a framework of structure/agency that they pose – to explore in greater detail the social and cultural organisation of gendered relations between different bodies.

Notes

1 The distinction between 'looks' and 'selves' in the art-work, then, is less one that the girls have made and more one that I have understood. This might be argued to be an abstracted form of analysis which I have been arguing against. However, I would ask if it any more abstracted than the understandings produced through how the girls talk about their bodies. As I argued in Chapter 2, there is something about using visual methods of research that opens up questions of research practice and ethics. I would argue that in both the 'verbal' and 'visual' interviews, as a social researcher, I have produced certain understandings and concepts from the 'data' that the girls do not use in their own explanations of their bodies; 'looks' and 'selves' are concepts that I have generated through how the girls express their bodies. In generating these concepts, though, I have attempted to argue that 'looks' and 'selves' are not the only or even most important ways in which bodies might be understood but rather that they are specific to the research relations. In this sense, I coincide with Deleuze who says, 'the empiricists are not wrong to present general ideas as particular ideas in themselves, so long as they add the belief that each of these can be replaced by any other particular idea which resembles it in relation to a given word' (2001b: 1).
2 I have blurred the faces of the girls who included Polaroid photographs of themselves in their art-work, both in this chapter and in the appendix, to help ensure their anonymity.
3 See, for example, Barnet-Weiser and Portwood-Stacer (2006) on the participants of make-over reality television programmes explaining their new look as revealing 'the real me'. See also McRobbie (2004) for the class and gender dimensions of such make-over programmes.
4 Interestingly, when we were talking about whether the girls wanted to be called by their own names or by aliases, Dionne jokingly remarked that she would like to be called 'Christina' after Christina Aguilera. Later she decided that she wanted to use her own name.
5 Note that Sammy and Tahsa spent most of their time together in the art-work workshop with Tasha helping Sammy to prepare (perform) her

Polaroid photograph. I do not remember if Tasha also straightened her hair but I do remember Tasha applying her own make-up. The art-work the girls produced 'fed off' each other and the girls often developed and repeated ideas from each other. Relations are therefore crucial to the bodies that emerge in the interviews – see Chapter 2.

6 I have associated looks with behaviour here because, like looks, this is the 'outside' of a body that is distinguished from the 'inside', who Casey is. I am not suggesting here that Casey's behaviour is that of a 'slag' – see Chapter 5 for more discussion on 'behaviour', particularly in terms of the relations between Casey's body and 'slag'.

7 This might be understood in terms of Ricoeur's (1992) argument that a person's identity requires a coherent, continuous and uninterrupted permanence in time (1992: 142).

8 Consider here Deleuze's point concerning how multiplicity should be understood not through one (set of) thing(s) but rather through the relation of AND: '[i]t is not the elements or the sets which define multiplicity. What defines it is the AND, as something which has its place between the elements or between the sets. AND, AND, AND – stammering' (Deleuze in Deleuze and Parnet 2002: 34).

9 This gap between how other people think Sammy looks and how Sammy thinks she looks might be understood through the performance of her body that I discussed above. For example, we might understand wearing 'tight clothes' that 'show off' her body as Sammy performing her body in such a way that repeats the expectations of the compliments she receives.

5

Fighting Back

BECKIE: do you think there's a difference between firstly what girls and boys say and secondly how it makes you feel?
[. . .]
FAY: I think girls can say it nastily
DIONNE: the opposite sex make you feel worse, basically
FAY: yeah cos they're the people you're trying to impress at the end of the day aren't they, you know you wanna look good for the boys
DIONNE: you can't live with them, can't live without them, ha ha
FAY: but there's yeah, I suppose, it hurts more if a boy says it, probably
BECKIE: do you all think that?
TASHA: but girls can, girls can argue back to girls, girls like, . . . if Fay like goes to me 'oh you look really ugly today'
FAY: you'd fight back yeah
TASHA: I'd just be like, 'well, Fay, that's well harsh' and we'd just like start having an argument and like, whereas boys like I don't know, 'oh ok then, boooo!'

> A body affects other bodies, or is affected by other bodies. (Deleuze 1992: 625)

According to Fay, Tasha and Dionne in the extract above, comments from boys hurt more than comments from girls[1]. One reason they give for this is that they feel unable to 'fight back' to comments from 'the opposite sex'. This chapter examines the relations between the girls' bodies and bodies of boys, girls and girl-friends.[2] It explores these relations through the ways in which the possibilities of the becoming of their bodies are limited or extended through the girls' *capacity* to 'fight back'. The concept of capacity is developed through Deleuze's (1992) work on *affect* where, drawing on Spinoza, bodies are defined not by what they are but by the affects of which they capable. Bodies are their capacities of affecting and being affected, capacities which are produced through, and cannot be known in advance of, the relations specific to an encounter. Focusing on the affective capacities of bodies is intended to draw attention away from bodies, or 'the girls', and pull it instead towards *the becoming of bodies through relations*. As I have argued in previous chapters, bodies do not pre-exist their relations but rather bodies are constituted through their affective relations. As such, I argue that the becoming of the girls' bodies is through their relations with other bodies.

This chapter engages most explicitly with the ways in which the girls' bodies become through gender. Gender is understood here not to pre-exist bodies but to constitute them. The girls' bodies become gendered *as girls' bodies*, and the boys' bodies become gendered as boys' bodies, through the affective relations they are involved in. Further, gender is understood as one of the ways in which the affective capacities of bodies become organised and produced. Bodies become gendered through the expansion or limitation of their affective capacities, through the capacities of those bodies to 'fight back'. In this sense, this chapter is another attempt to practise a transcendental empiricism, to trace the becoming of bodies through the ways in which affective intensity is extensively organised. Gender is an extensive organisation of a body, in that bodies become organised in socially and culturally recognisable ways. The chapter begins by exploring how the affective relations between the girls' bodies and the bodies of boys and girls limit or restrict the girls' bodily capacities and the possibilities of the becoming of the girls' bodies. It then moves to address the ways in which the relations between the bodies of the girls and their girl-friends unfix and expand the possibilities of becoming through trust, honesty and advice. At stake in this chapter, then, is a consideration of how the relations through which the girls' bodies become are organised in particular ways, through movement and stoppage, for example. In this sense, this chapter pushes Deleuze's concept of affect to examine what Ahmed (2001, 2004) calls the 'affective economy' in and through which relations are structured. In emphasising relationality, this chapter also thinks through in more detail how Deleuzian concepts of affect and intensity challenge the structure/agency distinction and produce a different kind of research ethics.

Fixing bodies

Boys fixing girls

In the extract with which this chapter opened, Fay, Tasha and Dionne discuss how they experience their bodies through images produced through their relations with boys, with girls and with girl-friends. In making the distinction between 'boys' and 'girls', Fay argues that comments from boys 'hurt more' than comments from girls because she is unable to 'fight back'. In the extract, Fay discusses how she experiences her relations with boys in terms of 'looking good' for them; 'you know you wanna look good for the boys'. If Fay does not look good for boys and boys make comments about this, Fay says that she is hurt. Tasha takes up Fay's point and argues that part of what makes boys' comments hurtful is that girls cannot 'argue back' to boys; 'girls can argue back to girls . . . whereas boys like I don't know, "oh ok then, boooo!"'. The distinction between comments from boys and girls was discussed at another point in this interview in terms of 'how far' boys go in making comments about how the girls look:

> FAY: if someone said that to me, like I don't know said something horrible to me, like a boy, then I'd just think 'well you've got a load of spots on your face today'
> [Laughter]
> DIONNE: yeah but girls don't say it, boys that are cocky and confident
> FAY: say it
> DIONNE: and popular sort of like say 'oh you look really fat' and then like the other boys laugh and
> KATIE: [inaudible]
> DIONNE: but if we were like to say something like 'oh you're really spotty' then they would be like 'oh shut up you big ugly cow' or something and then you wouldn't know what to say back because like it hits you harder than it hits them
> ANNA: that's what happens though, like you say one thing and they can say as much to you and you can't say anything back
> DIONNE: yeah
> ANNA: and the minute you say something back and they just flip and say
> DIONNE: yeah even if you said the same amount of stuff it still wouldn't hurt their feelings as much as it would hurt you
> KATIE: you don't know that
> DIONNE: huh?
> KATIE: you don't know that
> DIONNE: yeah but generally
> TASHA: yeah, if you said something back
> DIONNE: otherwise why would they say it in the first place?

While Katie does not agree, saying 'you don't know' how much a comment from a girl could hurt a boy, the rest of the girls in this extract say that comments from boys hurt more than comments from girls because boys say 'more'. Dionne, for example, argues that what boys say to her 'hits you harder than it hits them' so 'even if you say the same amount of stuff it still wouldn't hurt their feelings as much as it would hurt you'. For Dionne here, the 'same amount of stuff' hits the bodies of girls and boys differently; girls' bodies are hit by comments harder than boys' bodies. This is perhaps unsurprising given the discussions in Chapter 4, where the girls describe the reduction of their body to looks, and the judgements of people who 'don't really know' them. Dionne understands the distinction between how hard boys and girls are hit through her inability to say anything back, explaining that in response to a comment from a boy about her looks, 'you wouldn't know what to say back'. This is also the point that Anna makes; 'they can say as much and you can't say anything back'. There is a disparity in how hard comments hit the girls and boys, partly because the girls say that they are unable to hit back.

According to Deleuze's reading of Spinoza, 'a body affects other bodies, or is affected by other bodies; it is this capacity for affecting and being affected that . . . defines a body in its individuality' (1992: 625). If the relations between the girls' bodies and the bodies of boys are understood here in these terms – that is as relations where bodies affect and are affected by other bodies – what the girls are pointing to is the ways in which their bodies are affected by the bodies of boys but do not have the capacity to affect them back. The girls' bodies are hit by boys' bodies but are unable to hit them back; they are capable of being affected but not of affecting. According to the girls, the relations (of being hurt, for example) between their bodies and boys' bodies are not mutually constitutive; boys' bodies affect the constitution of the girls' bodies but the girls' bodies do not affect the ways in which boys' bodies are constituted. For the girls, the affective relations between their bodies constitutes the boys' bodies as capable of affecting but of not being affected; boys' bodies can hit but cannot be hit back.

Here, then, the girls are arguing that relations between bodies are not equal or equivalent; not all bodies are capable of the same affects. In this sense, relations of affect might be understood as operating through 'affective economy' (Ahmed 2001, 2004) where some affects are more likely to stick to certain bodies than others (see Chapter 1). In this case, hurtful comments concerning looks seem to stick harder[3] to girls' bodies than to boys'. Ahmed argues that the notion of the affective economy does not conceive affects as emanating from particular bodies but rather as bringing certain bodies into being. In Deleuze's terms, this might be understood as the way in which the 'capacity for affecting and being affected . . . defines a body in its individuality'. This is an important point – and is returned to at the end of the chapter – because it focuses attention not on the bodies themselves (that is, as conscious, intentional, active subjects) but on the relations between bodies. As I have suggested so far, bodies are constituted through their relations.[4] Here, then, the discussion is concerned with how, through relations, the girls' bodies become defined 'in its individuality'.[5] How does the capacity to be affected but not to affect extensively define the girls' bodies?

Importantly, arguing that a body is defined in its individuality through relations of affect is not to suggest that the body that is brought into being is the end of the story. The analysis of what bodies relations of affect constitute cannot finish here; the girls' bodies are not 'done'. Instead, drawing on and developing the ontology of becoming, bodies are never settled or complete. As such, the question that emerges is, what does the capacity to be affected but not to affect back do to the *becoming* of the girls' bodies? What does it make possible, and impossible? In Chapter 4, I introduced the notions of the possibilities of the becoming of the girls' bodies being *limited or expanded* through particular relations (through the attachment and detachment of looks and selves for example). Taking up these notions here, the girls' experiences of unidirectional relations of affect can be understood as the limiting of the possibilities of becoming. For example, Fay discusses how her relations with boys involve looking good for them. If Fay's body is experienced by the boys as looking good, the possibilities of her body are expanded. However, if Fay's body is not experienced as looking good, the possibilities of her body are limited. This limitation has a dual aspect. First, the possibilities of Fay's body are limited because she is understood as not looking good for boys. Second, and underpinning the first aspect, Fay's body is limited because her body is already reduced to the organ of looking good for boys. Fay's body is limited because she experiences her body as not looking good for boys and as reduced to the aspect of looking good for boys. That Fay's body has its limitations is not unique – as suggested in previous chapters, the becoming of bodies is not infinitely open or unbounded. However, the *inability to fight back* that Fay and the other girls experience genders and *fixes* the limitations of their bodies; Fay's limits become stuck to her body and come to define it (as spotty, fat, ugly; not looking good).

Girls fixing girls

The girls discussed the relations between their bodies and boys' bodies as limiting and fixing the possibilities of becoming through an understanding of looking good. The way in which girls were understood as limiting and fixing bodies were discussed by Casey, Hannah, Tina and Chloe in terms of fashion and clothes. For example:

BECKIE: so like comments and stuff are they worse from girls or boys, or different?
CASEY: it depends
HANNAH: say I was wearing

TINA: I'd probably say it's more from boys
CHLOE: no I think it's more from girls
CASEY: girls
CHLOE: because
TINA: no but say if you like a boy and then he started dissing you
CHLOE: no but that's a different thing, that's only one thing, cos say if you're walking down the street and a girl starts dissing you, or what you're wearing, a girl, a boy wouldn't know what a girls wears and stuff
HANNAH: yeah say a boy walked down the road and said, 'oh you tramp, why are you wearing those trousers?' I'd just be like 'oh shut up, you know nothing about fashion', say a girl did it, I'd like look at myself and say 'oh do I look trampy?'
CHLOE: yeah cos they'd actually know

According to Chloe and Hannah, girls make comments about clothes and fashion which are more powerful than comments boys might make about them because girls 'actually know' about fashion. Hannah points to a reversal of the affects of fixing where it becomes possible to 'shut up' a boy about comments he makes about clothes ('you know nothing about fashion') but difficult to 'fight back' to a girl who makes such comments ('I'd ... look at myself and say "oh do I look trampy?"'). Relations between the girls and girls can also 'fix' the girls' bodies.

One way to understand the 'fixing' of the girls' bodies through relations with boys and girls here is to conceive 'fixing' as the isolating of a body. If, as has been argued so far, a body is the affects that other bodies have on it and that it can have on other bodies, 'fixing' is the ways in which a body's affects are limited and reduced to that limitation. This can be demonstrated through how the girls say they are unable to 'fight back'. The affective relations that the girls are in only work one way. Other bodies can affect them but they cannot affect these other bodies; they cannot 'fight back'. Both boys and girls fix the possibilities of the girls' bodies, then. There is, though, a distinction between how fixing is produced through relations with boys and with girls. This distinction involves different kinds of knowledges which fix the limits of bodies in different ways. The girls argue that relations with girls fix their bodies through knowledges of fashion and clothes. Girls 'actually know' about fashion and clothes and this knowledge has the capacity to fix the girls bodies in terms of what the girls *don't know*. The girls describe girls' knowledges of fashion and clothes as potentially accessible, that is as potentially knowable; as girls, the girls could, and indeed should, know about fashion and clothes. While this understanding of knowledges of fashion and clothes as potentially knowable is discussed here in terms of how it is used to fix bodies, its potential knowableness also indicates that, with the 'right' knowledge, relations of fixing between girls are not necessarily one-way; with knowledge of fashion and clothes, the girls can 'affect-back'. This is discussed below in more detail in terms of how knowledge is shared and made knowable through friendships.

In contrast, some of the girls argue that relations with boys fix their bodies through sexualisation. For example, Hannah describes how her body is fixed through its sexualisation by boys as such:

> HANNAH: yeah and then when they say to me 'oh Hannah you've got competition, Sarah's got bigger boobs than you' I'm like, no offence to you [Sarah], but I'm like 'I'm fine with my body', I'm not like I want really big boobs, I don't care

Here, both Hannah's and Sarah's bodies are fixed through their sexualisation by boys. This sexualisation involves reducing their bodies to parts and putting these body parts into competition with each other; who has the bigger boobs? The possibilities of Hannah's and Sarah's bodies are therefore limited and then fixed; their bodies are only sexualised body parts and one of their body parts is 'better' by virtue of how 'big' it is. In the following extract the girls discuss how this limiting and fixing of their bodies is specific to their relations with boys and is not a mode of fixing which could be reversed:

> BECKIE: so boys make comments about girls' appearances, can girls do the same back to boys?
> TINA: no cos boys don't
> CASEY: boys don't really care
> CHLOE: no we can't
> CATHERINE: they'll just hit ya
> CHLOE: we can't just go up to someone and say 'you've got a smaller willy than him ain't ya, ain't ya?'
> TINA: cos then they'll be like 'ergh'
> CHLOE: 'why you looking at my dick for?' or they'll go 'c'mon let me show you it, what can you do with it'
> TINA: like 'stick it in your mouth'
> CHLOE: you don't wanna do anything with it
> TINA: 'it'll go right down your throat and that and come out your ear' and stuff like you don't wanna know
> CHLOE: it's sick innit
> TINA: disgusting

According to this extract, the girls argue that they cannot limit and fix boys' bodies through sexualisation. Indeed, the girls argue that attempts to sexualise the boys' bodies would result in their own bodies also becoming sexualised. The way in which boys' bodies limit and fix the girls' bodies, then, is not reversible. The different ways in which the girls' bodies are fixed through their relations with boys' and girls' bodies involves not only particular knowledges of their bodies but also particular understandings of the *possibilities* of the girls' bodies. The way in which girls fix the girls' bodies are in relation to the possibilities of the girls' own bodies. For example, Hannah's body is fixed by girls through knowledges of fashion and clothes in relation to the possibilities of Hannah's body. In contrast, the way in which the boys fix the girls' bodies are in relation to other girls' bodies; Hannah's body is in relation to, in competition with, Sarah's body. The relationality between bodies, then, differs for girls' and boys' bodies. So far, what this suggests is that the knowledges through which the girls' bodies are fixed through relations with boys are not equal or reversible relations of being affected but not affecting-back. The next section takes up the notion of possibilities in relation to the girls' 'own' bodies and explores it through the ways in which the limits of the girls' bodies can be 'unfixed' and opened up through relations with girl-friends.

Unfixing bodies

That's the thing about friendship

The girls discussed their relations with girl-friends as those which did not limit and fix the possibilities of their bodies but rather which expanded or opened what their bodies might do. Knowledges, for example, might be shared and made accessible rather than used to fix the limits to a body. The relations between the girls and girl-friends involved complex appreciations of *trust* and *honesty* where the limiting and fixing of a body (as ugly, fat, unfashionable, for example), could be unfixed. For example, Fay described the friendship between herself, Dionne and Sammy as trying to minimise the opportunity of being fixed:

> FAY: yeah like we have like an unspoken thing, us 3 as, I think we've never exactly come out and said it but we've got this unspoken thing where we'll tell each other if we think, 'mmm' you know, like 'mmmm, maybe not that top today or that way of wearing your hair or something' and I think you do go defensive, I go defensive when someone says something to me but I do listen, you listen to what they have said to you
> SAMMY: mmm
> DIONNE: like when I said that Fay's hair didn't look very nice up high
> FAY: I did go defensive
> DIONNE: you went like 'oh, well maybe I will wear it like this again' and like Sammy, oh, when your hair as well wasn't it?

> FAY: yeah, and you got really defensive on me when I said your hair had a kink in it
> DIONNE: and you were like 'well maybe I don't care, maybe I want to wear it down' like, and then when people say stuff to me
> FAY: but like we don't fall out over it I listen, actually, I do listen but I do get defensive
> SAMMY: mmm
> DIONNE: cos like Fay always wears her hair in a high ponytail and like Sammy always gets her hair straighteners out

The relations between Fay, Dionne and Sammy are concerned with unfixing or living with what of their bodies might be fixed. What might be fixed becomes possibility, so Fay can wear her hair up, and Sammy can straighten her hair. By listening to – defensively or not – what each other has to say, Fay, Dionne and Sammy can ensure they look nice and avoid being fixed through not looking nice. Knowledges that might be used by girls to fix each other's bodies are shared and made accessible to each other through friendships. Friendships in this sense entail not the limiting of a body's possibilities but rather the expansion of potential limits; what can a body do, and do to other bodies?

This possibility of a body becoming through friendship involves *trust*. Fay, Sammy and Dionne have to trust each other in order to follow their advice on what looks nice. Chloe's account of her friendship with Casey is also one which she experiences through trust:

> CHLOE: but when I got my trainers, cos I had to go to a different shop to what my mum was in I was telling Casey 'you wouldn't make me walk down the street like an idiot?' and she was like 'no, it looks really nice' so that's why I got them cos I felt really confident cos of Casey was telling me it looked alright, if I liked them I would have just got them cos that's what I'm like if I like it, I wear it and no-one else don't look at me but like with trainers and stuff like that I was wary but in clothes shops if something shows all my lumps and bumps and that I can see it but then I just go and get the bigger size and then once I've got the bigger size hopefully I look alright, I'll ask Casey for her opinion and then if it don't look alright then I won't get it but if I think it looked alright then I'd still get it anyway

Chloe says, 'I always depend on Casey if I look alright', which points to her trust in Casey. The trust here between Chloe and Casey convinces Chloe that she looks 'alright' so that Casey's understanding of Chloe's body becomes a way for Chloe to know and understand her body. Chloe experiences and lives her body through her 'dependence' on Casey. How Chloe knows and understands her body depends, at least in part, on how Casey knows and understands Chloe's body; if Casey says that Chloe's trainers 'look . . . really nice' and that Chloe's clothes 'look alright', then Chloe experiences them as such. The relations of trust between Casey and Chloe indicate how bodies are not just either fixity or possibility but are both. Chloe knows that her body can be fixed in certain ways – through 'lumps and bumps', 'look[ing] like an idiot' and being unable to afford clothes that she would like[6] – but also knows that this is not all that her body might be. Through her friendship with Casey and the knowledge that Casey has of Chloe's body, Chloe's body can potentially be unfixed.

This unfixing is more complicated than a simple 'freeing up' of what had or could be fixed. The relations of trust that Fay, Dionne and Sammy and Chloe discuss 'unfix' fixity but do it through a recognition of this fixity. Another way of putting this is that bodies have certain physical and imaginary limitations. Some examples of these limitations so far have been hair (Fay, Dionne and Sammy), 'lumps and bumps' (Chloe) and the inability to 'fight back'. What the friendships between the girls do is make these limitations possibilities, that is, *rather than being fixed, limitations become possibilities*. Chloe, for example, recognises her body as limited in certain ways and understands that these limits might become fixed to her body, so she might 'look like an idiot'. Through her friendship with Casey, Chloe's body can become through these limitations rather than be fixed by them. The trust involved here is complicated. It involves Chloe being able to 'fight back' against Casey, as Chloe says 'if I liked them I would have just got them cos that's what I'm like if I like it'. Here, Chloe is keen to assert how she lives through her limitations by herself. Her friendship with Casey where Casey tells Chloe that she looks 'really nice' makes Chloe feel 'really confident' about what she likes and that she will not look like an 'idiot'.

Chloe's friendship with Casey involves relations where it is not only Casey that can affect Chloe but also where Chloe can affect Casey, or can avoid the affects of Casey. This capacity for Chloe to not only be affected but also to affect is key to relations of trust. The friendship between Fay, Dionne and Sammy also works through this capacity to be affected and to affect as the 'unspoken thing' between them involves them all giving each other *advice*. The comments that they make about each other are not fixing each other's bodies but are unfixing bodies in certain ways through advice. The advice that the girls give their friends, then, is different to the comments that boys or girls who are not their friends make because advice is about living with and through – becoming – limitations.

Advice, then, is helping a friend's body become through its limitations. However, Casey discusses how a friend's limitations restrict the advice that it is possible to give. Casey describes how her advice to Chloe is given through what she thinks Chloe thinks:

> CASEY: I would tell the truth though but if they thought it looked really nice I would never cos I, they would think 'oh I thought I looked really nice and you're saying I don't', I'd be saying 'oh it looks nice, it looks nice'
> BECKIE: so does that depend on whether it's a friend saying it or –?
> TINA: yeah but some girls, like you've got to check for your friends cos like some girls will be like 'oh yeah it looks nice' just to make them look better than you
> HANNAH: that's the thing which has got nothing whatsoever to do with it but that's the thing about friendship, it's like if I ate pasta and it had pesto and like if I had a bit of pesto on my tooth, who would tell me
> [Laughter]

Here Casey describes how 'telling the truth' is dependent on the truth she thinks her friend will want to hear, so Casey will confirm her friend's opinion even if she does not agree. *Honesty*, that is 'telling the truth', in friendship is produced through the limits of possibility so what Casey tells Chloe looks nice on her is a possibility restricted through what Casey thinks Chloe thinks about her body's limitations and possibilities. This trust – advice and honesty – is limited through Chloe's own knowledge and understanding of her body which Casey is careful not to exceed. Casey's advice is not to limit Chloe's body but nor is it to exceed Chloe's experience through what (else or more) could be done to Chloe's body. What a body can do, in this sense, is limited not only through comments which fix a body but also through how a body is understood as only capable of being experienced in certain ways.

This knowledge and understanding of the potential possibilities of a body involves a genuine friendship, so a friend will know the limits of what can be done to a body. Casey is a genuine friend because she will give advice and truth which confirms the possibilities of a friend's body; 'I'd be saying "oh it looks nice, it looks nice"'. Being a genuine friend, crucially then, involves not only offering advice and truth with the best intentions but also knowing if a friend wants advice and truth and, if so, what kind. Being a genuine friend is not offering advice and truth if a friend does not want to hear such advice and truth. This understanding of a genuine friend is indicated by the experience that Anna describes in the following extract.

> ANNA: like today, at break some of my friends were like sitting there and they were like trying, actually saying what I should do to make myself look better, they'd say like 'take your hair down', like 'oh, do, you should put more weight on' blah blah and that

[The others are talking]
ANNA: at first it was insulting, then I realised they were trying to be helpful and like that and then I just suddenly
BECKIE: are you listening?
TASHA: don't don't talk
BECKIE: are you listening to what she's saying?
FAY/DIONNE/SAMMY: yeah yeah
ANNA: and it was just like
EMILY: is she crying?
FAY: no
EMILY: you look like you're crying, sorry
FAY: no I'm not
BECKIE: carry on Anna
ANNA: oh and I was just like, just let them say what they say cos you can't, as much as they, as much as you want to fight back you can't
BECKIE: ok
ANNA: yeah it's like you know they're being horrible about what you look like
EMILY: Fay did you hear the beginning?
DIONNE: no, could you repeat the start
EMILY: go on
ANNA: erm, I was having an argument today and – you know all that lot – they were saying that I should keep my hair down, put my hair down, cos it looks shiny and then they were saying that, going on about my weight and then they were going on about my fashion and, and at first I had a go back at them, and then I just had to, because they were saying 'we're only trying to be nice to you', and then that got us into another argument

In this extract, Anna describes how her friends offered her suggestions on how she could make herself 'look better'. Like Fay, Dionne and Sammy, Anna's friends gave suggestions about how Anna could style her hair and what clothes she could wear. However, unlike the friendships between Fay, Dionne and Sammy and Chloe and Casey where there is an agreement, or an 'unspoken thing', that friends will offer such suggestions and suggestions will be welcome (albeit with some 'defensiveness'), Anna describes how her friends' comments are not welcome. Anna describes how she experiences her friends' comments as 'at first ... insulting, then I realised they were trying to be helpful'. What Anna is pointing to is how her friends' comments are not 'advice' and 'truth' as conceived above because her friends have not understood the – physical and imaginary – limits of her body. Anna does not want to hear comments about how she looks and so experiences these comments not as possibilities which extend the limits of her body but as comments which themselves fix her body. Anna does not experience her friends' comments as possible ways of becoming through the limits of her body but rather experiences her friends' discussion of her limits as fixing her body. For Anna, discussing the limits of her body does not help her to live with and through these limits but rather confirms – fixes – these as limits; 'it's like you know they're being horrible about what you look like'.

Bitching

The ways in which Anna describes this conversation with her friends indicates how 'friends', 'trust', 'advice' and 'honesty' do not necessarily coincide. Anna's friendships, for example, do not involve advice and truth; Anna does not 'trust' her 'friends' in the same way that Dionne, Fay and Sammy and Chloe and Casey can trust each other as friends. Anna does not experience the suggestions that her friends make as genuine; she experiences these not as about giving possibility to the limits of her body but are rather as fixing her body to these limits. Tina also talks about how friendship and trust do not necessarily coincide, saying 'some girls will be like "oh yeah it looks nice" just to make them look better than you'. Indeed, Tina questions the coincidence of friendship and trust arguing that 'some girls have ulterior motives for saying their friends look nice'. Tina, Hannah and Anna, then, point to how friendships must be 'checked' or 'tested' (the 'pesto test') for 'truth' or 'ulterior motives' as this becomes crucial to how their bodies might be fixed or unfixed. Attempts to identify 'truthful' friendships that are based on the genuine desire to help a friend live with and through limits of their bodies as possibilities as opposed to friendships based on 'ulterior motives' were discussed by the girls in terms of 'bitching'. 'Bitching' is a means of limiting and fixing the possibilities of a body by restricting how a girl who is bitched about can respond to, can affect back, the girl who has 'bitched'. Anna's description of the encounter with her friends, then, can be understood in terms of 'bitching'; Anna's bodily possibilities are fixed through her body's limitations because as she says, 'just let them say what they say cos . . . *as much as you want to fight back you can't*' (my emphasis).

'Bitching' is a way of limiting the capacity to affect that the girls discuss as only involving relations between girls. The girls point to a distinction between how boys fix their bodies and how girls do:

> FAY: but it's generally boys like boys will come out with something really nasty
> EMILY: but girls can too

> FAY: but even if girls are bitchy they'll say it behind their back and like even though that's horrible
> EMILY: but no some girls can say it your face, I can
> FAY: yeah but it's not as nasty, boys are horrible about it
> DIONNE: I'd rather hear it to my face and nicely than have 'why do you think you're wearing that, you look a right idiot?' then erm, saying it like somebody – not you [Katie] then like someone saying it behind your back and then finding out from and feeling even worse so you're thinking
> EMILY: and you think like it's gone round the whole school
> FAY: but that's generally girls you know they don't really, they don't generally as a rule say it to your face

Whereas boys fix the girls' bodies explicitly and loudly (shouts, comments, car horns), girls are described as limiting and fixing in more implicit ways, through 'dirty looks' and 'saying things behind your back', for example. 'Bitching' as the girls discuss it here and in the following extract, is not easy to identify and therefore is not easy to 'fight back' against:

> FAY: a lot of the time you can tell when people [girls] are saying something falsely and that, yeah, most of the time you can tell but some people can hide it
> DIONNE: yeah but then it makes you think that if they've been lying then they're probably bitching about you behind your back and that's not very
> FAY: well, unless you trust the person that told you
> DIONNE: yeah, but if you don't
> EMILY: it's not like you can trust everyone
> DIONNE: yeah, don't trust anyone
> KATIE: you don't trust anyone?
> DIONNE: no, I said, some people, it's like, yeah, you can't trust anyone[7]
> [silence]

Bitching limits what a body can do through how it is not explicit. The girls do not necessarily know if they have been bitched about and it is this uncertainty – have they been bitched about or not? – that limits a body. Bitching is not the explicit fixing of a body to its limits but is the fixing of a body because it might have been bitched about. It is, then, the *possibility or capacity* for bitching that occurs in the relations between certain girls that fixes a body. Bitching fixes a body because it *might have* happened behind a girl's back. There is a limit that is put on a body prior to or despite of any relations that it might become involved in; bitching puts a limit on possibilities *in advance* of how these possibilities might be limited. The possibility that bitching might have or might not have happened puts a limit on a body partly because friendships might come under scrutiny in terms of trust. Dionne, for example, says 'you can't trust anyone' and Tina says that she always examines comments from friends for ulterior motives. Friendships between girls, then, are detached from trust and are questioned both for 'truth' (in the sense that Casey understands her friendship with Chloe as the recognition of how Chloe experiences the limits of her body) and also in terms of Tina's 'checking' of her friends.

Bitching, as saying things 'behind your back' as opposed to 'to your face', is, however, more complex than whether or not it is explicit. The girls talk about how friendships, experienced through multiple knowledges and understandings of trust and truth, involve saying things 'to your face' rather than 'behind your back'. Saying things 'to your face', though, is not a guarantee that friends are not being 'bitchy'. As Anna argues, friends who say things 'to your face' can still be bitchy. Bitching, then, is not the distinction between girl-friends and girls in general as girl-friends can be bitchy, nor the distinction between something being said to your face or behind your back. Rather, *bitching is the inability to know, judge or care about how a girl knows, understands and experiences the limits to the possibilities of her body*. For example, Fay discusses her friendship with Sammy and Dionne as one in which they tell each other the 'truth' 'to their face'. This truth, like Casey's, must not exceed the friend's physical and imaginary bodily limits and possibilities. To exceed these limits and possibilities, to go 'too far' in 'telling the truth', is to risk being understood as a 'bitch'. Fay describes it as such:

> FAY: but you could accept one thing somebody says, like, oh what is it like when, like you [Dionne] wore eyeliner, didn't you, and we said like 'don't wear as much eyeliner' but then if we'd gone and said, 'oh don't wear your hair like that' and you know, 'you need to wear more foundation'
>
> DIONNE: what, did I not need to do my hair like that, do I need to, when you're talking about?
>
> FAY: no, no, but if
>
> SAMMY: [annoyed] she just said that

Bitching, then, is not only the inability to fight back against what a girl might or might not have said behind your back but is also the inability to show consideration for a friend's limits and possibilities. Bitching can occur within friendships of trust and the girls are careful with friends who they trust not to be a bitch. They can say 'one thing' but not more as more than one thing is not the attempt to help a body's limits become (through) possibilities but is rather the fixing of a body to those limits. As Anna said, it is not being nice but being horrible.

Most of the girls describe their relations with girls as more complex than their relations with boys. Boys can usually either be deemed 'nice' and a friend, or not, whereas being a bitch does not necessarily designate that a girl is not nice or is not a friend. Indeed, the girls have the capacity to be bitches themselves, for example by saying things 'behind the back' of a girl or by 'going too far' with a friend. Being a bitch was a careful negotiation for the girls that was evident at points in some of the interviews. At some moments, the girls were keen not to be understood as a bitch by each other or by me while at other moments the girls described themselves as bitches. Hannah, for example, said: 'but then that's the thing that I don't like, I mean I'm not just sitting here slagging off [girl's name], well I am'. Katie described how she preferred to be friends with boys rather than girls because boys are 'not as bitchy' but justified this saying 'it's not that I'm saying I'm an angel or anything cos I'm like it as well but teenage girls, we're all just little bitches really [laughs]'. Within the relations of the interviews, the girls negotiated whether they were a bitch through being careful about who they bitched about and who would know whether they had bitched. In this sense, bitching, as the inability to know, judge or care about the limits of a friend's bodily possibilities, can be momentary; a friend might care at one moment but not in another set of momentary relations. Bitching could be 'sanctioned' within the interviews if the girls acknowledged it with a laugh (as with Hannah), or if the girls had a 'good reason' (see Chloe's comments below), or if it was a kind of 'therapy', as Dionne says 'I don't care, it makes me get everything out, no you keep in up inside and you bitch about someone in a pair it's much better to I'd much rather put it on tape'.

The sanctioning of bitching within the interviews involved a detaching of bitchiness from the girls who bitched. The girls could understand themselves and the others in the group as not 'really' bitching in comparison with the girls who were 'real' bitches and had bitchiness attached and fixed to their bodies. The detachment of bitchiness from the bodies of the girls involved in the research – they are not bitches but other girls are – involved understandings of trust and truth and saying things 'to your face' and 'behind your back' in different ways to what is examined above. Dionne, for example, who in the group interview speaks of her strong friendship with Fay and Sammy, in her individual interview talks about Sammy 'behind her back'.

DIONNE: but Sammy's sort of ditching us at the moment
BECKIE: ok, why?

DIONNE: cos [girl's name 1], you know my ex-best friend I was saying, erm from like primary school she's like the leader of the group and everyone like follows her and me, Fay and Sammy used to hang out with her and then we thought 'oh let's not' cos we just feel like tag-alongs so we stopped and now they're sort of paying interest to Sammy and she keeps going off with them but we think she's gonna get ditched again, she's our friend so we worry about her cos like Sammy's like such an easy follower she'll like go when they click their fingers, cos like she was like with [girl's name 2], cos like names probably don't mean anything to you, all the time, she was with us and then [girl's name 2] just ditched her cos she fell out with every one else and then went back to them and Sammy came back to us and that's happened so many times to her, that's also like friends are judgemental, I don't like that lot cos like they're really judgmental to all like, if you wore, if your trousers were slightly too short they'd be like 'you ankle basher' and they'd really make you feel bad and so that's why I worry about her cos she's in with all that lot and they hang around with people who are like way too old, people who are in year 11 and are like 18 and she's gonna get in with the wrong crowd and I just worry about her

Because she is talking about a trusted friend behind her back, Dionne is careful not to be understood by me as a bitch away from the sanctioned bitchiness in the group interview. In this extract, Dionne describes herself as 'worried' about Sammy so that talking about her behind her back is not bitching. Central to this negotiation of bitching is whether the friend is acknowledged in negative or positive terms. Dionne is not bitching in her individual interview because, although she is talking 'behind her back', she discusses Sammy in positive terms, as an 'easy follower' rather than as 'judgemental' like the 'real' bitches. This, then, is not to suggest that Dionne is 'really' bitching about Sammy but rather is pointing to how *bitching is relational*, that is to an understanding of bitching as negotiated within different spatial and temporal moments. Talking about a friend 'behind their back' might be bitchy at one moment, as in the group interview, but might be 'worry' or concern at another moment, as with Dionne's individual interview.

Bringing it on yourself

The negotiation of a body as 'bitchy' demonstrates the ways in which experiences of a body are attached to and detached from bodies through relations with other bodies. The girls are not 'really' bitches but rather 'bitchiness' becomes stuck to, and unstuck from, bodies through the relations those bodies are in. The girls in the focus group interviews are not 'bitches' because the relations of the interviews enable 'bitchiness' to be unfixed from their bodies. Dionne is not a 'bitch' in her individual interview because she is able to unfix bitchiness from her body through worry and concern. In this sense, bitchiness is attached and detached to a body not only through relations with other bodies but also through relations 'within' one body. Dionne's bitchiness is attached and detached from her 'own' body. If Dionne attaches 'bitch' to her body and this attachment fixes her body, Dionne has limited the possibilities of her 'own' body; she has 'brought it on herself'. The attaching and detaching of qualities to bodies to limit or create possibilities can also be explored in relation to how the girls talked about girls as 'slags':

> CHLOE: most girls do bring it on themselves though, I mean there is some girls that do go round sleeping with boys, backing em, I mean, just kissing anyone they see, they are classed as a slag but
> ?: [girl's name 1]
> TINA: [girl's name 1], she's slept with every boy

Here, Chloe talks about a girl being 'classed as a slag'. Chloe understands herself not so much as classing the girl as a 'slag' but more as describing the girl in terms of how she has made other people see her. The slag has 'brought it on herself'. 'Slag', in these terms, becomes fixed to the girl because of her own behaviour: the slag has fixed this understanding of her body to herself and thus has limited the possibilities of her body. The slag has fixed her own body. The girl who is classed as a slag in this extract is not a girl that the girls in the interview are in trust-friendships with. The behaviour of this girl, then, is not explored but is simply taken to be indicative of how she *is* a slag. It is through her behaviour that 'slag' becomes fixed to her body.

However, as with bitching, it is not the behaviour itself that fixes a body but rather it is the *relations* that body is involved in that fixes a body as 'slag'. In the following, lengthy, extract, the girls explore how 'slag' has become fixed to Casey's body and in the process of this exploration they unfix this understanding of Casey from her body.

> CHLOE: but yeah most girls are like that and they do bring it on themselves but if you're with a boy and you do love them, like, even if it's only 2 months and you really do think you love him and then you sleep with him you do still get called a slag, but if you feel you do love someone then it's got nothing to do with anyone but like, it's all the same but it does get on my nerves
> CASEY: and yeah there's like girls that are in year 10 and I don't know whether they do call me a slag but I just think sometimes they are cos of the way they stare at me and stuff but
> CHLOE: it's only because
> TINA: it's like jealousy and stuff

CASEY: no it's only because there's a boy in that year that I talk to and they all like him and they all like are all over him and cos like they see him hugging me and stuff they get all jealous about it and start like staring me out and it's like 'grow up'
HANNAH: that's the thing, you, Casey, she gets attention from boys and like I don't know, like this boy called [boy's name], say [boy's name] gives her attention and other boys in year 10 gives her attention, like all the year 10 girls are like 'oh stupid ho, what's she doing, what's she doing'
CASEY: but it's only cos of him
HANNAH: but she hasn't done a thing
CASEY: that those girls in year 10 hate me, cos of him, cos he waves, like I'll sometimes walk home with him and they all like him and there was a rumour going round that this girl [girl's name 2] saw me and [boy's name] kissing at the top of the road and they were all spreading it, it's just like
CHLOE: but like the girls in that year
CASEY: pathetic cos like the girls in that year, even if it was only a kiss it doesn't matter
CHLOE: but like the girls in that year spreading rumours, like [girl's name 2] she's an evil little cow, I mean I'm not being like horrible but she is
HANNAH: you are being horrible
CHLOE: no but she's poison,
CASEY: she can't really say much
CHLOE: like she can't really say much cos like she will go round saying that
CASEY: yeah like [girl's name 3] she was just going round saying that, she was just staring at me one day and I was like 'what you staring at you ho?' and ever since she ain't even looked at me, like she hasn't said anything about me, like when I see her she just looks away, she doesn't even look at me any more
CHLOE: but like [girl's name 2], she, it was [girl's name 2] who started the rumour about her and [boy's name] kissing and for people to go against [girl's name 2], she'll like start spreading rumours like 'oh yeah Casey', like '[boy's name] was fingering Casey at the top of the hill' and like '[boy's name] was doing this to Casey and Casey was doing this to [boy's name]'
HANNAH: but at the end of the day she can't talk cos like I know for like true that she has slept with a couple of boys
CHLOE: apparently it is true that she lost her virginity when she was 9 watching Grease
CATHERINE: who's [girl's name 2]?
HANNAH: [girl's name 2] the little one, with dark Adidas trainers
CASEY: and she walks around like that [sticking her chest out] and she goes like [boy's name]! [boy's name]!
[Laughter]

160   *The becoming of bodies: girls, images, experience*

As her friends, the girls here unfix Casey's body from 'slag'. They argue that Casey is not a slag because she has not 'brought it on herself' through her behaviour. Casey's behaviour is not that of a slag. Instead, the girls identify the ways in which 'slag' has become attached to Casey through rumours and stares because girls are jealous of Casey and the attention she receives from a popular older boy. Interestingly, one of the ways in which slag is unfixed from Casey is by fixing slag to one of the girls (girl 2) who has spread rumours about Casey; 'but at the end of the day she can't talk cos like I know for like true that she has slept with a couple of boys'. For this girl, behaviour can be understood to fix her body's limits. This distinguishes the girl's behaviour from Casey's and in doing so unfixes Casey's body.

The girls in this extract unfix the limits of Casey's body through detaching slag from her. Slag can be fixed and unfixed through the relations the body is in; in this case, the girls can unfix slag from a friend and can fix it to a girl who is not a friend. However, as with bitching, the girls are also aware that they can fix their 'own' bodies as 'slag'; they can bring it on themselves. Attaching slag to your own body was discussed not just in terms of behaviour but also in terms of clothes as Hannah, Tina and Chloe describe:

> HANNAH: cos I mean no-school-uniform day is like a really big thing
> TINA: cos like people get to see you
> HANNAH: cos it's just like it shows what you are, cos like say I came in with a pink fluffy dress on and like a big star and like a tiny bag people would think 'ok', and if I came in with like some henched trousers people would be like 'hey grungy' and if I came in with like a mini, a belt skirt and like a tiny top
> TINA: a little boob tube
> HANNAH: yeah a little boob tube people would be like 'slag' so
> CHLOE: what you wear is like
> HANNAH: like you get categorised, for like for what you're wearing so it does matter[8]
> TINA: that is so true

Certain clothes, then, limit the possibilities of a body through how they can be attached to that body. These are understood as limits not only in terms of other people fixing them but also in terms of the girls fixing themselves. As such, as Hannah indicates, the girls themselves must be *responsible* for the ways in which their bodies might be limited and fixed through clothes:

> HANNAH: yeah the other day I was like writing something on a piece of paper and [boy's name] came up to me and proper back-handed me and

slapped me on my bum and I was like 'that really hurt' and then all the time he's just like 'back me a slam' and it makes me feel so bad cos it's like, 'ok do I look like a slag?' and then I think about myself and I'm like 'ok', and I'm trying to think of my actions and I don't know, I don't want a reputation and if he says that twenty-four/seven then it makes me feel like 'ok have I done something to make me look like a slag?', you know 'why are you saying this to me?' and I'm like

Hannah's comments about being responsible for how her body might become limited and fixed is a way for her to attempt to avoid being limited and fixed. If she is not a slag in what she wears and how she behaves then she should not be fixed as a slag. If she is fixed as a slag undeservedly, that is if she does not 'bring it on herself', then it should follow that she should be able to unfix her own body without the need for her friends to support her. In short, she should be able to 'fight back'. However, as Hannah's comments indicate, she does not 'fight back' when her body is undeservedly limited as a slag, for example by being 'slapped' by a boy. Instead of fighting back, Hannah describes how she 'feel[s] so bad' and monitors her appearance and behaviour; '"ok have I done something to make me look like a slag?", you know "why are you saying this to me?"'.

What this self-monitoring of the possibility of being fixed as a slag, or a bitch, points to is how bodies become fixed and unfixed not only through relations with other bodies but also through the limits that the girls put on their own bodies, that is *through relations with their own bodies*. Hannah, for example, describes her body as involved in relations with clothes and behaviour that she is responsible for. She limits and fixes her own body through the clothes she does or does not wear and through what she will or will not do at particular spatial and temporal moments. The capacities or potentials of Hannah's body – what a body can do – are limited by the *relations* between different 'organs' of her body: 'selfhood', 'looks', 'behaviour', for example. However, the notion of responsibility that Hannah works through points to how the relations a body has with itself involve other bodies; Hannah monitors and becomes responsible for the relations of her body not because these are the possibilities of her body but in order to avoid the limiting of what her body can do. Hannah limits the possibilities of her body in advance to avoid other bodies limiting them. The monitoring and limiting of a body by that body, then, indicates a desire to *not be affected*; Hannah limits the affects that other bodies might have on her. This is in contrast with the notion of 'bringing it on yourself' which suggests that certain girls' bodies have opened themselves up to being affected by other bodies; 'slags' and 'bitches' encourage relations that limit and fix their bodies and through this encouragement restrict their capacity to unfix these limits, to 'fight back'.

Affect, intensity and ethics

Hannah's description of the responsibility that she must take for how her body is experienced by others and the relations with boys, girls and girl-friends that the girls explain as limiting, fixing and un-fixing their bodies can be understood in terms of the concepts of intensity and extensity. In focusing on the affective relations between the girls bodies and other bodies, my interest has been in how 'affect' is not located *in* bodies but rather but is constitutive of bodies. Importantly, this removes what is done by and to bodies *from subjects to relations*. Bodies cannot be understood only in terms of acting or being acted on. Indeed, as I argued in Chapter 4, a re-conception of bodies through relationality suspends the structure/agency dichotomy and draws attention instead to the becoming of bodies, where bodies are immanent processes of possibilities and impossibilities. Relations of affect are the capacities of bodies where these capacities cannot be reduced to any conscious or deliberate action. Relations of affect have affects that cannot be known in advance. One way to understand Hannah's discussion of responsibility, for example, would be to see it as an effect of the action of the boy who slapped her on her bum. The boy who slapped Hannah on her bum is the cause of the responsibility that Hannah experiences. However, understood through the concepts of affect and intensity, where there is a shift from structure/agency and subject/object, it is the relation between the boy who slapped Hannah on the bum and Hannah's body which *produces* the 'responsibility' through which Hannah experiences the possibilities of the becoming of her body. Indeed, conceived in terms of Deleuze's (1992) concept of affect as not knowable in advance of a specific arrangement, and in terms of Massumi's (2002a) notion of affect as the disruption of linear connections between things, the slap on the bum is not a deliberate attempt to limit and fix Hannah's body through responsibility; it has affects that were unknown.[9] Affects are 'the becoming of qualities' (Colebrook 2002: 39) and, as such, comments affect in ways which cannot be quantified and which exceed 'just' their quality; *comments become* and bodies become through this.

The subtle, but important, shift from subject/object, structure/agency to bodies draws attention both to intensity and extensity. As with the discussion of looks and selves in Chapter 4, in this chapter the reduction of the girls' bodies to looks indicates an extensive organisation of the intensive affective relations between the girls' bodies and other bodies.

In Chapter 4, I suggested that the reduction of the girls' bodies to looks, which are then judged, is itself an extensive organisation of a body in that it depends upon and works through an investment in looks as a meaningful signifier. The extracts discussed in this chapter indicate that the relations between different bodies organise intensity into gender(ed) extensity. The girls' bodies, and the boys' bodies, are organised to socially and culturally mean or signify. Further, Hannah's descriptions of the responsibility that she must take for how her body is experienced by others indicates that the girls organise their own bodies extensively; to not signify 'slag', for example. The relations with boys, girls and girl-friends that the girls explain as limiting, fixing and un-fixing their bodies would appear to be a usual subject matter for a feminist analysis. Feminist approaches to empirical material like that of this chapter have tended to understand the relations between the girls' bodies and other bodies through an underlying patriarchal and/or heterosexual logic. For example, the uni-directional relations between the boys and girls might be considered to be an instance of heterosexual power relationships, the relations between the girls and girls a consequence of a masculine system that places female bodies in competition with each other and the friendships between the girls as a strategy of resisting a patriarchal power structure. These ways in which the relations the girls experience between their own bodies and other bodies might be understood by feminist theory are discussed in detail in the Conclusion in terms of the ways in which notions of sex and gender, and conceptions of bodies, are mobilised. Here, and in relation to the discussion in the Conclusion, I want to make clear how the approach that I have taken in this chapter differs; what does an account that understands bodies through the capacities of affect do to the relations between different bodies?

As I have suggested in previous chapters, there is, I think, an ethical shift in conceiving bodies through affect and intensity. This shift is produced through the detachment of the affects of bodies – what bodies are capable of doing and of having done – from some kind of agency. As Deleuze says in his lectures on Spinoza's concept of affect, 'I am not the cause of my own affects, and since I am not the cause of my own affects, they are produced in me by something else: I am therefore passive, I'm in the world of passion' (1978: 6). Being (or becoming) in the world of passion does not mean being 'passive' in the sense that the term is usually understood through the structure/agency dichotomy. To be passive is not the inability to act nor the ability to be acted on. Rather the world of passion suggests the intensity of affect; affect is not located within us but it happens to and across us. This chapter, then, has traced the ways in which the girls' bodies become through their organisation into gendered extensity. As such, I have tried to understand the relations between the bodies of the girls, boys, girls and girl-friends outside of a model of structure and agency and instead in terms of the Deleuzian ontology of becoming. Indeed, in the empirical material of this chapter, the girls' can be understood as discussing experiences of their bodies as becoming gendered through their relations. It is, then, not that bodies or knowledges are gendered in advance of the particular relations that they are involved in. In this sense, knowledge can itself be understood as a relation through which bodies become and not as that which is inherent to different 'kinds' of bodies. In terms of this chapter, asking what the capacities are for a body affecting or being affected does not presume to know in advance what these capacities are. Instead, in beginning from affect and intensity, the chapter traces various ways through which the becoming of a body is extensively organised. This point is returned to and developed in the Conclusion and is taken up in the following chapter in relation to temporality; how do bodies become through the capacity of comments to endure, or not?

Notes

1 It should be noted here that the bodies of the boys, girls and girl-friends discussed here refer to the girls' *perceptions* of them.
2 It is important to note here the distinction between boys, girls and girl-friends and, more specifically, the distinction between girls and girl-friends. Not all girls are friends and not all relations with girl-friends enable the capacity to 'fight back'. In the extract above, Tasha discusses her ability to 'fight back' in relation to Fay, her friend.
3 And indeed, according to the argument in the Conclusion, might be understood to stick for longer.
4 It's worth noting, then, that my subheadings in this chapter draw attention not to how individual bodies fix or unfix other bodies but to how the relations between particular bodies fix and unfix the possibilities of becoming.
5 And not, for example, with the difficulty of defining the boundaries of individual bodies as in Chapter 3. However, see also section below on Unfixing bodies.
6 For example: Chloe says: 'yeah cos like all the girls, you see them walking down the street, like with trousers Casey's got on, like they're really nice but like they're really expensive as well and like my mum can't keep up with it all and like my sister doesn't really care but I do worry about what I'm looking like and like my mum can't keep up with it and then I feel like a tramp cos like I haven't got what everyone else has got and I don't know, it's like really expensive to get things that are in fashion and then when they're not [expensive] and you buy them and they're a bit cheaper you like get taken the mick out of like 'err, they went out ages ago' and stuff'.

7 Note it is Katie, who has boy-friends and a 'different point of view' to the rest of the girls, who questions Dionne's statement that she doesn't trust anyone. This is discussed below in terms of how it is not necessarily girls who are friends.
8 Hannah described, in her individual interview, particular experiences of the ways in which other people had categorised her as 'grungy' because of the clothes she wore and how she was sensitive to how 'now if I knew that something was gonna get the mickey taken out of me I wouldn't wanna go through it again cos its just effort and at the end of the day you literally feel like shit so, what's the point if everyone's gonna take the mickey out of you?'
9 This is discussed in the Conclusion in terms of the size and scale of comments; small, seemingly unimportant comments can stick.

6

Things that stay

BECKIE: do you [find], if people say something nice about you, it generally doesn't stick with you?
DIONNE: yeah
BECKIE: but if someone says something horrible about you?
FAY: it does
DIONNE: it stays in your mind
FAY: it completely, it will stay with you, it could be a little comment
DIONNE: and you'll think about it at least every day for at least a week and you'll concentrate on it
BECKIE: ok
FAY: and you'll think about it, 'oh god, someone said that about me', like Dan's given me a phobia about my bum, I knew I had a big bum but now I'm gonna have like all week I'll be like

In this extract, Fay and Dionne describe how they experience their bodies through comments that 'stay' or 'stick'. Fay and Dionne 'think about' and 'concentrate on' these comments and these comments become part of the possibilities of knowing and understanding their bodies; 'I knew I had a big bum but now I'm gonna have like all week I'll be like'. This chapter considers these 'things that stay' through a focus on the temporalities of bodies.[1] In particular, through this focus on temporality, the chapter takes up and develops further the concept of intensity. Understood as extensive, 'time' is 'a series of "nows" which are connected together' (Colebrook 2002: 41). In this sense, time is separated into spatially bounded units which are joined together in a linear progression.[2] In contrast, understood as intensive, time is not only an external organisation but is also an immanent becoming, is 'always taking the form of different and divergent "durations"' (Colebrook 2002: 41). The concept of duration here refers to the speed or rhythm that is particular to a becoming, and that, importantly, might differ from the speed or rhythm of time. The contrast between the notion of duration and the notion of 'time' is that while time is measured objectively and externally, duration is what Henri Bergson (1903/1999) calls 'intuitive'; duration is known from within. For Bergson, duration is theorised in relation to the becoming of bodies; what is particular to bodies is that they cannot be properly known through time (or 'Time') but rather can only be grasped through their duration, through the rhythm that is specific to them. This, though, is not to suggest that bodies have only one rhythm or speed. On the contrary, the reason that bodies are not knowable through Time is because Time has only one speed whereas, as becomings, bodies have different rhythms, different speeds. It is through these different rhythms and speeds that bodies become.

Indeed, Fay and Dionne's explanations above can be understood through this concept of duration. Bodies are experienced through comments which have different durational capacities; some comments stay, others do not. In this chapter, comments that stay are conceived as intense images of a body that *endure*. That is, in Massumi's terms, these are images that are intense in their 'strength or duration' (2002a: 24, see Chapter 4). They are an image of a body that stays and that produces the possibilities of becoming. This chapter begins by examining what comments stay and introduces Bergson's concepts of intuition and duration in more detail. The chapter then moves to consider the ways in which comments stay through memory and discusses how the girls explain that comments stay through (i) deliberate remembering and (ii) the shocks of memory. Through this discussion of memory, the relations between the past, the present and the future are explored and I argue that these relations are not linear or uni-directional – that is extensive – but rather intensive. The past does not determine the present and the future but rather the past, present and future assemble in ways which disrupt a model of linear progression. In this sense, this chapter draws on the notion of intensity that is developed in Chapters 4 and 5, and on the understanding of bodies as becoming through relations of affect where two or more points might not seem to have a logical connection. As durational becomings, different temporalities affect bodies, sometimes in novel and unexpected ways.

What things stay?

In the extract above, Fay and Dionne say that what 'stays' are horrible comments; 'nice' comments do not 'stick' but 'horrible' ones do. Comments are here distinguished not only in terms of their content (whether they are 'nice' or 'horrible') but also through their different capacities of staying and sticking. For example, at another point in the interview, Fay says:

FAY: yeah, it's like what you say, a good comment you don't really listen to, you do, you always say 'thank you' . . . but a bad comment will stay with you for ages and someone can put you down with one comment, one little thing can put you down, it can just make you so upset

'Good' and 'bad' comments are here given different rhythms of duration by Fay so that while good comments do not stay ('a good comment you don't really listen to'), bad comments 'stay with you for ages'. For Fay, bad comments endure and good comments do not. Bad comments can move from the space and time in which they happen and can happen again, become re-experienced, as other spatial and temporal assemblages. Bad comments become part of the possibilities of how a body can be experienced. The duration of bad comments is, then, for Fay an enduring one.

The distinction that Fay makes between the different rhythms of 'good' and 'bad' comments was not experienced by all the girls. Katie, for example, distinguished between good and bad comments but did not locate their durational rhythm in their 'goodness' or 'badness'. Katie gives good and bad comments different rhythms but experiences good comments as capable of endurance:

BECKIE: and is that what it means to feel good, like when someone's said something –?
KATIE: yeah it's nice when people are saying things to you, but, dunno, cos I don't, half the stuff they say they say it in passing so I don't really take it in, and so I dunno really
BECKIE: ok, so someone says something nice about you, how long do you remember that for?
KATIE: quite a while! [laughs] a long time! But I dunno, it's more when the boys say things to you, like 'you look really nice today', that sticks with you a lot longer than when your girls, like when your girl friends do, sort of the girls you just think 'yeah thanks' but when the boys it's like 'yeah!' I dunno so
BECKIE: and what about if someone says something bad about you, is that the same?
KATIE: that sticks with you a lot longer, cos you just like, you keep focusing, like say they've called you fat or something, like you focus on that a lot longer and you're like trying to change it all the time, but I dunno, like I don't really wanna change everything for everyone else, I wanna sort of get to the point where I just sort of think about me

For Katie, comments about how she looks each have their own durational rhythm. Some comments 'pass' ('half the stuff they say in passing so I don't really take it in'), some are recognised but do not really stay ('the girls you just think "yeah thanks"') and some 'stick' ('when the boys say things to you, like "you look really nice today", that sticks with you a lot longer than when your girls' and 'like say when they've called you fat or something, like you focus on that a lot longer and you're like trying to change it all the time'). What is important here, then, is not so much the distinction between good and bad comments – both good and bad comments are capable of staying – as the intensity of how comments are experienced. Comments that endure, according to Katie's explanation, are differentiated through their intensity.

Any comment can stay, but why do some endure longer than others? Why are some comments more intense than others? And what is the relation between intensity and endurance? Drawing on the argument made in Chapters 4 and 5, intensity is understood as the ways in which a body becomes through particular moments of experience that are in some way set apart from other experiences, for example through their affectivity. One way to understand how particular moments of experience are more intense than others is through the link that Massumi (2002a) makes between intensity and emotion; '[i]ntensity is qualifiable as an emotional state' (2002a: 26, see Chapter 1 above). For Massumi, while affect is intensive, a force, non-objectifiable and non-quantifiable, emotion is 'a *recognised* affect' (Massumi 2002a: 61), an intensive affect which becomes socially, or extensively, organised, for example. In this sense, certain moments become intense through their qualification into emotion. Intensive affect is organised into extensive emotion. In the extract above, Katie differentiates moments that stay from those that pass in terms of who they come from (girls, girl-friends, boys), how comments are directed (in passing or carefully) and how much she focuses on them. If moments endure through their intensity (rather than their goodness or badness, for example), then intensity is produced in many different ways and involves many different aspects; both good and bad comments might endure, both comments from boys and girls might endure, comments made both intentionally and in passing might endure. What seems important to the endurance of comments here, then, is not the size or scale of a comment (that is who it is made by, whether it is made intentionally or in passing) but how much Katie focuses on them, how they become recognisable as emotion.

Tasha describes the endurance of comments in a similar way to Katie:

BECKIE: ok, so if someone says something horrible about you, kind of, how long does that stay with you? How long do you think about that and remember that?
TASHA: oh I think about it for ages, I don't, yeah cos I'm really sensitive to things as well so like if someone says something like tiny and it's not nasty then I'll get upset about it so, like it lasts for like a long time

BECKIE: ok, and what about if someone says something nice about you? How long does that –?
TASHA: oh yeah I feel really happy when people say something really nice, like 'oh you look really nice today', 'oh your make-up looks really nice, you're really pretty', it makes me feel really happy and like it's really sweet cos this boy I fancied he said he thought I was pretty as well so that made me feel happy, I was just happy for days, my friends had never seen me so happy, but, yeah
BECKIE: so if someone says something nice about you, does that stay with you as long as someone saying something horrible about you?
TASHA: no, it's for somebody saying something nice it probably doesn't stay for as long because, erm, because somebody will say something horrible before, so say if somebody said something nice, a few days later someone will say something horrible so that will have gone out of my mind, so I'm just thinking about what somebody said, like horrible

Here, Tasha explains that the capacity for a moment to endure is not dependent on how a comment is directed towards her, that is whether or not a comment is made with the intention to hurt her. Neither is a comment's capacity of endurance dependent on its size or scale; apparently 'tiny' and 'not nasty' comments can stay. Instead, Tasha argues comments endure because of her 'sensitivity' to particular comments. But how does Tasha become sensitive to certain comments? And why would Katie focus on some comments more than others?

In the conversation from which the above extract is taken, Katie explained that she used to be bullied for being 'really fat' and that now she experiences comments about her weight more intensely than other comments about how she looks. Comments concerning her weight 'stay' with her and involve a lot of attention; 'like you focus on that a lot longer and you're like trying to change it all the time'. The intensity of moments of experience are produced through complex processes that are particular to each body. For Katie, comments about weight are experienced more intensely than other comments because of what she has experienced in her past. In terms of intensity as 'qualifiable as an emotional state' this indicates two things. First, as an emotional state, intensity is qualified by a past time. For Katie, the emotionality which makes a moment intense comes from her past. Moments are emotionally intense because of what Katie has experienced in her past. In this sense, the past qualifies intensity. Second, and relatedly, the qualification of intensity refers not to a pre-determined emotionality but to the ways in which emotionality is produced through durational rhythms rather than Time. For Katie, what makes a moment intense is its duration, and in this case whether or not it endures. In this sense, intensive time and space, where moments are affective rather than linked linearly, become qualified as extensive emotion. However, what is important here is that, although intensive affect becomes qualified as extensive emotion, this is not a notion of the past *determining* the intensity of a moment of experience. Rather, the past *qualifies* it. This distinction between determination and qualification is unpacked in the rest of this chapter. But for Katie, the qualification of the past involves the endurance of moments of experience; a past comment does not determine the intensity of a present comment but rather a past comment endures and qualifies the intensity of a present comment. Endurance here refers to the becoming of a moment of experience. A moment that endures is not a discrete unit but rather is a moment that becomes, and becomes part of other moments of experience.

What a notion of the past as qualifying rather than determining does, as Massumi points out, is disrupt or suspend 'the linear progress of the narrative present from the past to future' (2002a: 26). As such, the notion of linearity that many approaches to time take is avoided. Explanations that want to explore what *causes* particular bodies (body sizes and shapes, feeling about and because of bodies, for example) tend to assume time as an unproblematic, straightforward advancement from the past (cause) to the present (effect). Consider for example the notion of time that models of media cause-and-effect (see Introduction) assume, where the proposal is to correct the effect by changing the cause. This correction is understood as an intervention in the temporal progression from past-to-present-to future.[3] In contrast, here, such a model of cause-and-effect is suspended by an understanding of time not as what determines (Time) but as becoming (duration). An understanding of time as becoming conceives the past not as what has happened but as *what is happening*.[4] It is not, for example, that things that stay are taken *with* a body into the present and on into the future but rather things that stay become and it is through this becoming that a body's possibilities are produced.

Indeed, for Tasha, the movement and becoming of moments of endurance is through their emotional intensity, an intensity that does not work through the (extensive) linearity of intention and size but rather through the concentration and contraction of time.[5] Tasha's sensitivity is specific to her own durational experience. Time in this sense is not external to a body as it tends to be in models of causation. Time is not an organisational structure which exists outside of and regardless of a body's experience of it. Instead, as duration, time is peculiar to a body's experience of it. What this means is that enduring moments stay not as a *cause of* intensity but *because of* their intensity. Whereas models of cause-and-effect are located *in* time, duration cannot be externalised. As such, the shift from determination to qualification sees Tasha's sensitivity as the recognition of affect and, thus, the organisation of affect into emotion. Emotion is, here, the enfolding of the socially and culturally recognisable into Tasha's body where Tasha's body expresses a particularly intense aspect of the entire series.

Intuition and duration

The notion of temporality developed so far draws upon Bergson's (1903/1999, 1908/2002) concepts of *intuition* and *duration* and I am interested in these concepts insofar as they open up a feminist understanding of the girls' bodies.[6] In *An Introduction to Metaphysics* (1999) Bergson describes intuition as the 'entering into' a state in order to know it. Intuition, for Bergson, is in opposition to analysis for while analysis involves immobility, interpretation and representation, intuition involves mobility, adaptation and 'intellectual sympathy'. In trying to know a thing, Bergson argues that the thing must be grasped not from without but 'from where it is, from within, as it is in itself' (1999: 22):

> By intuition is meant the kind of *intellectual sympathy* by which one places oneself within an object in order to coincide with what is unique in it and consequently inexpressible. Analysis, on the contrary, is the operation which reduces the object to elements already known, that is, to elements common both to it and other objects. To analyse, therefore, is to express a thing as a function of something other than itself. All analysis is thus a translation, a development into symbols, a representation taken from successive points of view from which we note as many resemblances as possible between the new object which we are studying and others which we believe we know already. (Bergson 1999: 23–24)

Bergson's argument here has strong resonances with the argument developed in Chapter 2 concerning the methodological importance of *producing* ideas and concepts *through* empirical material rather than supposing in advance what ideas and concepts should be imposed on or applied to material.[7] However, in terms of this chapter, the case made above for an understanding of time not through a linear model of cause-and-effect, is also an attempt to 'place . . . oneself within an object in order to coincide with what is unique in it and consequently inexpressible'. For example, I have tried to understand Katie's experiences not through a notion of Time as external but though temporality understood as particular to her bodily experiences of it. Moreover, for Bergson, what is most unique and inexpressible is *temporality*, or, better, *duration*, as he says: 'There is one reality, at least, which we all seize from within, by intuition and not by simple analysis. It is our own personality in its flowing through time – our self which endures. We may sympathise intellectually with nothing else, but we certainly sympathise with our own selves' (1999: 24–25). There is, then, for Bergson, something particular about duration, about 'our self which endures', for which intuition rather than 'abstract, general or simple' conceptual analysis (1999: 27) is most appropriate.

For duration to be known, it must be entered into 'by an effort of intuition'. By entering into it, duration can be known as 'unity, multiplicity, and many other things besides' (1999: 31). With this, Bergson is pointing to the mobility of the body that flows through time, that is how duration cannot be 'caught' within one, pre-existing, model of understanding. For, as Bergson argues in *Matter and Memory* (1908/2002),

> In reality there is no one rhythm of duration; it is possible to imagine many different rhythms which, slower or faster, measure the degree of tension or relaxation of different kinds of consciousness and thereby fix their respective places in the scale of being. To conceive of different tensions is perhaps both difficult and strange to our mind, because we have acquired the useful habit of substituting for the true duration, lived by consciousness, an homogeneous and independent Time. (2002: 207)

Bergson's notion of duration, then, challenges the only knowledge of temporality as how it has been organised into Time and encourages the distinction 'between our own duration and time in general'. Time in general is understood in terms of 'abstract space' which is, 'by definition . . . outside us . . . a part of space appears to us to subsist even when we cease to be concerned with it' (2002: 206). However, this is not so with duration which has 'the capacity [to] go . . . beyond all our imagination'. Duration 'is not ours, assuredly, but neither is it that homogeneous and impersonal duration, the same for everything and for everyone, which flows onward, indifferent and void, external to all that endures' (2002: 207).[8] Bodies, which are also not ours (Deleuze and Guattari 1987: 164), have their own duration which is not the 'same for everything'; different bodies have different durations. Moreover, the durations of different bodies involve potentially many different rhythms of duration. A body, then, as the comments from Fay, Dionne, Katie and Tasha above suggest, is experienced through different durational rhythms, some of which pass, some of which endure and some of which are made to endure. It is to these different rhythms of endurance, and their relations with memory, that this chapter now turns.

'Shining points of memory'

So far, duration has been discussed in terms of its differences with an extensive notion of Time. What I want to do in the rest of this chapter is consider what duration does to understandings of the past, the present and the future, and the relations between them. This has been hinted at in previous sections in terms of the non-linearity of duration. Here, however, I want to consider this non-linearity in more detail and, more specifically, consider the relations between a non-linear temporality and memory. The focus on memory and remembering is important not only because it is in relation to memory that Bergson conceives duration but also because of the ways in which some of the girls explained the endurance of intense moments through remembering. Consider, for example, Tasha's account of how moments endure through their remembering:

> BECKIE: ok, so if, like you remember something someone said horrible, how do you remember it? I mean what are you doing?
> TASHA: I dunno cos most days, like I do like sit in my room and I dunno, just think about everything that's like happened in my life and I just remember things then
> BECKIE: ok, so it's kind of at a specific time when you sit and think about it or is it kind of with –?
> TASHA: well, I do think about it, it's weird, it suddenly just comes into my head, I'm not like doing anything to make me think of it but it just comes into my head

Here Tasha points to two different types of remembering. The first is Tasha's deliberate remembering which she describes as 'I . . . sit in my room and I dunno, just think about everything that's like happened in my life and I just remember things then.' The second type of remembering is when moments of intensity overtake Tasha and make themselves re-membered and re-experienced; 'it's weird, it suddenly comes into my head, I'm not like doing anything to make me think of it but it just comes into my head'. I will return to the second type of remembering below. In terms of the first type, when Tasha deliberately remembers intense moments, past moments are brought into and assembled as a present temporality. The past is not what *has* happened to Tasha but rather what *is* (still) happening, what she is (still) experiencing. This, then, is the *endurance* of moments rather than their continuation; the endurance of moments is not the linear accumulation of past event which survive into the present but rather are the ways in which certain moments of intense experience move from 'the past' and are re-experienced as a different assemblage of durations. Moments that endure, then, are not what a body has lived through but rather what a body *is* living (through) as non-linear durational rhythms.

For Bergson, a body has many different durational rhythms which exist alongside each other; as discussed above, a body is experienced through rhythms which pass and which endure. Through an understanding of a body's temporality not as an external state which has been organised for specific purposes but as an internal, unified and multiple, flow of difference, Bergson draws attention to how the past is mobile and dynamic, to how the past endures. The past for Bergson exists as a series of planes which contain 'the whole of the past' (Grosz 2000: 224) to greater or lesser extents. Grosz neatly sums up Bergson's notion of the past as such:

> Each segment [of the past] has its own features although each contains within itself the whole of the past. Memories drawn from various strata may be clustered around idiosyncratic points, 'shining points of memory', as Bergson describes them, which are multiplied to the extent that memory is dilated. Depending on the recollection we are seeking, we must jump in at a particular segment; in order to move on to another, we must do so through another leap. (Grosz 2000: 224, reference omitted)

Through the notion of 'shining points of memory', Bergson wants to draw attention to how memory works through a process of 'localisation':

> The process of localising a recollection in the past, for instance, cannot at all consist, as has been said, in plunging into the mass of our memories, as into a bag, to draw out memories, closer and closer to each other, between which the memory to be localised may find its place. By what happy chance could we just hit upon a growing number of intercalary recollections? The work of localisation consists, in reality, in a growing effort of *expansion*, by which the memory, always present in its entirety to itself, spreads out its recollections over an ever wider surface and so ends by distinguishing, in what was till then a confused mass, the remembrance which could not find its proper place. (Bergson 2002: 171)

The work of localisation, then, 'tracks down' a memory through the different planes of the past by its proximity to these shining points of 'dominant memories' (Bergson 2002: 171). The deliberate remembering that Tasha describes can be understood through this process of localisation; Tasha deliberately remembers 'everything that's like happened in my life'. At the centre of this kind of remembering is, as Grosz explains in the quotation above, the necessity for the past to be entered or 'jumped' into. For a particular memory to be sought, 'the past' must be jumped into. In this sense, to re-experience the past deliberately as Tasha describes is not to remain in the present and recollect or recount the past but to 'leap' into the past, to remember the past and experience its temporal intensity again.

In this sense, then, the past is not lying latent, ready to be tapped into, or 'plunged . . . as into a bag', but is to be re-experienced through its very intensity, through how that intensity enables a connection (a jump, a leap) between different durational rhythms. This connection is not a replacement of one durational rhythm with another, nor a move from one durational rhythm to another. Moments of intense experience are not self-contained or bounded units. Rather, the jump or leap involved in remembering and re-experiencing a past moment is a connection between different durations where these durations are assembled simultaneously.[9] As Bergson says, through intuition, that is the jumping into a state, 'we can picture to ourselves as many durations as we wish, all very different from each other' (1999: 47). Tasha's deliberate remembering, for example, does not involve the replacement of the one duration of 'sit[ting]' and 'think[ing]' 'in my room' with the duration of 'everything that's like happened in my life'. One duration cannot be subsumed by another but rather duration involves multiple rhythms, in this case of both sitting and thinking and of everything that has happened. What is involved in Tasha's remembering is the connection between the rhythm of her remembering and the rhythm of the past remembered. The jump or leap between them is a relation through which the intensities of the past and present are experienced at once.

Indeed, in defining the present in relation to the past, Bergson argues that the definition of the present 'as *that which is*' is 'arbitrary' (2002: 149). Instead, the present is,

> simply *what is being made*. Nothing *is* less than the present moment, if you understand by that the indivisible limit which divides the past from the future. When we think this present as going to be, it exists not yet, and when we think of it as existing, it is already past. If, on the other hand, what you are considering is the concrete present such as it is actually lived by consciousness, we may say that this present consists, in large measure, in the immediate past. (2002: 149–150)

Rather than ma(r)king the distinction between the past and the present in terms of what is and what has been, Bergson differentiates them through the actual and the virtual. The present involves the actual, *'that which is acting'* (Bergson 2002: 69) and the past involves the virtual, *'that which acts no longer'* (Bergson 2002: 68). As it involves that which acts, the present is a duration placed, both on this side and on that,...what I call 'my present' has one foot in my past and another in my future. In my past, first, because 'the moment in which I am speaking is already far from me'; in my future, next, because this moment is impending over the future: it is to the future that I am tending (Bergson 2002: 138).

The past and future have different rhythms of duration which can be experienced simultaneously through their assemblage in the present. As Grosz puts it, the present 'straddles both past and future, requiring the past as its precondition, while oriented towards the immediate future' (2000: 222–223). There is a *'simultaneity* of past and present. The past is contemporaneous with the present it has been. They exist at the "same" time. The past could never exist if it did not coexist with the present of which it is the past' (Grosz 2000: 223). Access to the past, and the future, are through the durational rhythm of the present, through the jump from the actual to the virtual: 'we shall never reach the past unless we follow and adopt the movement by which it expands into a present image' (Bergson 2002: 135). The connection that Tasha makes between the present and the past through deliberately remembering involves the past and the present existing simultaneously; the past is necessitated in the present, neither the past nor the present could exist without the other.

Enduring the past

What this notion of the simultaneity of the past and the present suggests is that the present is the present of the past, is *this* present of *this* past; *this* present and *this* past could not exist without each other. Tasha could not remember a specific past outside of a specific present and a specific present could not exist without a specific past. There is a particular and vital relation between them. The present, in Bergson's terms, 'contains virtually within it the whole of the past and present of the being experiencing it' (1999: 31). Grosz describes Bergson's understanding of the relation between the present/actual and past/virtual as such:

> Each moment carries a virtual past with it; each present must, as it were, pass through the whole of the past. This is what is meant by the past in general; the past does not come after the present has ceased to be, nor does the present somehow move into the past. Rather, *it is the past which is the condition of the present*, it is only through its pre-existence that the present can come to be. Bergson does not want to deny that succession takes place – one present (and past) replaces another: but such real or actual succession can only take place because of a virtual coexistence of

the past and the present, the virtual coexistence of all of the past at each moment of the present. (2000: 224–225, my emphasis)

Understanding the past as 'the condition of the present', the virtual of the actual, does not suggest that the past is the *pre*-condition of the present; the past does not *determine* the present. Rather, the relations between the past and present involve a 'coexistent' connection; the past and present are the conditions, or in Massumi's terms 'qualifiers', of each other. The 'whole of the past' is *this* past of *this present*. This is important in terms of not overlooking or ignoring what and how moments of intensity stay. All moments are capable of intensity but not all moments are intense. All moments are capable of staying but some moments pass. What an understanding of the relation of the past and the present as conditions of each other points to is how particular moments become experienced intensely.

For example, Katie's focus on comments about her weight which she says 'stay' longer than other comments and Tasha's 'sensitivity' to certain comments might be understood through this notion of the relations between the past and the present – the past as conditioning or qualifying the present. For Katie, the past can be understood as the condition of the present in that she experiences comments about her weight intensely because of her past. Katie discusses this past at another point in her individual interview and said that her past 'stays' in particular ways and is part of how she experiences her present. For example, despite her friends' encouragement that she should wear 'tight clothes' to 'look nice' all the time and not just on special occasions, Katie explains that she does not have the 'confidence' to:

BECKIE: ok, so even though you were bullied when you were younger
KATIE: yeah
BECKIE: do you think that stuff's kind of stayed with you or do you think it's kind of more to do with when you lost confidence or?
KATIE: it's probably more to do with when I lost confidence, cos my bullying, it wasn't like, it was bullying, but it wasn't like as stressful, cos we were only little and you couldn't really do much about it, it hasn't, I still remember like stuff that they did to me but it doesn't, it doesn't bother me anymore, cos we were only little cos we didn't really, well they did know what they were doing but, sort of if you know what I mean
BCKIE: ok yeah
KATIE: but it's just probably like losing my confidence, like before, but I still wore baggy clothes and everything but it didn't look as bad cos I was fat and like filled it out [laughs] but, I dunno really, it's probably my confidence

Katie's loss of confidence, although it 'happened' in her past, is not confined to the past, to the moment(s) when it was 'lost'. Instead, Katie's past qualifies or conditions the possible ways in which she can experience her body. Katie's past stays with her as how she experiences her body; losing her confidence endures. This is an understanding of 'losing confidence' not as something that happens once and is lost forever; Katie is not, for example, 'without confidence'. Rather, 'losing confidence' stays, it is an experience that is re-experienced. Each time Katie wears tight clothes, this present moment must 'pass through' what she experienced in her past. It is in this way that losing confidence stays; the past conditions the present.

In the following extract, Chloe discusses how her past conditions her present explicitly:

> BECKIE: so do you think you're really judged on your looks?
> CHLOE: yeah, very much so, everyone is I think but it's mainly bigger people cos like everyone wants to be skinny but I think if everyone wants to be skinny, the world will be boring, cos there wouldn't be different people, cos I think being big has made me what I am, I like to think I'm funny and bubbly but I think that's just through, I don't know, just being who I am now, just being who I was when I was younger and that's just going to stay with me for the rest of my life so if I wasn't like this now then I'd probably be a completely different person, I mean I might be one of those nasty people who took the mickey out of people when they walk down the street so I'm quite glad, I'm not glad I've been big all my life but I sort of am in a way
> BECKIE: ok, so you think that the things that you've been through, they make you think about other people?
> CHLOE: yeah, and people who shout things out about other people in the street, they're just so inconsiderate of their feelings, see, me, I'd think about it, like if I was gonna shout something out in the street I'd think about it and be like 'no' cos I wouldn't like that to be said to me, so I always have to stop and think before I do stuff, cos being like, having gone through what I have it's made me think, well, I wouldn't like it if it was done to me

In this extract Chloe says that what she has 'gone through' endures into the present and 'it's made me think'. Chloe says that her past means that she 'thinks' before 'shout[ing] something out in the street'. Chloe's past endures through this 'thinking' which acts as a stoppage to potential action, stops the actualisation of potential hurtful comments ('I wouldn't like it if it was done to me'). In this sense, the virtual past conditions the actual present through setting limits on what of the virtual might be actualised. As Chloe says, 'just being who I was when I was younger and that's going to stay with me for the rest of my life so if I wasn't like this now then I'd probably be a completely different person'. The possibilities of how Chloe's body might become are not endlessly open – the virtual is not a state of infinite possibility – but are limited or conditioned by what she has been through.

Here, then, what is important about 'experience' for Chloe is not (just) what she has been through but how what she has been through endures. This, for Bergson, is the duration of the present, an 'inner' duration which, while involving 'that which is acting', also involves 'that which acts no longer'.

> Inner duration is the continuous life of a memory which prolongs the past into the present, the present either containing within it in a distinct form the ceaselessly growing image of the past, or, more probably, showing by its continual change of quality the heavier and still heavier load we drag behind us as we grow older. Without this survival of the past into the present there would be no duration, but only instantaneity. (1999: 40)[10]

The past 'lives' through how memory endures into the present. This virtual life of the actual for Bergson grows 'heavier and still heavier' as a body 'goes through' more experience. Importantly, though, this is not the past understood as the accumulation of experience but rather as the endurance, the living of the past in a virtual state. Although it is only the present that 'acts', the past is not closed off from the present into a bounded unit; the past lives. As Bergson says, this is crucial to an understanding of the becoming of a body because it means that, despite a focus on the present, there is duration and not 'only instantaneity'. Understanding a body as becoming is to 'be in the present and in a present which is always beginning again' (Bergson 2002: 210). *But this is not to foreclose how the past is involved in this present.* In understanding the present, as discussed above, as *both* within the present and the (immediate) future, the present has a duration which is not instantaneous.[11] As this chapter indicates, the past endures, *things stay.*[12] This is a focus on the present that does not ignore how a body changes. The past conditions rather than pre-conditions the present. This therefore means that the present is not always-already determined by the past, nor that the past plays out in the present with a regularity which can be predicted in advance.

The past that lives through memory, then, is not knowable prior to how it is actualised through specific spatial and temporal assemblages. The past that lives through memory can be open, intuitive, creative. Chloe, for example, has not turned into 'one of those nasty people' because of the 'nasty' experiences she has been through as some models of causational temporality might suggest. However, neither can the way in which she deliberately thinks so as not to hurt people as she has been hurt necessarily be understood as the 'correction' to the past cause and present effect as other models of linear temporality might suggest. Instead, how the past *conditions* Chloe's present and future can be understood as 'a present which is always beginning again', as that which is 'simply being made'. The past does not determine the present but is made again through its repetition in the present:

> If matter does not remember the past, it is because it repeats the past unceasingly, because, subject to necessity, it unfolds a series of moments of which each is the equivalent of the preceding moment and may be deduced from it: thus its past is truly given in the present. But a being which evolves more or less freely creates something new every movement: in vain, then, should we seek to read its past in its present unless its past were deposited within it in the form of memory. (Bergson 2002: 222–223)

Chloe's becoming of the present might be understood as something of a mix between the past which is not remembered by matter but is repeated 'unceasingly' and the 'freedom' of 'creat[ing] something new every movement'. That is, Chloe's past is repeated in new and creative ways. Moreover, and interestingly, Bergson's final point in the above extract warns against attempting to 'read' a past in a present *'unless its past were deposited within it* in the form of memory'. The notion of memory that Bergson proposes here is not so much a deliberate remembering, that is an intentional attempt to track down a memory by jumping from the present to the past as it is *the past entering into the present*. Memory as open, new and creative is entered into not through a jump of the present into the past but of the past into the present. In this sense, this type of memory might be comparable to the second way in which Tasha says she remembers intense moments of experience, not through a deliberate remembering but through these moments making themselves remembered, depositing themselves in the present; when 'it suddenly comes into my head'. This second type of remembering is what is explored in the following section.

Shocks of remembering

In cases where moments make themselves remembered, the past 'enters' the present and is re-experienced as and through a 'shock'. Of course, given the argument made above, the past does not 'enter' the present as if both the present and the past exist as self-contained units. Indeed, the example of the 'shock' of remembering a memory draws attention to how the past and the present, as Bergson suggests, exist simultaneously, as rhythms of durations that move and become re-experienced through different assemblages. The understanding of a moment of experience as intense can also be clearly thought through the shock of remembering; moments of experience can be understood as 'shocks' which endure, moments of intensity move and remain shocking through their movement. In this sense, 'endurance' here refers not only to the capacity for moments of experience to move (not continue or survive) but also to how a moment retains its intensity. The moments that 'suddenly come into' Tasha's head overtake and shock her because their intensity is experienced again; a horrible comments can be as intensely horrible in the present as it was in the past. Things that stay endure because of their intensity where this intensity involves the collapse of the distinction between the past and the present. With deliberate remembering, although the past is re-membered in the present, they are distinct, held apart as different durational rhythms. However, in these cases of the shocks of remembering, this distinction dissolves; the past jumps into the present, the past *is* the present.

The endurance of the past through such shocks is a mode or rhythm of duration which involves the unexpected. In this sense it is a rhythm of duration which, as Grosz explains,

> proceeds not by continuous growth, smooth unfolding, or accretion, but through division, bifurcation, dissociation – by difference – through sudden and unexpected change or eruption. Duration is a mode of inflecting self-differentiation: difference is internal to its function, its modes of elaboration and production, and also its ramifying effect on those objects located 'within' its milieu. (1999c: 28)

Such a rhythm of endurance which proceeds through difference, change and suddenness involves the past and present in ways which disrupt linear temporality. Moments of the past are capable of retaining their intensity and 'shocking' the present through this intensity. What happens if, as suggested by shocks of remembering, the past is not jumped into from the present (as with deliberate remembering) but jumps into the present? What happens if the present cannot be a plane to be returned to in order to assemble with moments of the past but is instead a plane which is disrupted by the past? What happens if the past is not the *condition* of the present but is re-experienced *as* the present? What happens when intense experiences retain their intensity and through this intensity move and assemble with different durations?

The notion of endurance through shocks as a specific mode of duration disrupts linearity because of its capacity to disturb the lines between different durational rhythms. If a past moment of intensity is intense in the present, what is the past and what is the present? Where are the lines between the past and the present if a moment, through its intensity, moves and is re-experienced as part of an assemblage of a different duration? Is a particular assemblage 'within' the present if the past shocks 'into' it? The 'shock of memory' is discussed by Lury (1998) in relation to photographs which she argues contain within them, and at once, the possibility of the past, present and future. Lury develops Walter Benjamin's (1950/1999) concept of 'the flash', that is 'the spark of recognition', to suggest that the photograph disrupts the temporal progression from past-to-present-to-future by 'illumin[ating] the past in the present' (Lury 1998: 36). Linear temporality is thus disturbed by the shocks of remembering.[13] Benjamin suggests the impossibility of recognising the past 'the way it really was' and instead argues that: 'The true picture of the past flits by. The past can be seized only as an image which flashes up when it can be recognised and can never be seen again' (Benjamin 1999: 247). These points when the past 'flashes up' and can be 'seized' are what Benjamin terms 'moments of danger'. The 'past' that Tasha describes as 'suddenly coming into my head', then, might be understood as these moments of danger, that is as moments when the past shocks itself into recognition and demands re-experience.

Loops of temporality

The shock of remembering as a moment of danger suggests that temporality can be understood as 'flashes' of experience which become re-experienced through a different temporal assemblage.[14] Lury explores Benjamin's moment of danger through Barthes' notion of the photographic *punctum*, or wound (see Chapter 3), which she argues conceives moments of danger as the experience of different temporalities at once. The notion of the *punctum* draws attention to how the photograph occupies both 'the here and now' and a time and space other than this. This capacity for the photograph to be both here and now and elsewhere and elsewhen,[15] this simultaneity of a present and a past moment,[16] Lury suggests can be understood in terms of a 'photographic loop'. Although this is a loop between the past and the present, it also contains within it a moment of the future, a moment of 'anticipation and hesitation' (Lury 1998: 91). The moment of hesitation and anticipation can be understood as the *punctum*, as the wound or the recognition of danger that the photographic image casts open. Lury writes that for Barthes,

> the *punctum* is the effect not only of metamorphosis but also of coincidence. This coincidence is an encounter that has not been missed but is

184 *The becoming of bodies: girls, images, experience*

> waiting to happen. In other words, whereas the psychoanalytic notion of trauma is tied to the past, that which Barthes identifies is still in the future. This future, while it has not yet happened, is held in anticipation by the image. (1998: 103)

The illumination of the past in the present contains within it the future; the photographic image is the potential moment of shock where the past, present and future, as anticipation, are experienced at once. This is interesting in terms of the duration of the present explored above, that is of the duration of the present involving many different rhythms at once. The duration of the present involves not only the endurance of the past into the present but also the hesitation and anticipation of the future. The future, in this sense, endures.

Lury's argument is that the photographic image contains within it the past, the present and the anticipation of the future. Consider this in relation to the following extract in which Dionne, Tasha and Fay discuss looking at family photographs:

> DIONNE: I like looking at old photos, you know the little ones when they were just like that when you took them and got them developed cos like it's not just the people who were in it, it's like what everything was like, like I've got pictures of my mum's mum's parents when they got married and everything and it's just like nice to see how everything has changed as well
> TASHA: yeah, it's like when you look at your parents when they were children and you're like 'oh my god', you can't believe what they wore, what they looked like
> FAY: people say I look like my mum, cos we've got this picture of my mum like my age on the wall and people say I look like my mum now but when she was 14 I don't look like her then, it's like

In this extract, the girls understand themselves through the multiple temporalities that are contained within a photograph. Fay, for example, understands her body through 'this picture of my mum'. Here, then, Fay experiences her body through her mother's duration, that is another body's duration which has a rhythm different to her own; 'people say I look like my mum now but when she was 14 I don't look like her then'. Consider also Hannah's understanding of her body through the temporal assemblage with her mother's, and in particular the reversal of the conventional linear temporal relation between mothers and daughters:

> BECKIE: So do you ever imagine what you'll look like when you're older, or imagine yourself when you're older?
> HANNAH: I don't, I imagine what I'd look like reality-wise when I'm older

BECKIE: which is what?

HANNAH: I dunno cos the thing is with my mum I look I mean my mum now looks a bit like me but not much like me and I've seen pictures of her when she was younger and I put them to pictures of me when I was younger and we look like twins, I mean I look exactly the same as her, so I've seen pictures of her when she's twenty and so I just imagine myself to look like that, I don't know how I'd look like that cos I look kinda different now but that's how I'd think I would look cos I look so similar to how she looked at my age

Here, Hannah reverses temporal priority in saying that her mother 'looks a bit like me'. The duration of Hannah's body and her mother's body are different, as are the durations of Fay's and her mother's. What Hannah points to is the ways in which neither of these durational rhythms necessarily takes priority, that is, there is no linear temporality where, for example, the past or age should be considered prior or more significant; Hannah's mother can look like her.

Sammy also discusses how her own duration is different to her mother's:

BECKIE: so if you imagine yourself in the future, do you just imagine good things about you, so if there was something you didn't like about you know, would you think that would be gone when you're 20 or whatever?

SAMMY: erm, I dunno, I haven't really thought about it like if things will go or if things will change, I haven't really thought about it

BECKIE: ok, if you did think about it now?

SAMMY: erm, I dunno I suppose I do need a mirror cos then I could see things I don't know, I don't actually know what I would look like, I just don't know cos like you know when you see your parents as a child they look so much different to what they are now and like I look more like my mum now than she did as a child

BECKIE: ok

SAMMY: so I may change, I may stay the same, cos like she changed

As with Fay, Sammy says that she thinks she looks more like her mother at the age she is 'now than she did as a child'. Sammy thinks through this durational difference to consider her future; what will she look like, what will change and what will stay? What is apparent in both Fay's and Sammy's explanations is the way in which the future is understood through its anticipation in different kinds of images. For both Fay and Sammy, photographic images involve a temporal loop in that the future is contained, as a hesitation, within the past and present of the photograph. Looking at the past and present temporalities of a photograph help Fay and Sammy to anticipate what their bodies might become in the future through the duration of their mothers; how will they look like their mothers? This, then, is a relation of duration between different bodies, between Fay's and Sammy's bodies and their mothers' bodies. It is the combining of durations as a new assemblage which has its own duration. Duration is not a process of aging where aging can be understood as an extensive progression common to all but rather duration is the capacity for connections to be made between different temporalities (different ages and different people, for example).

For Sammy, the duration of her body might also be anticipated through a mirror image; 'I suppose I do need a mirror cos then I could see things I don't know'. The mirror, for Sammy, allows her to recognise, or anticipate, the possibilities of the future ('things I don't know') through considering 'if things will go or if things will change'. The future in this sense is not an inevitable event which the past and the present lead to but rather is a possibility that might be anticipated through the duration of the present. In his discussion of the glance, Edward S. Casey (1999), through Bergson, considers what the mirror makes possible for understanding the past and the present. He writes,

> The mirror-glance exemplifies that *dedoublement* whereby one present moment of our experience immediately and forthwith spawns a virtual image of itself. This image is the past of that present, and, instead of being deferred in its formation (as we all too often assume), is formed at the very moment of perception. (1999: 87)

Casey's argument is that the mirror-glance is both a present image and a virtual image of the past. This present and past do not exist as separate, nor as a slippage into each other, but simultaneously; the past and present exist at once through their production 'at the very moment of perception' through the mirror. The virtual image of 'the past of that present' that is formed through the mirror-glance exists with the present but cannot be contained within that image. The virtual is always elsewhere and elsewhen to the image, that is, is always *a* past of *that* present (not *the* past of *the* present). In terms of how Sammy discusses the temporalities involved in a mirror image of herself, it would also seem that the future, as well as the past and present, is involved. Indeed, the way in which Sammy thinks about her future is not as *the* future but is rather *a* future, a *virtual* future, anticipated by, and made possible through, *this* present. Sammy says that she does not and cannot know the future but is pushed by my question to anticipate a future. She considers this (possible and specific, that is *virtual*) future through the futures that might be anticipated in photographic and mirror images. For Sammy, the mirror creates a virtual image of her body that is a future of a particular present, a future that assembles with and is produced through this (interview) present.

Making things stay

The notion of the future developed here, then, is not of the future as determined by the past or the present but as *anticipated by* or *made possible through*, particular durational assemblages. The future is not an infinite possibility but nor is the future always-already knowable or plannable. As Grosz says, 'to know the future is to deny it as future, to place it as a given, as past' (1999b: 6). The notion of the anticipation of the future therefore draws attention to how the future can be *imagined* through the duration of the present. As explored above, the present as a duration involves the assemblage of different durational rhythms. So far the discussion has been concerned with how *the past* endures in ways which either involve the 'jump' from a present into a past (deliberate remembering) or the 'shock' of the past into the present (the suddenness of memory). However, some of the girls also discussed how they knowingly and carefully attempted to sustain particular moments from the past or the present into the future. In this sense, not only did things from the past endure into the present but they were also made, successfully or not, to endure into the present. The future also involves endurance. Consider, for example, the following three extracts taken from individual interviews with Chloe, Tina and Catherine and Fay:

BECKIE: ok and what about if someone says something good, does that stay with you, do you remember that?
CHLOE: yeah, I'll always remember that, like if someone said my hair looks nice in a certain way, like maybe a couple of days later I'll have it like that again cos someone's commented on me so yeah they stay with me

BECKIE: so if you get nice things said about you, do you remember them, do they stay with you and you remember them?
TINA: yeah
BECKIE: for how long, and how do they make you feel?
TINA: I dunno like, if someone says something really nice I'll like put my head up and be like 'oh', but if someone like said something mean you'd just like get in a mood
BECKIE: what about you?
CATHERINE: erm I think, say you're wearing a new top and they compliment you then you feel really good and you want to wear that top again and again but say if they said something bad about the top then you don't wanna wear it like ever again cos you feel really stupid sort of thing

FAY: what makes me feel bad is like when these two [Dionne and Sammy] say, oh, they've said something like erm, it's the end of the day and my hair just does not stay in the same place or it just doesn't, it just goes, and by the end of the day and like these two will say something and like that really puts me down

These extracts demonstrate how Chloe, Catherine and Tina and Fay want some moments to endure and so spend time and effort trying to make them stay. Chloe, for example, remembers 'nice' comments about her hair and attempts to make such nice comments endure by styling her hair 'in a certain way' that 'someone said . . . looks nice'. Similarly, Catherine discusses how she 'want[s] to wear that top again and again' if she has received a 'compliment' about it. Chloe and Catherine here point to how their future is anticipated in past and present moments. Compliments or 'nice' comments in the past and present can be made to endure in order to try to produce a future of compliments and nice comments, of looking nice. 'Nice' moments of experience can be made to stay through particular bodily practices, such as wearing a specific top or styling hair 'a certain way'.[17] Catherine and Chloe's remarks are therefore about the capacity of their bodies' duration to involve the past, present and future in complex and co-existent ways. The past neither remains locked in what has happened nor slips neatly into the present and future. Rather, the past and present can be made to stay. In Edward S. Casey's terms, then, 'we go out and meet [the future]; not because it already exists . . . but because our very duration is able to grow commensurately with anything that will happen to us' (1999: 91). The past can be made to endure as the present and the future; Chloe and Catherine go out and meet their futures.

In contrast to Catherine and Chloe, Fay's remarks above draw attention to how her attempts to make 'nice' moments endure are not successful in her eyes. Her hair, for example, will not 'stay in the same place, it just doesn't, it just goes'. This unsuccessfulness is reinforced because 'these two will say something' about it which 'really puts me down'.[18] For Fay, her attempts to make certain moments endure fail, she cannot go out and meet the future (indeed, might it be Dionne and Sammy who go out and meet Fay's future?). The future, then, is not a controllable thing but might be something that can be anticipated. Fay anticipates her future but cannot control it, she can anticipate how to style her hair but this style cannot be guaranteed to stay in place. The anticipation of the future connects different rhythms of duration; a past and a present are connected to a future through the attempts to make things stay through bodily practices. In the extracts immediately above, the connections between different durations are attempted deliberately; there are deliberate attempts to make things stay. There were also cases discussed by some of the girls where the anticipation of the future involved different durations which they did not know how to connect. The future was discussed as a possibility understood through the past and present but these different durations were not known as connectable in any clear sense. This was often discussed by the girls in terms of body size and shape and 'staying' or 'getting' slim. Consider for example the following extract from Sarah's individual interview.

> BECKIE: so if you did imagine yourself in the future, sort of, what clothes size would you be?[19]
> SARAH: erm, 8 now, I'm not sure, I'd like to stay at least 10 if I can

Sarah wanted the clothes size of her present to endure into her future. However, in her interview, Sarah did not give details of *how* she was going to 'stay at least a 10'; there were no specific bodily practices which could be engaged in to make 'size 10' stay. In the following extract, Dionne, Fay, Tasha and Emily discuss the possibilities of dieting in order to make a certain body size and shape endure:

> TASHA: girls that are like larger than others they're like, 'oh I need to go on a diet', but diets don't help at this age because they don't, your body
> FAY: your body
> TASHA: you can't stick to them cos like you need a diet and it's like nothing will help because if you lose it you'll just think 'oh I've lost it, oh I can start eating again' and
> FAY: and it piles on
> TASHA: and you put it back on but when you're older you have much more willpower
> DIONNE: most of us are on a diet about now anyway,
> FAY: it comes back on but like double quick
> TASHA: yeah exactly
> EMILY: I'm not
> DIONNE: you will though cos like in a couple of years time you like go
> FAY: yeah cos you haven't developed a metabolism or anything
> DIONNE: one way or the other, like you go fat you go thin, you go up you go down
> EMILY: I don't go up
> DIONNE: yeah but you don't know cos you're not there yet,
> EMILY: I know I will cos like the whole of my family is like six foot
> DIONNE: yeah but like
> EMILY: so I'll be really tall when I'm older but at the moment I'm not
> TASHA: but like kids they haven't developed properly and they're like
> FAY: they haven't developed a metabolism for the way their body works yet

TASHA: yeah exactly, and when you're older like you have much more willpower to like stick to something

This extract is interesting in terms of the different notions of the past, present and future held by Emily and by Dionne, Tasha and Fay. For Emily, the present connects to the future while for the other girls, the future is a durational rhythm that is *disconnected* from their pasts and presents. For example, Dionne, Fay and Tasha make comments about how their present and past is disconnected from their future, that is what they 'are' now is not what they will be(come) in the future; 'diets don't help at this age', 'you're not there yet', 'when you're older'. Emily, however, challenges this disconnection of the future from the present and past; 'I'm not [on a diet]', 'I don't go up [in weight]'. Indeed, for Emily, the present, although not the same as the future, is understood not as disconnected but as *connected* to the future through her family; 'I know I will cos like the whole of my family is like 6 foot so I'll be really tall when I'm older but at the moment I'm not'. The future of Emily's body does not so much involve making things stay, nor things making themselves stay but rather is an assemblage of different durations. As Emily points out, her present body is experienced through what she says she will become in the future. Emily's future is understood by Emily through the present of her family, but is not the experience of her 'own' present, 'at the moment I'm not'.

Emily's future is connected to her future because the present for Emily is *possible*.[20] She is not on a diet and her weight does not 'go up and down'. However, for Fay, Dionne and Tasha in this extract, the future is *disconnected* from their pasts and presents because their pasts and presents are not possible, that is their experiences of their bodies involve unhappiness, disobedience and futility. Their futures are therefore unlike their pasts and presents, the future is when things are different to how they are now. For example, in the future their bodies will have a 'properly developed' metabolism, diets 'will work', 'willpower' will be stronger and more effective. Metabolism, dieting and willpower are not, then, deliberate bodily practices through which things can be made to endure but rather are practices which are understood as not entirely conscious or deliberate. Metabolism, dieting and willpower are bodily processes through which the girls say their bodies will be experienced in the future but which are not controllable, their 'development' is outside of their bodies' intentional control. Tasha and Fay will develop 'proper' metabolisms 'for the way their bodies work' and Emily will grow tall because the rest of her family are.[21] They are bodily processes where the body is understood as an assemblage of different rhythms, some of which can be (attempted to be) deliberately sustained and others of which exist elsewhere and elsewhen to the body. Willpower, metabolism and dieting are rhythms (or organs?) of a body that develop at a different speed to deliberate bodily practices. They are involved in the future possibilities of the girls' bodies in this extract but in ways where those futures are disconnected from the consciously experienced pasts and presents. In this way, through the disconnection of the past, present and future, the future is somehow held open as a possibility, that is as more possible than the present.

Indeed, the disconnection of the future from the past and present is pointed to most explicitly by Tasha in the extract above. Her remarks about willpower being more powerful in her future understands this future as when the past *does not stay*. The future is when the body 'settles down' and no longer, in Dionne's words, has the capacity to go up and down. This notion of the future is also similar to the one described by Fay when asked to imagine her future: 'hopefully it, all the things I don't like just go away and it like just works out that I look really good'. Fay's future is one where 'you just see yourself as perfect and how you want to be'; it is an imagination of a future that ignores or forgets the past and the present ('all the things I don't like just go away') and is instead 'perfect'. This break from the past and present is also how Katie imagines her future as 'hopefully [when] it will all get better'. Katie describes her future in terms of a complete disconnection from her past and present. She will leave her home town and the people she knows and 'start again, start again as an adult, sort of, well not an adult but an 18 year old at uni and stuff, just to have a good time'. The futures that Katie, Fay and Tasha imagine are perfect, settled, secure. They are hopeful. This is in contrast to the disruption and instability of how they experience their pasts and presents. Their futures are imagined to become not *through* their pasts and presents but somehow *in spite of* or *without* them. Whereas for Emily the future is connected to the past and present because they are possible, for Fay, Tasha and Katie, the future is disconnected from this past and this present because they are not possible. The future is disconnected as a fantasy or an escape.[22]

The future of the past and the present

The understanding of a body's past, present and future as different rhythms which might, or might not, assemble as that body's duration offers an alternative notion of temporality from those offered by models which see time as in some way linear or synthetic. The past does not work here as an experience to correct or become opposite to. The future is not the *continuation* or *survival* of the past and present into the future but is a, conditioned or qualified, durational rhythm involving them. Conceiving the future in terms of duration, then, does not necessarily imply that the desire to break from the past results in the discarding of the past. The duration of a body is that body's movement and flow. Things stay, even if the desire is to disconnect them. The past cannot be discarded because a break from the past is the condition of the future. As such, becomings can be understood as a focus on the present which is *future-oriented*. The future that is conditioned or anticipated is not the succession of the past and present nor the inevitable consequence of the past and present but rather is a new which involves the past and present in complex relational rhythms. Taking up such a conception of the future, what might be involved for an understanding of the becoming of the girls who participated in this project? The concluding chapter takes up this notion of becoming and considers it in relation to feminist theory through issues that have been raised in this and the previous two chapters; structure and agency, difference and repetition, heterosexuality, sex and gender. The focus of the concluding chapter is to ask, what might a feminist ontology of the becoming of bodies do with and to these models? What might feminist theory become?

Notes

1 Deleuze's work on becoming has most often been taken up in relation to space; perhaps unsurprisingly since he describes becoming as geography (Deleuze and Parnet 2002, see also Introduction above). As such, Grosz argues in a discussion of the notion of becoming, '[a]lthough temporal concepts are rarely absent from any discourse, these concepts are not usually discussed or framed explicitly or self-consciously' (1999b: 3).
2 For example, through the understanding of the living of a life as the progression from past to present to future.
3 Consider here also the notion of time as progressing linearly in Brown and Gilligan's (1992) understanding of adolescence. For these authors, adolescence is for girls a potentially troubling and damaging time where the bodily knowledges of childhood are lost to the more abstract, masculine discourses of adulthood.
4 Consider, for example, Deleuze's point that '[a] scar is the sign not of a past wound but of "the present fact of being wounded": we can say that it is the contemplation of the wound, that it contrasts all the instants which separate us from a living present' (Deleuze 2001b: 77).
5 See Edward S. Casey (1999) for an interesting discussion of how 'the glance' 'puts us both into and out of time – into an intense momentary time and out of a continuous distended time' (1999: 82).

Things that stay 193

6 By this, I mean to indicate that this is not a strict interpretation of Bergson's work. Rather this chapter engages with how some of his concepts have been taken up in feminist theory, particularly by Grosz (1999c, 2000), and provides ways of understanding the empirical material outside of a model of cause-and-effect.
7 See Coleman (2008c) for a discussion of how intuition as method might be a way to explore this empirical research project.
8 Consider this definition of duration in relation to Butler's understanding of discourse that is discussed in the Conclusion below.
9 In this sense, the jump can be understood in terms of affect, that is as the potentially ambiguous and unclear connections or jumps between things. See in particular Massumi 2002a.
10 It should be noted here that Bergson's use of the terms 'continuous', 'continual' and 'survival' do not involve the same connotations that such terms used in psychoanalytic and some narrative theory touched on above do. Indeed, Bergson is critical of approaches which try to 'analyse' duration in terms of unity and synthesis. See, for example, Bergson (1999: 46–49).
11 Consider here the distinction between judging as instantaneous and knowing as enduring that is discussed in Chapter 5.
12 In this sense, then, the notion of instantaneity is not the same as the notion of simultaneity. Durations can exist simultaneously (the past can be experienced simultaneously with the present) but are not instantaneous. Durations involve flows of temporality, which may, as discussed above, involve particularly intense spatial and temporal moments, 'shining points of memory'. Moments of intensity, though, also have duration; they are not instantaneous but enduring.
13 It should be noted that Lury's discussion is interested in questions of mimesis. See Introduction above.
14 As argued in Chapter 3, experience is therefore not a moment that can be recounted as it happened but rather through each recounting, experience is re-made, re-known, re-experienced.
15 Consider at this point the discussion in Chapter 3 about the temporalities of different 'types' of images and of the girls' explanations of mirror images as depicting their bodies as they are 'there and now, there and now'.
16 Lury argues this is the perpetual and necessary mimesis of the past into the present, and therefore of the present into the past.
17 In this sense, the attempt to make things stay through particular bodily practices is similar to the 'unfixing' or 'extending' of a body, discussed in Chapter 5, where specific clothes of hairstyles are understood by the girls, through friendships involving trust, honesty and advice, as opening up the possibilities of what a body might become.
18 In this sense, the impossibility of making things stay into the future might be understood as similar to the fixing of bodies, discussed in Chapter 5, where the possibilities of becoming are limited.

19 This question about clothes size was to provide more detail about what 'slim' meant to Sarah as she had said earlier in the interview that she wanted to stay slim.
20 This understanding of the present as possible, or indeed impossible, might be understood in Butler's terms as 'liveable'. See Butler (2004).
21 However, Emily's understanding of her body through her family is different to the above comments made by some of the girls about their resemblance to their mothers. For Emily, resemblance is not biologised but is remarked upon almost as a coincidence.
22 Compare this desire to break from the 'horrible' past and present with Chloe's remarks that the past and present have 'made me what I am'. Chloe's present and future is possible not in spite of but because of what she has been through.

Conclusion: become what you want?

There is a paradoxical desire at work in a feminist politics that aspires to change, to innovation, to the future (and it seems clear that any politics that seeks the designation of 'feminist' must have this as a minimal defining condition): to think the new entails some commitment to and use of the past and the present, of what prevails, what is familiar, the self-same. The terms by which something can be judged new, radical or innovative must involve some repetition, and some recognition of the old, such that this new departs from it. How can the new, the radical, the transgressive – the 'post-feminist' – be understood except as a departure from what it is, and in the terms of what is? This is the general challenge of any political transformation or upheaval, and most especially, that to which feminist, anti-racist and other minoritarian struggles are directed: to somehow generate a new that is not entirely disconnected from or alien to the old, which nevertheless overcomes its problems, its oppressions, conflicts or struggles. Politics is in fact always intimately bound up, in ways that are not always self-recognised, with the question of time, becoming, futurity and the generation of the new (Grosz 2000: 214).

In Chapter 1 I suggested that at stake in an ontology of becoming is the question of what and how a body becomes. That is, the central question that I have explored so far is not 'what is a body?' but 'how do bodies become through their relations with images?' Exploring this question has involved thinking through the capacities of images (what can images do?), examining the relations of affect and intensity through which bodies are constituted and exploring the temporality of moments of experience. According to the analysis of the empirical material of this book, bodies and images exist not as distinct units but rather as intricate and sticky processes of becoming; bodies become known, understood and lived through images. As such, 'bodies' and 'images' become re-conceived as 'entities' not according to a model of subject(ivity)/object(ivity) but rather through a logic of process and becoming. That is, as 'entities' bodies and images are not closed, unified, autonomous beings but are always becoming through their relations with other 'entities'. Mariam Fraser, Sarah Kember and Celia Lury (2005) describe this logic as:

> a view that entities are constituted in relations. Process, in other words, is characterised by a radical relationality: the (social and natural) world is understood in terms of constantly shifting relations between open-ended objects. This is not to suggest that there are relations *between* pre-existing entities or objects. Instead, objects, subjects, concepts are composed of nothing more or less than relations, reciprocal enfoldings gathered together in temporary and contingent unities. Furthermore, since a relation cannot exist in isolation, all entities can be understood in relation to one another. (2005: 3)

In this sense, in this book, bodies and images are 'open-ended' entities that are composed of, or better are enfoldings of, 'nothing more or less' than the relations between them. In the chapters that deal with the empirical material, it is the relations between bodies and images that constitute these very bodies and images: there are no entities that pre-exist these relations.

This point, that entities do not pre-exist the relations through which they become, was perhaps made most clearly in Chapter 2 in methodological terms. Drawing on Deleuze's (1992) argument concerning immanence, affect and ethics, one point I stressed was that the relations between bodies through which those bodies' affective capacities are produced *cannot be known in advance of* 'a given encounter, a given arrangement, a given combination' (Deleuze 1992: 627). In this concluding chapter, I want to take up this argument again in order to consider, in theoretical and empirical terms, the ways in which a commitment to 'transcendental empiricism' (Deleuze 2001a) re-works, or re-directs, feminist research on the relations between girls' and young women's bodies and images. The concepts of affect, intensity and temporality, or duration, have emerged as key to understanding the empirical material produced in this research according to an ontology of becoming and I consider these concepts in light of some of the 'problems' that have been raised in the empirical chapters. The term 'problem' is understood and taken up here in a specific sense. In a discussion of Bergson's 'method of intuition', Deleuze and Parnet (1977/2002) describe 'the stating and creating of problems' (2002: 14) as a first step in understanding the becoming of a thing. Deleuze suggests that problems should be posed in such a way that the solution emerges through the becoming of the thing, rather than the becoming of a thing being fitted into and understood through, a prior solution.[1] The problems created in this book involve the dichotomy of structure and agency (raised in Chapter 4 through the discussion of relationality), the framework of heterosexuality that often underpins feminist research on girls' and young women's bodies (raised in Chapter 5 through an analysis of affective relationality) and a model of linear, progressive time (critiqued in Chapter 6 through the concept of duration and the argument that temporality is a becoming). Here, I pose these problems and begin to explore them through a particular focus on the virtual, and on the relationship between the virtual, becoming and the future.[2] In the terms that Grosz describes above, in what ways might the virtual account for 'the new' in and of feminist research, a new that is both future-oriented, and hence concerned with change, and committed to an examination of 'what prevails, what is familiar, the self-same'?

The chapter begins with a discussion of how some feminist theoretical and empirical work has understood girls' and women's bodies in terms of sex, gender and heterosexuality. I focus on two tendencies within this work: (i) social constructionist and; (ii) social constructivism.[3] The purpose of this discussion is to explore *how* feminist work has tended to be underpinned by a focus on sex, gender and heterosexuality, a focus which, in the terms of understanding 'the problem' briefly explained above, might be understood as a preoccupation with being rather than becoming. That is, taking seriously Deleuze's arguments on not knowing in advance and on the creating and posing of problems, sex, gender and heterosexuality might be understood as a solution that exists prior to a 'given arrangement'. I unpack what I mean by this, and how a feminist Deleuzian approach might approach the problem differently, by considering the way in which a social constructionist and social constructivist perspective might interpret an extract from my empirical research and explaining instead how I have attempted to understand it. Based on this discussion, the chapter then moves to the problem of structure and agency, a dichotomy that itself, in different ways, underpins social constructionist and social constructivist models. By considering the mapping of this dichotomy onto the distinction between passivity and activity, and by pulling through the concepts of affect and intensity, I argue that one of the appeals of this dichotomy is its accounting for the ways in which bodies are restricted and reproduced. Thinking through the empirical chapters, and drawing on Deleuze's (1968/2001b) work on difference and repetition and on the virtual, I suggest that to understand bodies as becomings is not to ignore the ways in which becomings are limited and repeated. Here, I turn to examine in more detail the virtual as a structure; not a determining structure, as with the structure/agency dichotomy, but as a *condition*. Indeed, taking up the argument made in

Chapter 6 concerning temporality, I argue that, understood as a temporal process, a body's past does not determine a body's future but rather conditions it. As the virtual, a body's past conditions the possibilities of becoming. Furthermore, what this notion of conditioning implies is a sense of novelty, creativeness. Bodies become, often in repetitive – for example, gendered – ways, but as future-oriented processes.

The problem of sex,[4] gender and heterosexuality

In an essay on developments in Anglo-European feminist theory, and social theory more generally, Michèle Barrett (1992) notes a shift from 'things to words'. Citing Foucault, Derrida and Lacan as key influences on contemporary theory, Barrett argues that feminist sociology 'has shifted away from a determinist model of "social structure" (be it capitalism, or patriarchy, or a gender-segmented labour market or whatever) and deals with questions of culture, sexuality or political agency – obvious counterbalances to an emphasis on social structure' (1992: 204). Two prominent strands of feminist sociology that can be identified as part of this literary turn are social constructionism and social constructivism and it is these trends that this section addresses. It is worth noting here the ways in which the work of Foucault is taken up by these two approaches with differing rigour. The feminist social constructionist arguments discussed below use what might be termed a general Foucauldian approach; Foucault's work is understood in terms of an emphasis placed on construction. Bodies, in this sense, are understood as what are constructed *by* the workings of power. In contrast, Judith Butler's (1990/1999, 1993) social constructivism understands bodies and power in a more complex sense where bodies are conceived not as constructed but as *materialised through* power. According to Butler, Foucault's work has been misunderstood as 'personifying' power whereas his work should be seen to be proposing that '[t]here is no power that acts, but only a reiterated acting that is power in its persistence and instability' (Butler 1993: 9). These points are returned to below.

It is also worth noting here that despite social constructionism and social constructivism having different understandings of Foucault's work, the notion of 'the social' that they both imply is strikingly similar, not least in its non-theorisation. In an article called, interestingly in relation to Barrett's essay, 'When Things Strike Back', Bruno Latour (2000) critiques the usual social scientific understanding of 'Society':

> If we have a Society that is *already composed as one single whole* and which can be used to account for the behaviour of actors who do not know

what they are doing, but whose unknown structure is visible to the keen eyes of the trained social scientist, it then becomes possible to embark on the huge task of social engineering in order to produce the common good, without having to go through the painstaking labour of composing this commonality through political means. (Latour 2000: 118)

Latour notes how this notion of society has become problematic for social sciences: 'It has become clear over the years that the existence of society is part of the problem [of social sciences] and not of the solution. "Society" has to be composed, made up, constructed, established, maintained, and assembled. It is no longer to be taken as the hidden source of causality which could be mobilised so as to account for the existence and stability of some other action or behaviour' (Latour 2000: 113). Following Gabriel Tarde over Emile Durkheim, Latour argues that 'society explains nothing but has to be explained. If it is to be accounted for, it will be, by definition, through the presence of many other little things that are not social by nature, but only social in the sense that they are *associated* with one another' (2000: 113, references omitted). In Latour's sense, the social must be understood not as a pre-existing and external 'thing' but instead as the associations between things through which things become known.[5] As such, the social cannot be known, 'objectively', in advance. As the association of things, Society is not 'what manipulates the people in spite of themselves' (Latour 2000: 118).[6] With these critiques of 'the social' in mind, the sections that follow pull out at various points how the notion of society as that which 'manipulates the people in spite of themselves' underpins some aspects of social constructionism and social constructivism.

The construction of bodies

The feminist social constructionist tradition, where it is interested in bodies, takes as its starting point their social construction, that is the way in which bodies must be conceived not as naturally given but as socially inscribed. For some feminist social constructionists, bodies are socially inscribed by sex and gender in the terms of a heterosexual power structure. Of interest to the arguments of this book is the strong trend within feminist social constructionism of studying how girls and young women experience (hetero)sexuality. Much of this research takes heterosexuality to be an unequal power relation between boys and girls where girls are subordinated to boys through social and cultural practices. Janet Holland, Caroline Ramazanoglu, Sue Sharpe, and Rachel Thompson (1998), for example, take what they describe as a Foucauldian approach to young people's sexuality and argue that power is exercised through everyday, mundane bodily practices. Placing their work within the context of apparently progressive changes in young people's sexual behaviour, and in particular young women's sexuality, Holland *et al.* explore how young people experience sex, gender and heterosexuality. Their research suggests that, far from a liberalisation of sexuality where young women could engage in sexual behaviour from equal positions of power, young women are still subordinated to young men. Their Foucauldian approach to sexuality refuses to understand these power relations as individualised in personal relationships but rather conceives power as '*social*', that is personal relationships are also social relationships. Heterosexuality, then, is 'socially negotiated and constructed in social relationships' (Holland *et al.* 1998: 23) and what is personally unequal is also socially unequal.

According to Holland *et al.*, young women do not, and cannot, experience sexuality in the same way as young men; indeed they argue that young women's 'agency and desire are silenced and subordinated to those of the male, and it is the male body and its needs that shape the normalised heterosexual encounter' (1998: 108). They write,

> Young people are actively engaged in constructing their own femininity/ masculinity and sexuality, but in social situations in which they are both produced and constrained by discourses of power, and by the way power relations between women and men are socially organised. In response to this gendering of sexuality young women are under pressure to construct their femininity in relation to men's construction of masculinity. (1998: 24)

For Holland *et al.*, heterosexuality is a process of both gendering and sexing whereby girls are (hetero)sexualised according to the pressures of an already-existing notion of femininity which is defined in relation to a dominant masculinity. It is what they term a 'passive' and 'conservative' femininity that defines how heterosexuality can be experienced by young women. Gender and sexuality are separable but are also integral aspects of how heterosexuality is experienced and reproduced.

Holland *et al.*'s argument is supported by feminist explorations of gender and sexuality at school. Becky Francis (2000), for example, addresses the differences in educational achievement in secondary schools between girls and boys in terms of how gender and sexuality are played out in the classroom. Francis' study was explicitly influenced by Holland *et al*'s research; Francis recognises her own experiences of gender and sexuality at school in Holland *et al.*'s account and reports how she 'was struck by how little these constructions of heterosexual sexuality and the sexist regulation of girls had changed since I was a

Conclusion: become what you want? 201

secondary school pupil' (Francis 2000: 35). Francis neatly sums up feminist understandings of heterosexual relations at schools as such:

> Many studies have shown the secondary school to be an environment fostering compulsory heterosexuality and the sexist objectification, surveillance and regulation of girls and their sexuality. The issues of heterosexual sexuality and of sexism often overlap or are bound up together in the classroom. For example, Lees (1993) and Holland *et al.* (1998) discuss how heterosexual sexual relations invest power and action in the male: girls are expected to be sexually passive, and any female assertion can be labelled as 'slaggish'. Thus, boys expect to be able to give comments on girls' sexual attributes and to exert their own sexuality, whereas girls are expected to remain inert. Girls who do not remain passive, or conversely appear too compliant in relation to male sexual desire, risk being branded 'slags' – significantly, *not properly feminine* – and ostracised or harassed as a consequence. (2000: 35)

In her study, Francis identifies this behaviour where boys assert their sexuality over girls, and in doing so subordinate girls' sexuality, in terms of girls' maturity and boys' immaturity. This distinction is understood not in terms of psychological development (so girls are psychologically more mature than boys) but rather as a kind of social maturity; teachers, and adults in general, see girls dealing with 'immature' comments from boys 'maturely'. For example, Francis uses the instance of one boy deliberately walking into a girl in a classroom and calling 'Sure I bounced of [*sic*] your chest' to which the girl responded in a 'wearied, mildly irritated' way as demonstrating 'how common such incidents are, and also how such behaviour is constructed as illustrating boys' immaturity and the way in which "boys will be boys", rather than as anything more harmful' (Francis 2000: 38–39). Francis argues that such exchanges *are* serious and harmful and discusses how boys often used male sexuality to embarrass or intimidate girls. That girls respond to boys as 'wearied' and 'bored' is because girls and feminine sexuality in general have been subordinated and this is a strategy for dealing with, if not overcoming, these unequal power relations.

There are extracts from my empirical material which could be used to support arguments such as those that Francis makes. For example, in the following discussion the girls talk about how boys use masculine sexuality to try to intimidate and embarrass them and understand their reaction as 'mature' in the way that Francis describes:

> TINA: and boys are like 'oh suck my dick, suck my dick' then it will always go into a competition like 'oh mine's bigger than yours' and all this
> CHLOE: yeah

TINA: and they'll somehow bring us into it like 'you wanna check?' and all this and we're like 'we don't wanna know' and
HANNAH: and I just look at them and like 'do I look like I care?' its like I've got better things to worry about then who's got the biggest dick
[. . .]
CASEY: yeah like [boy's name] was like 'oh I put some girl way last night' and I just look at him and like 'you think we really care?'
HANNAH: we're not impressed or anything
CASEY: we don't really care what you do
HANNAH: yeah you're like 14, it's not really a good thing to be like sleeping around when you're 14
CHLOE: and when the boys are all sitting there like 'oh my dick's bigger than yours innit innit' that's like me saying to Hannah or 'my tits are bigger than yours'
CASEY: yeah like 'my dad's dick's bigger than yours' and
CHLOE: yeah 'I'm your dad, I'm your dad, I'm your granddad'
TINA: yeah 'I've f'ed your mum' and all this
CHLOE: they tell Casey, they tell Casey they're her dad but yet Casey's older than everyone d'you know what I mean, do a little bit of maths and then you'll realise that you're not

According to the conception of heterosexuality discussed above, the exchanges here between Casey, Chloe, Tina and Hannah could be conceived in terms of how gender and sexuality are social power relations which exist both within and outside of individual relationships between boys and girls. The comments that boys make about and to these girls are not isolated cases but, as demonstrated by the similar findings in Francis' study, are part of more widespread social expectations and understandings of what gender and sexuality are, and how they should be part of the interactions between girls and boys. For example, the ways in which the boys know and understand their bodies as gendered and sexed result in the ways they interact with girls through sexualising their own bodies ('my dick's bigger than yours') and the girls' bodies ('you wanna check?'). The girls in turn respond to these comments 'maturely' ('we don't wanna know', 'you think we really care?', 'do a little bit of maths'). The girls here reverse the gender and sexual relations that they experience as subordinating from boys and consider how their own knowledges and understandings of their bodies are different. As discussed in Chapter 5, girls do not compare their sexual organs with each other to assert their femininity ('that's like me saying to Hannah or "my tits are bigger than yours"') and do not sexualise their own bodies by involving boys ('yeah like "my dad's dick's bigger than yours"').

There is here, then, clearly a disparity between how boys and girls gender and sex themselves and others; boys gender and sexualise themselves through comparisons with each other and through involving girls in these comparisons whereas girls can be seen as being sexed and gendered through these unequal interactions with boys. Understanding gender and sex through an approach such as this enables an examination of how power relations are unequally accessible to and adoptable by girls and boys and how, consequently, girls' femininity and (hetero) sexuality are made passive and reliant on boys' masculinity and (hetero) sexuality. These approaches to gender and sex work through an understanding of power relations as that which *effect* boys' and girls' bodies. Boys and girls already have bodies on to and through which power relations such as gender and sex work. Indeed, in Fraser *et al*'s terms, the relations are between pre-existing girls' and boys' bodies. There is a separation between 'boys'/'girls', bodies and power. Bodies are pre-existing entities *on to* which power works and the effects of power are what are constructed as 'boys' and 'girls'. Bodies are therefore neutral spaces which are constructed as boys and girls through heterosexual power relations. A feminist notion of social construction therefore works through an understanding that (i) there is something that can be constructed (a body) and (ii) that this thing that can be constructed can be constructed through something else (the power relations of gender and sex). Moreover, (iii) these power relations are located in 'the social' where the social is that which exists prior to and externally to bodies. Bodies are constructed through being socially sexed and gendered.

This last point might be what Francis is pointing to when she discusses the gender and sexual 'expectations' of girls and boys; girls and boys are the results of certain social expectations that we know about in some way and through which we construct ourselves and each other. These expectations are both what are imposed on 'us' (as girls or women) – boys asserting their sexuality over girls for example – and what 'we' (as girls or women) do to ourselves – girls acting passively in intimate heterosexual relationships. 'Social constructionist' approaches such as the ones discussed above, then, begin from knowing *in advance* what a body is, what power is, and what the social is. From this, they trace the construction of gendered and sexed bodies into boys and girls, and men and women. There is something (a neutral entity) which is constructed (through power) into something else (an unequally sexed and gendered body).

'From construction to materialisation'[7]

In *Bodies That Matter* (1993), Butler critiques social constructionist approaches to sex and gender and instead proposes what she terms 'a return to the notion of matter' (1993: 9). Butler's objection to constructionism is that the distinction between 'nature' and 'culture' on which some approaches to sex and gender depend 'implies a culture or an agency of the social which acts upon a nature, which is itself presupposed as a passive surface, outside the social and yet its necessary counterpart' (1993: 4). Through a rigorous conception of Foucault's notion of power, Butler argues that 'the question is no longer, How is gender constituted as and through a certain interpretation of sex? (a [social constructionist] question that leaves the "matter" of sex untheorised), but rather, Through what regulatory norms is sex materialised? And how is it that treating the materiality of sex as a given presupposes and consolidates the normative conditions of its own emergence?' (1993: 10). In other words, and as I have also indicated above, Butler suggests that social constructionism understands sex as a 'passive surface' onto which gender is socially mapped; a neutral body is inscribed upon by power. Instead, Butler develops a notion of 'materialisation' through which bodies are made into intelligible, or not, subjects. Butler argues that contemporary poststructuralist feminist theory 'dissolves' the matter of bodies by emphasising instead 'textual play' (1993: 27). As a critical practice Butler suggests that feminism has recently tended to concentrate on this textual play of gender while maintaining 'the material irreducibility of sex' (1993: 28). Butler's project is to interrogate the 'materiality' of 'sex' by asking how materiality is constructed, that is, how is sex not an irreducible natural category but is itself constructed?[8] Butler's project is therefore not to deconstruct the 'matter' of sex so that it becomes redundant[9] but rather to investigate how this matter might be returned to as a tactical ground for feminism without becoming a reified shorthand for 'woman'.

According to Butler's argument, the materiality of sex must be examined in terms of its production; how is sex produced as matter that is socially intelligible, or how are bodies materialised as sexed?[10] For Butler, bodies become socially intelligible through their materialisation into subjects. Butler argues that bodies are materialised into intelligible subjects, that is subjects that are recognisably sexed and gendered, through what she terms a 'heterosexual matrix'. The heterosexual matrix is a conceptual framework that Butler developed in her earlier book *Gender Trouble* (1990/1999) and refers to the ways in which,

> the 'unity' of gender is the effect of a regulatory practice that seeks to render gender identity uniform through a compulsory heterosexuality. The force of this practice is, through an exclusionary apparatus of production, to restrict the relative meanings of 'heterosexuality', 'homosexuality', and 'bisexuality' as well as the subversive sites of their convergence and resignification. (1999: 42)

The 'exclusionary apparatus' produces a 'compulsory heterosexuality' through which bodies become historically, socially and politically recognisable, or not, as sexed subjects. As such, Butler argues that 'sex' is not 'material difference' but rather sex itself is 'a regulatory ideal whose materialisation is compelled, and this materialisation takes place (or fails to take place) through highly regulated practices' (1993: 1). That is, 'sex' is not a 'raw material' onto which gender is inscribed; there are not material, physical female bodies which are then constructed as socially feminine. Instead, '"sex" is an ideal construct which is forcibly materialised through time' (1993: 1).[11]

The materialisation of sex takes place through what Butler terms 'gender performativity'. Performativity in Butler's sense refers not to a performance of gender which makes social sense of physical sex but rather to 'the reiterative and citational practice by which discourse produces the effects that it names ... [T]he regulatory norms of "sex" work in a performative fashion to constitute the materiality of bodies and, more specifically, to materialise the body's sex, to materialise sexual difference in the service of the consolidation of the heterosexual imperative' (1993: 2). It is the performativity of gender, then, that materialises sex as socially intelligible. Butler defines 'gender' and 'sex' not as 'power' that works on bodies but rather 'sex' and 'gender' are the *effect* of power through which bodies become socially recognisable. Butler argues,

> In this sense, what constitutes the fixity of the body, its contours, its movements, will be fully material, but materiality will be rethought as the effect of power, as power's most productive effect. And there will be no way to understand 'gender' as a cultural construct which is imposed upon the surface of matter, understood either as 'the body' or its given sex. Rather, once 'sex' itself is understood in its normativity, the materiality of the body will not be thinkable apart from the materialisation of that regulatory norm. 'Sex' is, thus, not simply what one has, or a static description of what one is: it will be one of the norms by which the 'one' becomes viable at all, that which qualifies a body for life within the domain of cultural intelligibility. (1993: 2)

It is clear, then, that Butler's account of sex, gender and heterosexuality differs from those social constructionist approaches explored above. While social constructionism understands bodies as constructed by the unequal power relations of sex and gender, Butler argues that bodies are materialised into intelligible subjects as sex and gender as *effects* of power. For social constructionists, bodies are constructed by sex and gender but can be understood as in some way *prior* to sex and gender while, for Butler, bodies are only intelligible *through* sex and gender.

Bodies, as matter, are 'unthinkable' without sex and gender; bodies are transformed through something else (the heterosexual matrix) into something else (a socially intelligible subject).

How, then, might Butler's approach be a means to understand, to 'think', the bodies of the girls in this research? How might the girls' bodies be understood as primarily thinkable through sex and gender? What is the relationship between sex and gender and 'compulsory heterosexuality'? An approach to the girls' bodies such as that proposed by Butler's work might take account of how the girls' bodies become intelligible through sex and gender within a wider framework of the heterosexual imperative. The relations between the girls and boys and girl-friends might be understood through the notion of the heterosexual matrix which restricts the possible meanings of 'sex' and gender'. With regards to the notion of the heterosexual matrix, the girls' bodies are materialised as sexed through the regulatory and normative practices involved in gender performativity. Take, for example, the extract that is explored above through a social constructionist approach. According to the argument proposed by Butler, this extract might be understood to demonstrate how the heterosexual matrix restricts the possibilities of gender identity. The boys' comments that Tina, Chloe, Casey and Hannah discuss here 'sex' their body through gender performativity ('"oh I put some girl away last night"', '"you wanna check?"') where 'masculinity' is reiterated through discourses that are available to them (boasting of masculine sexuality for example). These discourses, which 'produces the effects that it names', regulate the 'sex' of the boys and also, crucially, regulate how sex is materialised through the girls' bodies ('and when the boys are all sitting there like "oh my dick's bigger than yours innit innit" that's like me saying to Hannah or "my tits are bigger than yours"').

Central to Butler's argument is not only how bodies are made intelligible but also, and relatedly, how certain bodies are therefore made unintelligible, or abject. The girls' bodies here are made *socially intelligible* through the regulatory power of the heterosexual matrix, they are materialised into intelligible subjects through the comments that the boys make which depend upon normative notions of what sex and gender, and consequently heterosexuality, are and can be. The girls' bodies are materialised into intelligible subjects because the gender performativity of their bodies, that is the exchanges between boys and the girls in this case, are historically, socially and politically recognisable and acceptable ('extensive', in the terms of this book). In this sense, an effect of the heterosexual matrix might be the materialisation of girls' bodies which are unable to 'fight back' (Chapter 5), that is the heterosexual matrix materialises bodies that are unable to refuse or resist its power and pervasiveness. For example, the at once individual and social gender performativity of 'maturity', 'not caring', 'weariness' discussed above, or the emphasising of personality over looks discussed in Chapter 4, reinforces rather than subverts the regulatory ideals of the compulsory heterosexuality.[12]

Bodies, therefore, can only be made socially intelligible through 'sex' and 'gender'. As such, I suggest, at stake in both the social constructionist and social constructivist approaches discussed above is an examination of the sexing and gendering of bodies. In both approaches to bodies, the question that is asked is: how are bodies known, understood, and experienced in terms of sex and gender? For Holland *et al.* and Francis, gender constructs bodies which are, in some way, already sexed. For Butler, bodies are materialised as 'sex' through gender performativity which produces them as intelligible or unintelligible subjects. At the heart of both these approaches then is an understanding of bodies as constructed or thinkable *in terms of sex and gender*. For Holland *et al.* and Francis, it is through sex and gender that bodies are constructed and for Butler bodies are principally thinkable through sex and gender; 'sex' is a norm which makes a subject 'viable', is that which qualifies a body for life within the domain of social intelligibility. Without sex and gender, then, in these terms, what a body *is* cannot be accessed.[13] Moreover, in terms of the argument above concerning the notion of the social, both social constructionism and social constructivism conceive sex and gender as social 'facts' which make bodies intelligible; what bodies are can only be accessed through the social nature of sex and gender. In this sense, sex, gender and heterosexuality are assumed as explicatory models *in advance*. In Deleuze's sense, the problem of the body is not created and stated but is known in advance to its becoming, and it is therefore 'solvable' in terms other than its own. I return to this point below. Here, however, I want to ask, what might an approach which was interested not so much in what a body *is* as in what a body *might become* emphasise? And in order to begin to answer this question, I turn to the problem of the dichotomy of structure and agency.

Structure and agency

Social constructionism and social constructivism have been critiqued above because of the ways in which bodies are understood primarily in terms of sex, gender and heterosexuality. Another critique that can be made of these approaches is the way in which bodies are understood through a, usually implicit, framework of structure and agency.

In feminist social constructionist approaches, structure and agency figure in terms of the power relations that girls and young women find themselves in, where power relations (for example, heterosexuality) are understood as structures and the girls and young women are considered as, in some sense, agents. Take as an example the quotation from Holland *et al.* (1998: 24) above concerning the heterosexualisation of young people. According to the argument put forward by the authors here, young people are agents whose agency (their capacity to 'actively engage ... in constructing their own femininity/masculinity and sexuality') is determined and restricted by particular social structures ('but in social situations in which they are both produced and constrained by discourses of power, and by the way power relations between women and men are socially organised'). There are (power) relations *between* men and women but these relations are structurally determined in advance of the agency of men and women; the agency of men and women cannot, for Holland *et al.*, change the structure. Moreover, Holland *et al.* argue that structures are socially organised according to a dominant masculinity and that girls and young women 'are under pressure to construct their femininity in relation to men's construction of masculinity'. From this position, it would seem that masculinity enables men more agency than femininity enables women; as agents, men have more power.

As I have indicated above, Butler's account of materialisation complicates the relationship between structure and agency that social constructionism implies by refusing to see sex (male and female) as constructed through the agency of gender (masculine and feminine); sex is not the passive surface on to which gender becomes inscribed through human subject(ive) activity. Butler's notion of performativity seeks to demonstrate how bodies are matter made intelligible through the heterosexual matrix. In the Introduction to *Bodies That Matter*, Butler (1993) lays out her answers to the question that was asked of her notion of performativity in *Gender Trouble*, namely, 'If gender is constructed, then who is constructing the subject?' (1993: 6). Butler argues that this question misunderstands performativity in two ways. First, critiques of performativity misunderstand the concept by equating performativity with performance, that is by assuming that performativity is an action or an activity carried out by a prior 'I' or 'we'; 'How can there be an activity, a constructing, without presupposing an agent who preceded and performs that activity?' (1993: 7). She counteracts this objection by arguing that gendered subjectivity cannot precede its construction:

> For if gender is constructed, it is not necessarily constructed by an 'I' or a 'we' who stands before that construction in any spatial or temporal sense

Conclusion: become what you want? 209

of 'before'. Indeed, it is unclear whether there can be an 'I' or a 'we' who has not been submitted, subjected to gender, where gendering is, among other things, the differentiating relations by which speaking subjects come into being. Subjected to gender, but subjectivated by gender, the 'I' neither precedes nor follows the process of this gendering, but emerges only within and as the matrix of gender relations themselves. (1993: 7)

Accordingly, and as discussed above, there is no 'blank space' or 'prior subject' onto which gender can be constructed.

The second objection to performativity that Butler deals with is the 'claim . . . that constructivism forecloses agency, presumes the agency of the subject, and finds itself presupposing the subject that it calls into question' (1993: 7). Her answer to this claim is as follows:

> To claim that the subject is itself produced in and as a gendered matrix of relations is not to do away with the subject, but only to ask after the conditions of its emergence and operation. The 'activity' of this gendering cannot, strictly speaking, be a human act or expression, a wilful appropriation, and it is certainly *not* a question of taking on a mask; it is the matrix through which all willing first becomes possible, its enabling cultural condition. In this sense, the matrix of gender relations is prior to the emergence of the 'human'. (1993: 7)

For Butler here, while the activity of an agent does not rest on or emanate from a pre-existing body/subject/human it is structured by a pre-existing set of power relations; *'the matrix of gender relations is prior to the emergence of the "human"'*.[14]

Butler understands the relationship between the agent and the structure in terms of reiteration, or the repetitive and citational acts that constitute performativity. Reiteration refers to how subjects act in ways which reproduce social contexts which involve inequality and injustice. However, as citational acts, the notion of reiteration seeks to disconnect the acts from the consciousness of subjects; as suggested above, the way in which subjects act in repetitive ways (performativity) is established through the power matrix which pre-exists them. Through the notion of reiteration, and through maintaining the concept of agency, Butler's work suggests the possibility of the subversion of the power matrix. For example, at the end of *Gender Trouble* Butler argues:

> The task is not whether to repeat, but how to repeat or, indeed, to repeat and, through a radical proliferation of gender, to *displace* the very gender norms that enable the repetition itself. (1999: 189)

Explaining this position in *Gender Trouble* that '[c]onstruction is not opposed to agency; it is the necessary scene of agency', Sara Salih suggests that 'construction and deconstruction . . . are the necessary – in fact the *only* – scenes of agency. Subversion must take place within an already existing discourse, since that is all there is' (Salih 2002: 67–68).

This argument that discourse is always-already the scene of any subversion illuminates the crux of the problem of the structure and agency distinction in Butler's work. In moving from structure to a reconceived notion of agency as reiteration, firstly Butler sees the possibility of agency as necessarily located within structure (or discourse) – as Salih says, 'that is all there is'.[15] It is as if reiteration is both structure *and* agency. In proposing reiteration as the way in which bodies are materialised into subjects, Butler reconceives the limits and possibilities of structure and agency but maintains them as the limits of possible conceptions of bodies; structure and agency limit the conditions of possibility of bodies. Second and relatedly, Butler sees subversion as only possible through agency. In the vocabulary used here, is 'structure' capable of subverting itself?[16] Butler recognises subversion only in agency because agency is materialised through structure and therefore might be materialised differently. Structure exists prior to and in spite of agency. For Butler it is through the heterosexual matrix that the possibilities of structure, agency and reiteration are conceived.[17] The heterosexual matrix can be understood in terms of a (human) body 'being installed in a historicity that is not my own, but which is the condition of my own' (Butler in Bell 1999: 166). According to Butler here, 'condition' refers to a specific time into which, in the terms of this section, agents are installed.[18] In this sense, 'condition' involves some kind of structure which both precedes and limits the possibilities of agency; conditioning is a determining time, a causal time.

Butler's notion of condition is therefore at odds with the notion of condition that is developed in Chapter 6, through Grosz's work, in relation to temporality. In that chapter I suggested that rather than being some kind of (pre-)determining 'time', condition might be understood as the *coexistence* of temporalities. Condition refers not to a determining time but rather involves the ways in which different moments of temporality move and assemble; *condition might be understood as what of the virtual is actualised* through the particularities of the becoming of bodies. Such an understanding draws on the concept of duration, where temporality is not (only) an external structure (clock time for example) but is to be grasped through the becoming specific (or, better, singular) to a body.[19] It also draws on the concept of the fold, whereby the world is folded in a body and a body is folded in the world. A body is a particularly intense expression – or perhaps experience is better here – of the world and a particularly intense expression or experience of the world is a body. Following this logic of the fold, the distinction between structure and agency that both feminist social constructionism and feminist social constructivism rely upon in different ways is put to one side. Bodies, for example, are not agents who construct or are constructed (feminist social constructionism) but nor are they inserted into an always-already existing discursive structure (feminist social constructivism). Instead, bodies become through the assemblage of temporal, and spatial, moments of experience.

One way to think about this distinction between the models of structure/agency and becoming is in terms of how the focus on relationality offers ways of examining bodies which do not take issue with the girls (or boys, girls, images) themselves. Indeed, the focus throughout the book has not been on *the girls* but on the *relations* that *bodies* are involved in and that are constitutive of these bodies. What this suggests is that what is at stake is not whether the girls are, or are not, the victims of or unwitting participants in an overarching heterosexist power structure which is controlled by and perpetuated by other people and other images.[20] In terms of the argument developed in Chapter 5 concerning affective relations between bodies, for example, it is not that these relations always-already exist as power structures but nor are they the result of the girls' actions; affect does not pre-exist these relations between bodies and it does not emanate *from* bodies. Affective relations constitute bodies (as open-ended entities) and are also constituted through other relations so that, as Deleuze suggests, the world is, potentially, infinitely connected. In examining the connections between things through specific becomings, it becomes possible to identify the assemblage of different temporal moments of experience: novelty and endurance, fixing and extending, sticking and moving, difference and sameness. The question that Chapter 6 was interested in concerned the ways in which the different moments of experience that are assembled condition each other and condition the possibilities of what might become; how does the past condition the present and the future where this conditioning does not involve linear time? What is of interest now is the kinds of possibilities that this notion of conditioning offers a feminist analysis of the becoming of bodies.

Repetition and sameness

The critique of feminist models of structure and agency concerns not only how bodies are figured (as a blank space or as discursively materialised) but also the way in which time is understood as somehow linear and causal. One point that I have tried to make throughout the book is that we do not necessarily know in advance what connections there might be between different temporal moments and that connections between different temporal moments might be vague, ambiguous, non-linear. Time, then, is not the ordered succession of occurrences but the shifting experience of duration. However, in arguing that time is not linear and that the past does not have pre-determined effects, focus must not be drawn away from how some temporal moments are experienced and re-experienced in particular ways, that is the ways in which certain moments of experience become stuck and are repeatedly experienced. How might the approach that I have put forward address this if not through a model of structure and agency? One appealing feature of the model of structure and agency is the attention it pays to (social) reproduction. However, in so doing (social) reproduction is conceived in terms of stasis, of the same thing being done again and again. In a discussion of the conceptual possibilities of 'intensity', Brian Massumi critiques the stasis of such arguments by opposing structure to the event:

> Approaches to the image in its relation to language are always incomplete if they operate only on the semantic or semiotic level, however that level is defined (linguistically, logically, narratologically, ideologically, or all of these in combination, as a Symbolic). What they lose, precisely, is the expression *event* – in favour of structure. Much could be gained by integrating the dimension of intensity into cultural theory. The stakes are the new. For structure is the place where nothing ever happens, that explanatory heaven in which all eventual permutations are prefigured in a self-consistent set of invariant generational rules. Nothing is prefigured in the event. It is the collapse of structured distinction into intensity, of rules into paradox. It is the suspension of the invariance that makes happy happy, sad sad, function function and meaning mean. (2002a: 27–28)

Conceived as 'the place where nothing ever happens', structure is understood as an over-arching framework where 'all eventual permutations are prefigured in a self-consistent set of invariable generational rules'. Instead, Massumi proposes 'the new' that is involved in the event; 'nothing is prefigured in the event'. In focusing on the new of the event, Massumi is pointing to the creativity of becomings, even when that becoming becomes not different but the same: *there is newness and creativity in becoming the same.*

The girls' bodies that I have discussed in this book often become the same, that is are often experienced and re-experienced in ways which do not seem to offer anything new or different. The typical ways in which feminist sociology has tried to deal with this has been to cite agency (less frequently) and structure (more frequently) as 'at fault'; there is a particular heterosexual logic 'to blame'. However, in holding structure

Conclusion: become what you want? 213

and agency to one side, what becomes apparent is not so much the *reproduction* of the same as the *repetition* of the same. Repetition here can be understood in the terms developed by Deleuze (1968/2001b) in *Difference and Repetition* where it refers not to generality and reproduction but to *difference and particularity* – as he puts it on the first page of his Introduction, '[t]o repeat is to behave in a certain manner, but in relation to something unique and singular which has no equal or equivalent' (2001b: 1). According to this argument, repetition is not the reproduction of the same because *repetition is a unique and singular behaviour with no equal or equivalent*. The concept of repetition is, in James Williams' (2003) view, Deleuze's attempt to theorise questions that emerge from his conception of the world as characterised not by sameness (or indeed reproduction) but by difference; 'How do things acquire any determinacy at all, given the founding role of pure difference? Why is there this world or set of things and not another, given the apparently chaotic and random nature of differences in themselves?'[21] (Williams 2003: 84).

Of interest to the discussion here is the way in which Deleuze conceives repetition and difference in terms of 'passivity' and 'action' in relation to time. Briefly, Deleuze opposes the reproduction of the same through three forms, or what he terms 'syntheses', of repetition. These three syntheses involve repetition in the present through habit, repetition in the past through memory and repetition in the future through action. It is this third synthesis of repetition in the future through action that fundamentally shifts repetition from reproduction to difference and the new, as Deleuze argues, '[r]epetition is a condition of action before it is a concept of reflection. We produce something new only on condition that we repeat' (2001b: 90). Deleuze accounts for these three syntheses as such:

> We see, then, that in this final synthesis of time, the present and future are in turn no more than dimensions of the future: the past as condition, the present as agent. The first synthesis, that of habit, constituted time as a living present by means of a passive foundation on which past and future depended. The second synthesis, that of memory, constituted time as a pure past, from the point of view of a ground which causes the passing of one present and the arrival of another. In the third synthesis, however, the present is no more than an actor, an agent destined to be effaced; while the past is no more than a condition operating by default. *The synthesis of time here constitutes a future which affirms at once both the unconditioned character of the product in relation to the conditions of its production, and the independence of the work in relation to its author or actor.*(2001b: 93–94, my emphasis)

What is at stake for this book in this third synthesis of repetition is both the focus on 'the future' and the conception of the possibilities of the agent in this future. In the last sentence of the quotation above, Deleuze points to the ways in which his notion of repetition in the future involves 'at once' a product produced through particular conditions which do not necessarily determine it ('the unconditioned character of the product in relation to the conditions of its production') and conditions which are produced through but are independent from this product ('the independence of the work in relation to its author or actor').[22] What I think this does is radically reconceive structure and agency, and the relations between them. For Deleuze, repetition involves not reproduction through the determining role of structure, nor reproduction through the actions of agents, nor reproduction through reiteration as the performativity of both structure and agency. Rather, repetition is understood as conditioned and unconditioned, as dependent and independent, *as produced through but not determined by its relations*.

The notion of condition that I have been developing in this and the previous chapter, is an attempt to point to such a repetition and/of difference. Bodies become through relations which are neither random nor inevitable but which assemble through the intensity of experience. These experiences can neither be located in structures or agents but rather are *folded through bodies* in particular ways. Understood in temporal terms, the notion of condition sees the future as enfolding through (the intensity of) the past and present. Enfolding, as I suggested in the Introduction and Chapter 1, is not the *un*folding of the past and the present into the future but rather is the non-linearity, the multiplicity, the assemblage, of a temporality. As Grosz puts it, there is a 'virtual coexistence' (2000: 225) of different temporalities. In this sense, then, the becoming of bodies is through the actualisation of the virtual; as I explored in Chapter 6, 'past' temporalities exist as a virtual condition on how it is possible for a body to become. The virtual is, as Fraser (2007) puts it, '[m]inimally defined as a dimension of the actual that's neither observable nor accessible *in itself*, the virtual offers a "beyond"-actual-states-of-affairs for the social scientist to look at' (2007: 6–7). In this sense, then, as a 'beyond', the virtual can be conceived as the excess, as the (finite) possibilities of a becoming which are not actualised. As such, the virtual *conditions* rather than determines. Indeed, Fraser goes on to argue that, '[u]nlike *social* structures, . . . virtual structures or patterns can't do "explanatory work", because they're not determining in the way that social forces, or the material sedimentation of such forces over time, are often understood to be in sociology. The concept of the virtual, in other words, doesn't allow me to replace sociology as **the** *articula-*

tor of problems, with sociology as **the** *determining-agent* of problems' (2007: 7). Instead she suggests:

> Virtual structures are not determining **not** because the virtual has *no* relation to the actual (it's not an unintelligible outside), but because processes of actualisation introduce many contingent divergences. Indeed, if the relations between the virtual and the actual were understood to be the ontological counterpoint of the epistemological relations between the problem and the solution, then one might say that a virtual problem has many different solutions. These solutions can never be true though, because there is no true solution to a virtual problem; there's only the development of the problem in particular ways. (Fraser 2007: 7)

It may seem that such an argument places me (the sociologist, social scientist, cultural researcher) in a position where to do research, to pose and solve problems, is impossible; if the virtual cannot be accessed 'in-itself' and if there is not a 'true solution to a virtual problem', where does research go, what does it *do*? Pulling through Deleuze's project of transcendental empiricism is helpful here, because, as I discussed in Chapter 2, this project traces the actualisation of the virtual, 'beginning from singular, partial or "molecular" experiences, which are then organised and extended into "molar" formations' (Colebrook 2002: 82). The virtual, then, as Fraser points out, is not accessed *in-itself*. Rather, the virtual is accessed through its (finite) possibilities, through its conditioning, through its actualisation. In this book, this has involved beginning with the partial, relational, immanent, intensive experiences produced through the research and tracing these to their conditions of possibility. The virtual, in this sense, does not determine the becoming of bodies but conditions it in particular ways.

Such a project accounts both for how 'processes of actualisation involve many contingent divergences' *and* how these contingent divergences are limited, or finite. What has become clear through the girls' experiences of their bodies is that bodies do not become what they want but rather certain becomings of bodies are repeated. Deleuze's concept of repetition, as that which might reproduce the same but which is, simultaneously, directed to the future or is novel, is important here. The becoming of the girls' bodies is undoubtedly repetitive; what is possible are the same experiences of bodies that feminist research has been long attending to. In another way, though, what I have tried to do in this book is attend to the immanence of the girls' experiences, that is to not presume in advance what and how bodies might become. In this way, the becoming of the girls' bodies are novel and creative. To conceive the becomings of bodies as novel and creative, even in their repetition, seems a necessary point for feminist work to hold on to, for, as Colebrook states, 'to repeat is to begin again, to renew, to question, and to refuse remaining the same (2002: 8).

The becoming of feminism?

The notion of repetition as creative that is developed here has emerged through the becoming of this book. It provides a way to address the ethical questions raised through the empirical material. Why are the girls involved in the repetition of becoming in ways which limit and fix, rather than open and expand, both their own bodies and other bodies? Why do the ways in which bodies are opened and expanded often replicate relations which the girls describe as simultaneously limiting and fixing (looks, selves, personalities, for example)? Why are these patterns repeated? Why is the virtual actualised in these ways? Are there ways out of these becomings? Although it is beyond the scope of this chapter to resolve these emerging questions, the Deleuzian notion of repetition points to ways in which such questions might begin to be explored by feminism through an understanding of the world, and of bodies, not as static entities but as necessarily involved in movement, process, becoming. Indeed, I hope that the renewal, questioning and refusal to remain the same that Colebrook points to has become apparent through the chapters that deal with the empirical material. This book has explored how bodies are involved in particular relations with other bodies, or other parts of that body, in which certain repetitions can be identified: the repetition of the emphasis of one aspect of a body over another (Chapter 4); the repetition of unhappy relations between 'different' bodies (Chapter 5) and different kinds of images (Chapters 3 and 5); the repetition of 'the past' (Chapter 6). However, rather than dealing with these repetitions as the reproduction of the same, through an ontology of becoming the book has tried to focus on the creativeness of the relations that the girls' bodies are involved in. In so doing, I have tried to point to the difference and novelty of the becoming of the girls' bodies, even when these becomings involve the becoming of the same. As immanent becomings, the relations of becoming that bodies are involved in and produced through are always 'singular'. In terms of Deleuze's notion of repetition then, time is understood as always new, different, unfolding. As Deleuze says, folds 'give ... the world the possibility of ... beginning over and again' (2003: 26); this is how time and repetition are always about the future.

One criticism that is often made of the concept and/or ontology of becoming is its focus on the future at the expense of the past. I hope in the chapters which deal with the empirical material and above I have demonstrated that this is a misunderstanding of becoming and that, through the notion of 'condition', a focus on the future does not mean the rejection or overlooking of the past. Instead, to concentrate on the future is, as Grosz argues in the quotation with which this chapter opened, to 'aspire to change, to innovation' while maintaining 'commitment to and use of the past and the present, of what prevails, what is familiar, the self-same'. This simultaneous aspiration to the future and commitment to the past is difficult but necessary; it is the challenge to which all minoritarian politics are directed (Grosz 2000). Another, linked, criticism that is made of the concept and/or ontology of becoming is that the emphasis is placed on what is provocative, exciting, different. I hope I have demonstrated that this is also a misunderstanding, at least in relation to the girls' bodies that were involved in this research. Indeed, what I have attempted to make clear throughout the chapters that deal with the empirical material is precisely how becomings are not necessarily exciting but instead often involve the (re)creation of the mundane, the ordinary, the same. However, as suggested above, the (re) creation of the same is not understood as a reproduction of what has been but rather is taken in its own, immanent, terms and explored not for what it is but for what it *does*. The shift from what an entity is to what an entity does or might do conceives that entity as constantly in process, as constantly becoming.

Another criticism often made of the concept and/or ontology of becoming, and which is related to the previous two criticisms, is that in focusing on the future and on creativity and change, attention is drawn to what is possible, rather than what is not. One point that should be noted again here is that bodies cannot become anything. The possibilities of the becoming of bodies are not infinite. As such Braidotti's point that 'the point [of feminism] is not to know who we are, but rather what, at last, we want to become' (2002: 2) is not a voluntarist understanding where women and feminism can shake off the past and become whatever they want. The notion of what 'we' want, as the girls' experiences of their bodies show, is limited and fixed in certain ways, that is, is *conditioned*. There is a virtual rather than a possible, and only particular aspects of this virtual are actualised. Deleuze argues that the actualisation of the virtual refers to 'an objectively real world' (see Chapter 1), that is to *the immanent specificities of a particular becoming*. As particularities, bodies are understood in ways which do not try to pre-empt what are and what will be important. This is to focus on the enfolding of bodies (and the world) and to account for what emerges as immanence. What I think this ontology of becoming and the concepts that it involves –

relationality, repetition, intensity, affect, folds – might do to feminist theoretical and empirical work is open up the ways in which bodies, and the world, might be understood and might be explored. This, then, is not to set in advance the ways in which bodies might be understood and nor is it to reproduce the ways in which feminism has tended to understand bodies. Instead, feminism might be understood in terms of the notion of repetition that is introduced above, that is as creative, novel, questioning: becoming.

Notes

1 See Coleman (2008c) for a discussion of how this research project might be understood through a method of intuition, de Landa (2002) for a discussion of philosophical 'problems' and Fraser (2006) for a discussion of the 'problem' in sociology.
2 Again, it is worth noting that 'solving' a problem does not necessarily mean resolving or finishing with it. Instead, solving here can be understood as a means, or better, a method, of understanding and exploring a problem that has been created.
3 There is, then, a shift of emphasis in this chapter from the feminist media and cultural studies work on the relations between girls' and young women's bodies and (popular media) images discussed in the Introduction to consider feminist sociology and 'the social' here. In making this shift, I am not intending to suggest that feminist media and cultural studies should be replaced with a feminist sociology. Rather I am attending to how feminist sociology engages with a similar set of ideas. This book is an interdisciplinary project which, in exploring the relations between bodies and images, draws on research from a number of interconnected areas.
4 The term 'sex' here refers to multiple 'things'; the category of 'the biological' onto which gender is mapped, (hetero)sexual practices and the sexaulisation of girls through heterosexual relations, for example.
5 Indeed, Latour begins his article with a definition of sociology's work as 'begin[ning] and end[ing] with socially relevant topics. If a cyclist falls off his bicycle because it has hit a rock, social scientists confess, they have nothing to say. It is only if a policeman, a lover, an insurance agent or a Good Samaritan enter the scene that a social science becomes possible, because we are now faced, not only with a causal sequence of occurrences, but also with a string of socially meaningful events.' In contrast Latour offers STS, which 'deem[s] sociologically interesting and empirically analysable, the very mechanisms of the bicycle, the paving of roads, the geology of rocks, the physiology of wounds and so on, without taking the boundary between matter and society as a division of labour between the natural and the social sciences' (2000: 108).

6 See also Adkins and Lury (1996) for a discussion of the ways in which 'the social' is increasingly being abandoned and replaced with 'the cultural' in feminist accounts of the gendering of the labour market.
7 This heading is taken from Butler (1993: 4).
8 However, there have been criticisms of Butler's 'return to matter' which suggest that, despite her claim to oppose 'textual play', Butler's understanding of 'matter' is anthropomorphic; it is a human matter. See Cheah (1995), Kirby (1997) and Fraser (2002).
9 Indeed, Butler draws on Spivak who argues that deconstruction critiques 'something that we cannot do without' to demonstrate how matter is a necessary recourse for feminism (Spivak, quoted in Butler 1993: 27).
10 The slippage here between 'matter', 'materiality' and 'materialisation' is documented by Kirby (1997) who, as part of her critique of Butler's anthropomorphism, argues that it is central to Butler's argument. Kirby writes:

> 'the initself of matter, the substantive something that Butler's minimal, if qualified, concession to hormonal and chromosomal difference acknowledges, is not the object of her analysis. Indeed, its absence is required in order for her thesis to have some purchase. Our sense of the materiality of matter, its palpability and its physical insistence, is rendered unspeakable and unthinkable in Butler's account, for the only thing that can be known about it is that it exceeds representation. Beyond cultural intelligibility, the existence of this external stuff ensures that our understanding of an outside, inasmuch as it is discourse dependent, can only be the dissimulation of an outside that *appears* as matter' (1997: 108).

11 Butler's point that sex is materialised *through* time is interesting here given the argument made in Chapter 6 where I argued that 'time' emerges (or becomes) with an assemblage. In this sense, time does not exist prior to or externally to its assemblage; there is no time through which something could be materialised. See also below on Butler's notion of time and discourse.
12 I return to the question of resistance and subversion in Butler's work in note 17 below.
13 It should be noted here that this chapter, perhaps unfairly, concentrates on the arguments made in *Gender Trouble* and *Bodies That Matter* which concern viability in relation to *subjectivity*. Here there is a slippage between the body, the subject and the human which produces some of the problems I go on to explore. In her more recent work, Butler (2004) addresses these problems by moving to consider viability in relation to life and the human. See also note 16 below.
14 Indeed, in an interview with Vikki Bell, Butler describes her notion of discourse through recalling Foucault's point, 'Discourse is not life, its time is not yours'. Butler suggests that, as subjects, we are always-already inserted into discourse which has a temporality that we both have and cannot

control; we are 'installed in a historicity that is not my own, but which is the condition of my own' (in Bell 1999: 166).

15 It is not my intention here to use structure and discourse interchangeably but rather to point to the ways in which discourse is conceived by Butler as that which precedes and extends beyond agency in a similar way to which structure is often understood by social constructionists.

16 This point relates to Butler's focus on humanness. See note 10 above. It also relates specifically to Butler's understanding of the human through subjectivity. See note 13 above.

17 As well as the problem of the relationship between structure and agency that I raise here, it is also worth noting the 'key tension' in the notion of agency that Saba Mahmood identifies in her careful reading of Butler in relation to her ethnography of a woman's piety movement in the mosques of Cairo: 'while she emphasises the ineluctable relationship between the consolidation and destabilisation of norms, [Butler's] discussion of agency tends to focus on those operations of power that resignify and subvert norms. Thus, even though Butler insists time and again that all acts of subversion are a product of the terms of violence that they seek to oppose, her analysis of agency often privileges those moments that "open possibilities for resignifying the terms of violation against their violating aims", or that provide an occasion "for a radical rearticulation" of the dominant symbolic horizon. In other words, the concept of agency in Butler's work is developed primarily in contexts where norms are thrown into question or are subject to resignification (2005: 21, references omitted). Mahmood's argument, which traces the tendency more generally within feminism as a progressive political movement to seek out and attend to 'expressions and moments of resistance that may suggest a challenge to male domination' (Mahmood 2005: 8), is that 'a theory of linguistic signification (as necessary to its articulation)' is not adequate 'for thinking conceptually about forms of corporeality that, while efficacious in behaviour, do not lend themselves easily to representation, elucidation, and a logic of signs and symbols' (Mahmood 2005: 165–166). As I have suggested, to think the becoming of bodies through images, an alternative series of concepts is required.

18 See Chapter 1 on the fold and the impossibility of insertion into an already-existing world.

19 See Geller's (2005/2006) interesting argument on feminist cinematographic philosophy where Butler's work on the temporality of gender performativity is thought through in relation to Deleuze's work on cinema and the movement-image. For Geller, Deleuze's argument that the movement-image 'subordinates time to movement' (2005/2006: paragraph 15) through editing 'temporally to force the set of images into a narrative whole' is 'very similar to Butler's description of the way a unified narrative of identity is formed in the organising of our bodily experiences through time' (2005/2006: paragraph 16). Geller's argument is also interesting for 'think[ing] Deleuze *and* Butler together despite their palpable differences'

(2005/2006: paragraph 14), instead of, as with this chapter, thinking through their differences.
20 Indeed, the girls are not always girls to themselves but rather are gendered through particular relations with other bodies. For an illuminating case of the process through which women become sexed and gendered *as women* from a different perspective, consider Denise Riley's example: 'what about another classic example of . . . a kind of precipitation into a sexed self-consciousness? You walk down the street wrapped in your own speculations; or you speed up, hell-bent on getting to the shops before they close: a car slows down, a shout comments on your expression, your movement; or there's a derisively hissed remark from the pavement. You have indeed been seen "as a woman", and violently reminded that your passage alone can spark off such random sexual attraction-cum-contempt, that you can be a spectacle when the last thing on your mind is your own embodiedness. But . . . the first thought here is not, "Now, humiliatingly, I've become a woman", but rather that you have been positioned antagonistically as a woman-thing, objectified as a distortion' (1988: 96–97).
21 In their discussion of process ontology Fraser *et al.* refer to a similar point posed by Haraway concerning 'change – both novelty and endurance – in a world which "might be different but is not"' (Haraway quoted in Fraser *et al.* 2005: 3).
22 See here Lury (2005) for an interesting discussion of the ways in which branding reorganises the relations between the artist and the work of art.

Appendix A: additional images

Figure A.1 Casey's art-work

Appendix A: additional images 223

Figure A.2 Catherine's art-work

Figure A.3 Chloe's art-work

224 *Appendix A: additional images*

Figure A.4 Dionne's art-work, front

Figure A.5 Dionne's art-work, back

Figure A.6 Emily's art-work

226 Appendix A: additional images

Figure A.7 Fay's art-work

Appendix A: additional images 227

Figure A.8 Hannah's art-work, front

Figure A.9 Katie's art-work, front

Figure A.10 Tina's art-work, front

Bibliography

Acker, Joan, Barry, Kate and Esseweld, Johanna (1991) 'Objectivity and Truth: Problems in Doing Feminist Research' in Fonow, Mary Margaret and Cook, Judith A. (eds) *Beyond Methodology: Feminist Scholarship as Lived Experience* Indiana: Indiana University Press
Adams, Parveen (1996) *The Emptiness of the Image: Psychoanalysis and Sexual Differences* London and New York: Routledge
Adkins, Lisa (2000) 'Mobile Desire: Aesthetics, Sexuality and the "Lesbian" at Work' in *Sexualities* Vol. 3, No. 2, 201–218
—— (2001) 'Cultural Feminisation: "Money, Sex and Power" for Women' in *Signs: Journal of Women in Culture and Society* Vol. 26, No. 31, 669–695
—— (2002) *Revisions: Gender and Sexuality in Late Modernity* Buckingham and Philadelphia: Open University Press
Ahmed, Sara (2000) *Strange Encounters: Embodied Others in Post-Coloniality* London and New York: Routledge
—— (2001) 'Communities that Feel: Intensity, Difference and Attachment' in Koivunen, Anu and Paasonen, Susanna (eds) Conference Proceedings for *Affective Encounters: Rethinking Embodiment in Feminist Media Studies* University of Turku, School of Art, Literature and Music, Media Studies, Series A, No. 49, pp. 10–24. E-book at http://www.utu.fi/hum/media tutkimus/affective/proceedings.html. Media Studies, Turku 2001. Accessed 17th July 2004.
—— (2004) *The Cultural Politics of Emotion* London: Routledge
——and Stacey, Jackie (2001) (eds) *Thinking Through the Skin* London: Routledge
Alcoff, Linda and Potter, Elizabeth (1993) (eds) *Feminist Epistemologies* London: Routledge
Ali, Suki (2003) *Mixed-Race, Post-Race: Gender, New Ethnicities and Cultural Practices* London and New York: Berg
Antliff, Mark (1999) 'The Rhythms of Duration: Bergson and the Art of Matisse' in Mullarkey, John (ed.) *The New Bergson* Manchester and New York: Manchester University Press, pp. 184–208
Badiou, Alain (1994) 'Gilles Deleuze, *The Fold: Leibniz and the Baroque*' in Boundas, Constantine V. and Olkowski, Dorothea (eds) *Gilles Deleuze and the Theatre of Philosophy* New York: Routledge, pp. 51–69

Barad, Karen (2007) *Meeting the Universe Halfway: Quantum Physics and the Entanglement of Matter and Meaning* Durham and London: Duke University Press

Barnet-Weiser, Sarah and Portwood-Stacer, Laura (2006) '"I Just Want to be Me Again!": Beauty Pageants, Reality Television and Post-Feminism' in *Feminist Theory* Vol. 7, No. 2, 255–272

Barthes, Roland (1980/2000) *Camera Lucida* London: Random House

Barrett, Michèle (1992) 'Words and Things: Materialism and Method in Contemporary Feminist Analysis' in Barrett, Michèle and Phillips, Anne (eds) *Destabilising Theory: Contemporary Feminist Debates* Cambridge: Polity, pp. 201–219

Barry, Andrew (2005) 'Pharmaceutical Matters: The Invention of Informed Materials' in *Theory, Culture and Society*, Vol. 22, No. 1, 51–70

Bell, Vikki (1999) 'On Speech, Race and Melancholia: An Interview With Judith Butler' in Bell, Vikki (ed.) *Performativity and Belonging* London: Sage, pp. 163–174

Bendelow, Gillian and Williams, Simon J. (eds) (1998) *Emotions in Social Life: Critical Themes and Contemporary Issues* London: Routledge

Benjamin, Walter (1950/1999) 'Theses on the Philosophy of History' in *Illuminations*, translated by Harry Zorn, London: Random House, pp. 245–255

Benthien, Claudia (2002) *Skin: On the Cultural Border Between Self and the World* New York, Chichester, West Sussex: Columbia University Press

Bergson, Henri (1903/1999) *An Introduction to Metaphysics*, translated by T.E. Hulme, Indianapolis: Hackett Publishing Company

—— (1908/2002) *Matter and Memory*, translated by N.M. Paul and W.S. Palmer, New York: Zone Books

Betterton, Rosemary (1987) 'How do Women Look? The Female Nude in the Work of Suzanne Valadon' in Betterton, Rosemary (ed.) *Looking On: Images of Femininity in the Visual Arts and Media* London: Pandora Press, pp. 217–234

—— (1996) *An Intimate Distance: Women, Artists and the Body* London: Routledge

Black, Paula (2004) *The Beauty Industry: Gender, Culture, Pleasure* London and New York: Routledge

Blackman, Lisa and Walkerdine, Valerie (2001) *Mass Hysteria: Critical Psychology and Media Studies* Basingstoke: Palgrave

Boundas, Constantine V. (1993) (ed.) *The Deleuze Reader* New York: Columbia University Press

Braidotti, Rosi (1991) *Patterns of Dissonance* Oxford: Polity Press

—— (1994) *Nomadic Subjects: Embodiment and Sexual Difference in Contemporary Feminist Theory* New York: Columbia University Press

—— (2002) *Metamorphoses: Towards a Materialist Theory of Becoming* Cambridge: Polity Press

—— (2006) *Transpositions: On Nomadic Ethics* Cambridge and Malden MA: Polity Press
Bray, Abigail and Colebrook, Claire (1998) 'The Haunted Flesh: Corporeal Feminism and the Politics of (Dis)Embodiment' in *Signs: Journal of Women in Culture and Society* Vol. 24, No. 1, 35–67
British Medical Association (2000) *Eating Disorders, Body Image and the Media* London: British Medical Association
Brown, Lyn Mikel and Gilligan, Carol (1992) *Meeting at the Crossroads: Women's Psychology and Girls' Development* Cambridge, Massachusetts and London: Harvard University Press
Buchanan, Ian and Colebrook, Claire (2000) (eds) *Deleuze and Feminist Theory* Edinburgh: Edinburgh University Press
Burkitt, Ian (1999) *Bodies of Thought: Embodiment, Identity and Modernity* London: Sage
Butler, Judith (1990/1999) *Gender Trouble: Feminism and the Subversion of Identity* London: Routledge
—— (1993) *Bodies That Matter: On the Discursive Limits of Sex* London: Routledge
—— (2004) *Undoing Gender* New York: Routledge
Casey, Edward S. (1999) 'The Time of the Glance: Toward Becoming Otherwise' in Grosz, Elizabeth (ed.) *Becomings: Explorations in Time, Memory, and Futures* Ithaca and London: Cornell University Press, pp. 79–97
Cheah, Pheng (1996) 'Mattering' in *Diacritics* Vol. 26, No. 1, 108–139
Cockburn, Claudia and Clarke, Gill (2002) '"Everybody's Looking at You!" Girls Negotiating the "Feminine Deficit" They Incur in Physical Education' in *Women's Studies International Forum* Vol. 25, No. 6, 651–665
Colebrook, Claire (2000) 'Introduction' in Buchanan, Ian and Colebrook, Claire (eds) *Deleuze and Feminist Theory* Edinburgh: Edinburgh University Press, pp. 1–17
—— (2002) *Gilles Deleuze* London and New York: Routledge
Coleman, Rebecca (2008a) '"Things That Stay": Feminist Theory, Duration and the Future' in *Time and Society* Vol. 17, No. 1, 85–102
—— (2008b) 'The Becoming of Bodies: Girls, Media Effects and Body-Image' in *Feminist Media Studies*, Vol. 8, No. 2, 163–178
—— (2008c) 'A Method of Intuition: Becoming, Relationality, Ethics' in *History of Human Sciences*, Special Issue on Intimacy in Research, Vol. 21, No. 4, 104–123
Conley, Verena Andermatt (2000) 'Becoming-Woman Now' pp. 18–37 in Buchanan, Ian and Colebrook, Claire (eds) *Deleuze and Feminist Theory* Edinburgh: Edinburgh University Press
Cosslett, Tess, Lury, Celia and Summerfield, Penny (2000) (eds) *Feminism and Autobiography: Texts, Theories, Methods* London and New York: Routledge
Csordas, Thomas J. (1994) 'Introduction: The Body as Representation and Being-in-the-World' in Csordas, Thomas J. (ed.) *Embodiment and Experience: the*

Existential Ground of Culture and Self Cambridge: Cambridge University Press, pp. 1–24

Cussins, Anne Marie (2001) 'The Role of Body Image in Women's Mental Health' in *Feminist Review* No. 68, 105–114

Davies, Kathy (1995) *Reshaping the Female Body: The Dilemma of Cosmetic Surgery* New York and London: Routledge

De Beauvoir, Simone (1949/1997) *The Second Sex* London: Vintage

De Landa, Manuel (1999) 'Deleuze, Diagrams, and the Open-Ended Becoming of the World' in Grosz, Elizabeth (ed.) *Becomings: Explorations in Time, Memory, and Futures* Ithaca and London: Cornell University Press, pp. 29–41

—— (2002) *Intensive Science and Virtual Philosophy* London and New York: Continuum

Deleuze, Gilles (1968/2001b) *Difference and Repetition*, translated by Paul Patton, London and New York: Continuum

——(1978–1981) *Lecture Transcripts on Spinoza's Concept of Affect* http://www.goldsmiths.ac.uk/csisp/source/authors/deleuze.html, accessed 15th September 2005

—— (1986/2005) *Cinema 1* London: Continuum

—— (1988) *Foucault*, translated by Seán Hand, London: The Athlone Press

—— (1991) *Bergsonism*, translated by Hugh Tomlinson and Barbara Habberjam, New York: Zone

—— (1992) 'Ethology: Spinoza and Us' in Crary, Jonathon and Kwinter, Sanford (eds) *Incorporations* New York: Zone, pp. 625–633

—— (1995) *Negotiations* New York: Columbia University Press

——(2001a) 'Immanence: A Life' in *Pure Immanence: Essays on A Life*, translated by Anne Boyman, New York: Zone, pp. 25–33

—— (1993/2003) *The Fold: Leibniz and the Baroque*, translated by Tom Conley, London and New York: Continuum

—— and Guattari, Felix (1987) *A Thousand Plateaus: Capitalism and Schizophrenia*, translated by Brian Massumi, London and New York: Continuum

—— and Parnet, Claire (1977/2002) *Dialogues II*, translated by Hugh Tomlison, Barbara Habberjam and Eliot Ross Albert, London: The Athlone Press

Despret, Vinciane (2004) 'The Body We Care For: Figures of Anthropo-zoo-genesis' in *Body and Society* Vol. 10, No. 2–3, 111–134

Diawara, Manthia (1998) 'Homeboy Cosmopolitan: Manthia Diawara interviewed by Silvia Kolbowski' in *October* 83 (Winter), 51–70

Doane, Mary Ann (1992) 'Film and the Masquerade: Theorising the Female Spectator' in *The Sexual Subject: A Screen Reader in Sexuality* London: Routledge, pp. 227–243

Driscoll, Catherine (2000) 'The Woman in Process: Deleuze, Kristeva and Feminism' in Buchanan, Ian and Colebrook, Claire (eds) *Deleuze and Feminist Theory* Edinburgh: Edinburgh University Press, pp. 64–85

—— (2002) *Girls: Feminine Adolescence in Popular Culture and Cultural Theory* New York and Chichester: Columbia University Press

Duke, Lisa (2000) 'Black in a Blonde World: Race and Girls. Interpretations of the Feminine Ideal in Teen Magazines' in *Journalism and Mass Communication Quarterly*, Vol. 77, No. 2, 367–392

Durham, Meenakshi Gigi (1999) 'Girls, Media, and the Negotiation of Sexuality: A Study of Race, Class and Gender in Adolescent Peer Groups' in *Journalism and Mass Communication Quarterly*, Vol. 76, No. 2, 193–216

Eagleton, Terry (1983) *Literary Theory: An Introduction* Oxford: Blackwell

Edwards, Anne (2002) 'Responsible Research: Ways of Being a Researcher' in *British Educational Research Journal*, Vol. 28, No. 2, 157–168

Fisher, Pamela and Goodly, Dan (2007) 'The Linear Medical Model of Disability: Mothers of Disabled Babies Resist with Counter-Narratives' in *Sociology of Health and Illness* Vol. 29, No. 1, 66–81

Francis, Becky (2000) *Boys, Girls and Achievement: Addressing the Classroom Issues* London: Routledge

Fraser, Mariam (1997) 'Feminism, Foucault and Deleuze' in *Theory, Culture and Society* Vol. 14, No. 2, 23–37

—— (1999) *Identity Without Selfhood: Simone de Beauvoir and Bisexuality* Cambridge: Cambridge University Press

—— (2002) 'What is the Matter of Feminist Criticism?' in *Economy and Society* Vol. 31, No. 4, 606–625

—— (2006) 'The Ethics of Reality and Virtual Reality: Latour, Facts and Values' *History of the Human Sciences* Vol. 19 No. 2, 45–72

—— (2007) 'Experience and Sociology', paper presented at the 'What is the empirical?' conference, Goldsmiths College, June 2007, http://www.goldsmiths.ac.uk/sociology/papers/experience-and-sociology.pdf, accessed 27th March 2008

—— and Greco, Monica (eds) (2004) *The Body: A Reader* London: Routledge

——, Kember, Sarah and Lury, Celia (2005) 'Inventive Life: Approaches to the New Vitalism' in *Theory, Culture and Society*, Vol. 22, No. 1, 1–14

Freud, Sigmund (1914/1995) 'On Narcissism: An Introduction' in Peter Hall (ed.) *The Freud Reader* London: Vintage, pp. 545–562

——(1927/1978) 'Fetishism' in James Strachley (ed.) *The Complete Psychological Works of Sigmund Freud* Vol. XXI (1927–1931) Toronto: Howgarth Press

—— (1930/1978) 'Civilisation and Its Discontents' in James Strachley (ed.) *The Complete Psychological Works of Sigmund Freud* Vol. XXI (1927–1931) Toronto: Howgarth Press

Frost, Liz (2001) *Young Women and the Body: A Feminist Sociology* Hampshire and New York: Palgrave

Furman, Frida Kerner (1997) *Facing the Mirror: Older Women and Beauty Shop Culture* New York: Routledge

Gauntlett, David (2005) *Moving Experiences: Media Effects and Beyond* Eastleigh: John Libbey Publishing

—— and Holzwarth, Peter (2006) 'Creative and Visual Methods for Exploring Identities' in *Visual Studies*, Vol. 21, No. 1, 82 – 91

Geller, Theresa L. (2005/2006) 'The Cinematic Relations of Corporeal Feminism: Towards a Feminist Cinematographic Philosophy' in *Rhizomes:Cultural Studies in Emerging Knowledge* Issue 11/12, Fall 2005/Spring 2006, http://www.rhizomes.net/issue11/geller.html, accessed 27th March 2008

Giddens, Anthony (1991) *Modernity and Self-Identity: Self and Society in the Late Modern Age* Cambridge: Polity

Gimlin, Debra L. (2002) *Body Work: Beauty and Self-Image in American Culture* Berkeley, Los Angeles, London: University of California Press

Glucksmann, Miriam (1994) 'The Work of Knowledge and the Knowledge of Women's Work' in Maynard, Mary and Purvis, June (eds) *Researching Women's Lives from a Feminist Perspective* London: Taylor & Francis, pp. 125–148

Goodman, J. Robyn (2002) 'Flabless is Fabulous: How Latina and Anglo Women Read and Incorporate the Excessively Thin Body Ideal into Everyday Experience' in *Journalism and Mass Communication Quarterly* Vol. 79, No. 3, 712–727

—— and Walsh-Childers, Kim (2004) 'Sculpting the Female Breast: How College Women Negotiate the Media's Ideal Breast Image' in *Journalism and Mass Communication Quarterly* Vol. 81, No. 3, 657–674

Gray, Ann (1992) *Video Playtime: The Gendering of a Leisure Technology* London: Routledge

Grogan, Sarah (1999) *Body Image: Understanding Body Dissatisfaction in Men, Women and Children* London and New York, Routledge

—— and Wainwright, Nicola (1996) 'Growing Up in the Culture of Slenderness: Girls' Experiences of Body Dissatisfaction' in *Women's Studies International Forum* Vol. 19, No. 6, 665–673

——, Williams, Zoe and Connor, Mark (1996) 'The Effects of Viewing Same-Gender Photographic Models on Body-Esteem' in *Psychology of Women Quarterly* Vol. 20, 569–575

Grosz, Elizabeth (1994) *Volatile Bodies: Towards a Corporeal Feminism* Bloomington and Indianapolis: Indiana University Press

—— (1999a) (ed.) *Becomings: Explorations in Time, Memory, and Futures* Ithaca and London: Cornell University Press

——(1999b) 'Becoming...An Introduction' in Grosz, Elizabeth (ed.) *Becomings: Explorations in Time, Memory, and Futures* Ithaca and London: Cornell University Press, pp. 1–11

—— (1999c) 'Thinking the New: Of Futures Yet Unthought' in Grosz, Elizabeth (ed.) *Becomings: Explorations in Time, Memory, and Futures* Ithaca and London: Cornell University Press, pp. 15–28

—— (2000) 'Deleuze's Bergson: Duration, the Virtual and a Politics of the Future' Buchanan, Ian and Colebrook, Claire (eds) *Deleuze and Feminist Theory* Edinburgh: Edinburgh University Press, pp. 214–234

—— (2001) *Architecture From the Outside: Essays on Virtual and Real Space* Cambridge, Massachusetts and London: The Massachusetts Institute of Technology Press

Hall, Stuart (1980) 'Encoding/Decoding' in Hall, S., Hobson, D, Lowe, A., Willis, P. (eds) *Culture, Media, Language* London: Hutchinson

Haraway, Donna (1990) 'A Manifesto for Cyborgs: Science, Technology, and Socialist Feminism in the 1980s' in Nicholson, Linda (ed.) *Feminism/ Postmodernism* London: Routledge

—— (1991) *Simians, Cyborgs and Women: The Reinvention of Nature* London: Free Association Books

—— (1992) 'Ecce Homo, Ain't (Ar'n't) I a Woman, and Inappropriate/d Others: The Human in a Post-Humanist Landscape' in Butler, Judith and Scott, Joan W. (eds) *Feminists Theorise the Political* London: Routledge, pp. 86–100

—— (1997) *ModestWitness@Second_Millennium.FemaleMan©_Meets _ OncoMouse™ Feminism and Technoscience* London and New York: Routledge

Hey, Valerie (1997) *The Company She Keeps: An Ethnography of Girls' Friendships* Buckingham: Open University Press

Holland, Janet and Ramazanoglu, Caroline (1994) 'Coming to Conclusions: Power and Interpretation in Researching Young Women's Sexuality' in Maynard, Mary and Purvis, June (eds.) *Researching Women's Lives from a Feminist Perspective* London: Taylor and Francis

—— and Blair, Maud with Sheldon, Sue (1995) (eds) *Debates and Issues in Feminist Research and Pedagogy* Clevedon, Philadelphia, Adelaide: Open University Press

——, Ramazanoglu, Caroline, Sharpe, Sue and Thompson, Rachel (1998) *The Male in the Head: Young People, Heterosexuality and Power* London: The Tufnell Press

Irigaray, Luce (1977) 'Women's Exile' in *Ideology and Consciousness*, May 1977, No. 1, 62–76

Jay, Martin (1994) *Downcast Eyes: The Denigration of Vision in Twentieth-Century French Thought* Los Angeles and London: University of California Press

Jung, Hwa Yol (1996) 'Phenomenology and Body Politics' in *Body and Society* Vol. 2, No. 2, 1–22

Keenan, Thomas (1993) 'Windows: of Vulnerability' in Robins, Bruce (ed.) *The Phantom Public Sphere* London, Minneapolis: University of Minnesota Press, pp. 121–141

Kennedy, Barbara (2004) *Deleuze and Cinema: The Aesthetics of Sensation* Edinburgh: Edinburgh University Press

King, Josephine and Stott, Mary (1977) *Is This Your Life? Images of Women in the Media* London: Quartet Books for Virago

Kirby, Vicky (1997) *Telling Flesh: The Substance of the Corporeal* London: Routledge

Kwinter, Sanford (2002) *Architectures of Time: Toward a Theory of Event in Modernist Culture* Cambridge, Massachusetts and London: The Massachusetts Institute of Technology Press

Latour, Bruno (2000) 'When Things Strike Back: A Possible Contribution of "Science Studies" to the Social Sciences' in *British Journal of Sociology* Vol. 51, No. 1, 107–123

Lawler, Steph (2000) *Mothering the Self: Mothers, Daughters, Subjects* London and New York: Routledge

Letherby, Gayle (2003) *Feminist Research in Theory and Practice* Buckingham and Philadelphia: Open University Press

Lupton, Deborah (1998) 'Going With the Flow: Some Central Discourses in Conceptualising and Articulating the Embodiment of Emotional States' in Nettleton, Sarah and Weston, Jonathon (eds) *The Body in Everyday Life* London: Routledge, pp. 82–99

Lury, Celia (1998) *Prosthetic Culture: Photography, Memory and Identity* London: Routledge

—— (2005) 'Contemplating a Self-portrait as a Pharmacist: A Trade Mark Style of Doing Art and Science' in *Theory, Culture and Society*, Vol. 22, No. 1, 93–110

McLaren, Margaret A. (2002) *Feminism, Foucault, and Embodied Subjectivity* Albany, New York: State University of New York Press

McLuhan, Marshall (1964) *Understanding Media: The Extensions of Man* London: Routledge & Kegan Paul

McNay, Lois (1992) *Foucault and Feminism: Power, Gender and the Self* Cambridge: Polity Press

McRobbie, Angela (1999) '*More!* New Sexualities in Girls' and Women's Magazines' in McRobbie, Angela (ed.) *Back to Reality? Social Experience and Cultural Studies* Manchester: Manchester University Press, pp. 190–209

—— (2000a) 'The Culture of Working Class Girls' in *Feminism and Youth Culture* Hampshire and London: Macmillan Press, 2nd Edition, pp. . 44–66

—— (2000b) 'The Politics of Feminist Research: Between Talk, Text and Action' in *Feminism and Youth Culture* Hampshire and London: Macmillan Press, 2nd Edition, pp. 118–136

—— (2004) 'Notes on "What Not To Wear" and Post-Feminist Symbolic Violence' in Adkins, Lisa and Skeggs, Beverley (eds) *Feminism after Bourdieu* Oxford: Blackwell, pp. 99–109

—— (2007) 'Top Girls? Young Women and the Post-feminist Sexual Contract' in *Cultural Studies* Vol. 21, Nos. 4 -5, 718 -737

Mahmood, Saba (2005) *Politics of Piety: The Islamic Revival and the Feminist Subject* Princeton and Oxford: Princeton University Press

Massumi, Brian (2002a) *Parables for the Virtual: Movement, Affect, Sensation* Durham and London: Duke University Press

—— (2002b) 'Navigating Movements: A Conversation with Brian Massumi' in Zournazi, Mary (ed.) *Hope: New Philosophies for Change* Sydney: Pluto, pp. 210–242

Maynard, Mary and Purvis, June (1994) (eds.) *Researching Women's Lives from a Feminist Perspective* London: Taylor and Francis

Merck, Mandy (1987) 'Introduction – Difference and Its Discontents' in *differences* Vol. 28, No. 1, 2–9

Merleau-Ponty, Maurice (1962/1989) *Phenomenology of Perception* London: Routledge

—— (1968/1997) *The Visible and the Invisible* Evanston, Illinois: Northwestern University Press

Morgan, David (1997) *Focus Groups as Qualitative Research* London: Sage.

Mulvey, Laura (1989) *Visual and Other Pleasures* Basingstoke: Macmillan

Munster, Anna (2006) *Materializing New Media: Embodiment in Information Aesthetics* University Press of New England

Nichter, Mimi (2000) *Fat Talk: What Girls and Their Parents Say about Dieting* Cambridge, Massachusetts: Harvard University Press

Olkowski, Dorothea (2000) 'Body, Knowledge and Becoming-Woman: Morpho-logic in Deleuze and Irigaray' in Buchanan, Ian and Colebrook, Claire (eds) *Deleuze and Feminist Theory* Edinburgh: Edinburgh University Press, pp. 86–109

Orbach, Susie (2003) 'Therapy from the Left: Interview with Susie Orbach' in *Journal of Psychotherapy, Counselling and Health*, Vol. 6, No. 1, 75–85

Parisi, Luciana (2004) *Abstract Sex. Philosophy, Biotechnology and the Mutations of Desire* London and New York: Continuum

Patton, Paul (1996) *Deleuze: A Critical Reader* Oxford: Blackwells

Pisters, Patricia (2003) *The Matrix of Visual Culture: Working with Deleuze in Film Theory* Stanford CA: Stanford University Press

Pollock, Griselda (1987) 'What's Wrong with Images of Women?' in Betterton, Rosemary (ed.) *Looking On: Images of Femininity in the Visual Arts and Media* London: Pandora Press, pp. 40–48

Potts, Annie (2004) 'Deleuze on Viagra (Or, What Can a "Viagra-body" Do?)' in *Body and Society* Vol. 10, No. 1, 17–36

Prendergast, Shirley (1995) '"With Gender on My Mind": Menstruation and Embodiment at Adolescence' in Holland, Janet and Blair, Maud with Sheldon, Sue (eds) *Debates and Issues in Feminist Research and Pedagogy* Clevedon, Philadelphia, Adelaide: Open University Press, pp. 196–213

Probyn, Elspeth (1993) *Sexing the Self: Gendered Positions in Cultural Studies* London: Routledge

Puwar, Nirmal (2004) *Space Invaders: Race, Gender and Bodies Out of Place* Oxford and New York: Berg

Ramazanoglu, Caroline (1993) (ed.) *Up against Foucault: Explorations of Some Tensions between Foucault and Feminism* London and New York: Routledge

Renold, Emma (2001) '"Square-girls", Femininity and the Negotiation of Academic Success in the Primary School' in *British Educational Research Journal* Vol. 27, No. 5, 577–588

Ricoeur, Paul (1992) *Oneself As Another* London and Chicago: Chicago University Press
Riley, Denise (1998) *Am I That Name? Feminism and the Category of "Women" in History* Basingstoke: Macmillan
Rose, Jacqueline (1986) *Sexuality in the Field of Vision* London and New York: Verso
Salih, Sara (2002) *Judith Butler* London and New York: Routledge
Scott, Joan W. (1992) 'Experience' in Butler, Judith and Scott, Joan W. (eds) *Feminists Theorise the Political* London: Routledge, pp. 22–40
Sedgwick, Eve Kosofsky (2003) *Touching Feeling: Affect, Pedagogy, Performativity* Durham and London: Duke University Press
Simmonds, Felly Nkweto (1997) 'My Body, Myself: How Does a Black Woman Do Sociology?' in Mirza, Heidi Safia (ed.) *Black British Feminism: A Reader* London: Routledge, pp. 226–239
Skeggs, Beverley (1995) 'Theorising, Ethics and Representation in Feminist Ethnography' in Skeggs, Beverley (ed.) *Feminist Cultural Theory: Process and Production* Manchester and New York: Manchester University Press
—— (1997) *Formations of Class and Gender: Becoming Respectable* London: Sage
—— (2004) *Class, Self, Culture* London and New York: Routledge
Stacey, Jackie (1994) *Star Gazing: Hollywood Cinema and Female Spectatorship* London: Routledge
Stanley, Liz (1990) *Feminist Praxis: Research, Theory and Epistemology in Feminist Sociology* London: Routledge
—— (1995) *The Auto/ Biographical I: The Theory and Practice of Feminist Auto/ Biography* Manchester and New York: Manchester University Press
—— and Wise, Sue (1983) (eds) *Breaking Out: Feminist Consciousness and Feminist Research* London and Boston: Routledge and Kegan Paul
Sturken, Marika and Cartwright, Lisa (2001) *Practices of Looking: An Introduction to Visual Culture* New York: Oxford University Press
Thrift, Nigel (2007) *Post-representational Theory: Space, Politics, Affect* London and New York: Routledge
Tomlinson, Hugh and Habberjam, Barbara (2002) 'Translators' Introduction' in Deleuze, Gilles and Parnet, Claire *Dialogues II* London and New York: Continuum
—— and Habberjam, Barbara (2005) 'Translators' Introduction' in Deleuze, Gilles *Cinema 1* London: Continuum
Tyler, Carole-Ann (1994) 'Passing: Narcissism, Identity, and Difference' in *differences* Vol. 6, No. 2–3, 212–248
Turner, Bryan S. (1996) *The Body and Society: Explorations in Social Theory* London: Sage
Vasseleu, Catherine (1998) *Textures of Light: Vision and Touch in Irigaray, Levinas and Merleau-Ponty* London: Routledge
Walkerdine, Valerie (1989) *Counting Girls Out* London: Virago
—— (1991) *Schoolgirl Fictions* London: Verso

—— (1993) 'Daddy's Gonna Buy You a Dream to Cling to' in Buckingham, David (ed.) *Reading Audiences: Young People and the Media* Manchester: Manchester University Press

—— (1997) *Daddy's Girl: Young Girls and Popular Culture* Basingstoke and London: Macmillan

——, Lucey, Helen and Melody, June (2001) *Growing Up Girl: Psychosocial Explorations of Gender and Class* Basingstoke: Palgrave

Weiss, Gail (1999) *Body Images: Embodiment as Intercorporeality* London: Routledge

Willett, Rebekah (2007) '"What You Wear Tells a Lot About You": Girls Dress Up Online' in *Gender and Education* pp.1–14, http://www.dx.doi.org/10.1080/09540250701797242, accessed 28th March 2008

Williams, James (2003) *Gilles Deleuze's 'Difference and Repetition': A Critical Introduction and Guide* Edinburgh: Edinburgh University Press

Williams, Susan L. (2002) 'Trying on Gender, Gender Regimes, and the Process of Becoming Woman' in *Gender and Society* Vol. 16, No. 1, 29–52

Wilson, Elizabeth A. (2004) *Psychosomatic: Feminism and the Neurological Body* Durham and London: Duke University Press

Woodall, Trinny and Constantine, Susannah (2002) *What Not to Wear* London: Weidenfeld & Nicolson

Young, Iris Marion (1990/1998) 'Throwing Like a Girl' in Welton, Donn (ed.) *Body and Flesh: A Philosophical Reader* Oxford: Blackwell, pp. 259–290

Zagala, Stephen (2002) 'Aesthetics: A Place I've Never Seen' in Massumi, Brian (ed.) *A Shock to Thought: Expression After Deleuze and Guattari* London and New York: Routledge, pp. 20–43

Websites

www.edauk.com accessed 15th June 2005

www.cabinet-office.gov.uk/women's-unit/WhatWeDo/BodyImage.Lastaccessed in the autumn of 2001; this site is no longer live.

Index

actual, the 25, 36–8
  mirror images 93–5, 97
  photographic images 89–92
  see also virtual, the
actual/virtual 51–2, 63–5, 71, 92, 113, 117, 126, 138–9, 176–8, 179–80, 214–17
Adams, Parveen 15–16
affect 20, 27, 42–8, 50, 137–9, 141–2, 144–5, 162–4, 167, 196, 211
  cause and effect 20, 44, 92, 100, 171–2
  emotion 45–8, 169–72
  see also relations
age 59
agency *see* structure and agency
aging 186
Ahmed, Sara 46–8, 144
airbrushing 103–4
appearance *see* looks
archive 78–9, 121–2
art-work 116–24
assemblage 26, 32–3, 113, 136, 183
see also Bodies without Organs

Barrett, Michèle 198
Barthes, Roland 109–10 n.3, n.5, 183–4
becoming 19–24, 101–2, 166–7, 171, 180, 195
  comparison with psychoanalysis 23, 69–71
  feminism 21–4, 216–18
  geography 20, 23
  ontology 48–52
  process 1, 33
becoming-woman 21–3
  the girl 22–3
behaviour 126–7, 157–62
Benjamin, Walter 18, 183
Bergson, Henri 27, 167, 172–3, 175–8, 180, 181
Betterton, Rosemary 9
'bitching' 106, 153–8
bodies
  affect 42–8
  Bergson 173, 180
  comparison with subjectivity 69–71
  Deleuzian conceptions of 23, 33–4, 38, 49, 63, 211–18
  see also becoming
  experience 59
  participants in research 2, 68–9, 76–8
  phenomenology 38–42
  relations 27
  subject/object 49–50
Body without Organs 33–4
see also assemblage
Body Image Summit 3–5
boys 112, 127–9, 141, 142–5, 146, 147–8, 153–4, 156, 168, 199–203, 206–7
  judgment 124–7, 129
  see also friends and judgement

see also heterosexuality
Braidotti, Rosi 217
Brown, Lyn Mikel and Gilligan, Carol 192n.3
Butler, Judith 99, 198, 203–10

capacity 141–2
Casey, Edward S. 186, 188, 192n.5
Colebrook, Claire 63, 64, 66, 67–8, 71, 137, 166, 216
comments 27, 74, 141–74, 187–8
concepts 62, 79–80
condition *see* past, the; virtual, the
creativeness 61, 79, 180–1, 198, 215–16
see also new, the

de Beauvoir, Simone 9–10
Deleuze, Gilles: *see* actual, the; actual/virtual; affect; assemblage; becoming; bodies; Body without Organs; concepts; creativeness; Deleuzian feminism; difference; duration; empirical, the; ethics; endurance; event, the; experience; extensity; fold, the; immanence; intensity; intuition; monad, the; new, the; relations; repetition; singularity; temporality; transcendental empiricism; virtual, the
Deleuzian feminism 1–2, 19–24, 27–8, 48–52, 64, 70–4, 136–9, 162–4, 195, 216–18
dieting 104
difference 42, 58, 72, 213
see also creativeness; repetition
Doane, Mary Ann 12–13
Driscoll, Catherine 21, 22
Duke, Lisa 6–8
duration 27, 67, 126, 166–7, 173, 174, 176–92, 210, 212

empirical, the 28, 56, 61–2, 139n.1
sociological categories 74–5

see also transcendental empiricism
endurance 126–7, 131–3, 167, 168–72, 174–5, 178–81, 182–5, 187–92
ethics 27, 71, 162–4, 216
event, the 212
experience 25, 56, 117, 183
actualisation 66, 67–8
feminist methodologies of 56–60
immanence 60–5
intensity 65–8, 136–9, 171, 180, 182
as a methodology 59–61, 64–6, 71–5
narrative 80–1 n.2
trickster 57–8
extensity 66, 87, 136–9, 166–7, 171–2
gender 142, 162–4, 169, 206
looks 113, 123–4

fashion 123, 130, 145–6, 160–1
feminine spectatorship 8–19
psychoanalysis 10–16
figuration 57
mimesis 16–19
fold, the 1, 34–8, 138, 210–11, 214, 216
see also actual/virtual
Foucault, Michel 198–200, 204
Francis, Becky 200–3, 207
Fraser, Mariam 196, 214–15
Freud, Sigmund 10–12
friends 77, 124–34, 141, 147, 148–57, 168
advice 150–3
honesty 151–3
judgment 124–7, 129, 131, 133, 155
knowing 124–36
trust 124–36, 149–57, 158
see also bitching; boys; endurance; looks and judgement; temporality and immediacy

future, the 177, 184–92, 197, 213–14, 216–17
see also becoming; duration; past, the; present, the; temporality

Gauntlett, David 6
Geller, Theresa L. 82n.8, 220–1n.19
gender: see boys; extensity; girls; heterosexuality
girls 141, 143, 145–8, 153–4, 199–203, 206–7, 211
  psychoanalysis 10–13, 69–71
see also becoming-woman; bodies; friends; heterosexuality
Grace, Della 15
Grogan, Sarah and Wainwright, Nicola 5–6, 8
Grosz, Elizabeth 23, 38–41, 175–8, 182, 187, 192n.1, 210, 214, 217

Haraway, Donna 30–1n.16, 56–9
heterosexual matrix 204–6
heterosexuality 197, 198–207
Holland, Janet 199–200, 207–8, 211

images 66–8, 73–4, 85–8, 107–9, 112, 195
see also art-work; comments; mirror images; photographic images; popular media images
immanence 21, 60–5, 75, 166, 217
intensity 25, 26, 45–6, 52, 65–8, 113, 136–9, 162–4, 166–7, 169–72, 174, 176, 178, 182–3, 212, 214
interpretation 71–2
intuition 27, 84n.26, 167, 172–3, 176, 196
invention 25, 79–80
Irigaray, Luce 30n.13, 40

Kember, Sarah 196
Kirby, Vicky 219n.10

Latour, Bruno 198–9, 218n.5
looking 18
looks 26, 86, 88–109, 112–40, 143, 145
  judgement 124–7, 130, 132, 179
see also extensity and looks; selves
Lury, Celia 16–19, 109, 119, 183–4, 196, 221n.22

McRobbie, Angela 4, 73
Mahmood, Saba 220n.17
make-up 95–7, 100, 103–6, 130–1
Massumi, Brian 44–6, 63, 81n.6, 80, 112–13, 167, 169, 171, 178, 212
materialisation 204–8
see also Butler, Judith; heterosexuality; performativity
media cause and effect 3–8, 50, 92, 100, 102–3, 105–6, 109, 171
  representation 19
see also affect and cause and effect
memory 167, 174–84
Merleau-Ponty 38–44
methodology 25, 73–80, 172
see also experience as a methodology
mimesis 16–19
mirror images 9–10, 90, 93–9, 107–9, 114, 134, 135, 185–7
monad, the 34–7
see also fold, the
money 104, 106, 164n.6
Mulvey, Laura 30n.14

narcissism 9–16
narrative 45–6, 58, 59, 80–1n.2, 169, 171
see also temporality
new, the 79, 197, 212–13, 214–15
see also creativity

Index

Parisi, Luciana 21–2, 80–1n.7
past, the 25, 27, 59, 88–92, 109, 130, 167, 170–1, 174–92, 213
  as condition 178–81, 182, 192
  see also duration; endurance; narrative; temporality
performativity 119–21, 205–9, 214
personality 112–13, 127–9, 132–3
  see also looks; selves
phenomenology 38–42
photographic images 15, 88–92, 93–5, 101, 102, 105–6, 107–9, 115, 119, 183–7
  ways of seeing 15, 18
Pollock, Griselda 9
popular media images 3–8, 100–6
present, the 27, 45, 93–9, 167, 171, 176–92, 213
  see also duration; endurance; narrative; temporality
problems 196–7, 215
Probyn, Elspeth 72–3

race 57–9
Ramazanoglu, Caroline 199–200, 207–8, 211
relations 1, 26, 42–3, 50, 61, 71, 74, 113, 196, 211
  bodies, images 2, 3
  see also affect
remembering *see* memory
repetition 211–17
reproduction *see* repetition
Ricoeur, Paul 110n.8
Rose, Jacqueline 13–14

Salih, Sara 209–10
sameness *see* repetition
school 68, 76–7, 200–1
Scott, Joan W. 64

Sedgwick, Eve 44
selfhood 112–40
  see also looks; personality
sex: *see* heterosexuality
sexual difference
  psychoanalysis 9–16
sexualisation 147–8, 158–62, 200–3
  see also heterosexuality
Sharpe, Sue 199–200, 207–8, 211
shopping 108–9
Simmonds, Felly Nkweto 58–9
singularity 57–8, 63, 81n.6, 67
Skeggs, Beverley 74–5, 82n.12
social, the 198–9, 203–4, 207
social constructionism 199–204, 205–8, 211
social constructivism 203–11
Stacey, Jackie 30n.14
structure and agency 28, 51–2, 138, 162–4, 197, 200, 207–11, 212, 214–15
  see also repetition and sameness; virtual, the
subject(ivity)/object(ivity) 3, 8, 85, 109, 162
  feminist methodologies of experience 56
  narcissism 11–16
  mimesis 17–19
  phenomenology 38–42
  photographic images 16–17
  transcendental empiricism 62–3
  see also feminine spectatorship

Taussig, Michael 18
temporality 27, 52, 87, 126, 166–94, 197, 210–18
  becoming 20–1
  determination and qualification 171, 178
  immediacy 126, 131–3
  linear progression 20–1, 166, 171, 174, 181–3, 211–12

mirror images 93–9
photographic images 16–17, 88–93
see also affect; duration; future, the; intensity; intuition; narrative; past, the; present, the
Thompson, Rachel 199–200, 207–8, 211
transcendental empiricism 25, 62–5, 113, 196, 215
see also empirical, the
Tyler, Carole-Ann 31n.17

Vasseleu, Kathryn 40–2
virtual, the 35–8, 87, 186–7, 197, 214–16
  condition 197, 210–11, 214–15
  experience 64
see also actual, the; actual/virtual; past, the; condition

Walkerdine, Valerie 69–71
weight 5, 120, 170, 178, 190
Williams, James 213

Young, Iris Marion 29n.12, 53.n8

Lightning Source UK Ltd.
Milton Keynes UK
UKHW022200220620
365402UK00004B/379